IMAGES of America
BUTTE

ON THE COVER: The Butte High School band at one time consisted of a 140-piece marching band and an 85-piece orchestra. The well-known band was under the tutelage of Henry Schiesser from 1939 to 1957. His wife, Jean, was in charge of the majorettes, band formations, and musical arrangements. The group was selected as the Honor Band at the Tournament of Roses Parade in Pasadena in 1948, and shown on the cover is the band leaving for Portland, Oregon, where it led the Rose Festival Parade in 1949. (Courtesy of the Schiesser Collection.)

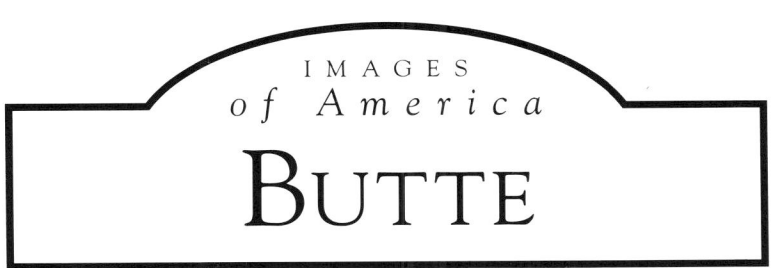

IMAGES of America
BUTTE

Ellen Crain and Lee Whitney

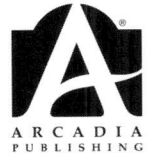

Copyright © 2009 by Ellen Crain and Lee Whitney
ISBN 978-0-7385-7186-7

Published by Arcadia Publishing
Charleston SC, Chicago IL, Portsmouth NH, San Francisco CA

Printed in the United States of America

Library of Congress Control Number: 2009926443

For all general information contact Arcadia Publishing at:
Telephone 843-853-2070
Fax 843-853-0044
E-mail sales@arcadiapublishing.com
For customer service and orders:
Toll-Free 1-888-313-2665

Visit us on the Internet at www.arcadiapublishing.com

This book is dedicated to the men, women, and children who came before us and influenced the cosmopolitan, strenuous, unique, and prosperous character of our community.

Contents

Acknowledgments   6

Introduction   7

1. Butte the Cosmopolitan   11
2. Butte the Strenuous   43
3. Butte the Unique   73
4. Butte the Prosperous   103

Acknowledgments

The authors would like to acknowledge the manuscript and photograph collections of the Butte-Silver Bow Public Archives, an award-winning facility whose collections document the impressive history of Butte, Montana. Established in 1981 to be the keeper of the historical record of the Butte-Silver Bow local government, the Archives is housed in the Butte Fire Department building that was constructed in 1900. Butte people are extremely proud of their history and heritage, and the Archives was honored in 2007 to receive the support of the citizens authorizing a significant bond initiative to renovate its existing facility and construct a new, environmentally sound vault. The people of Butte have contributed their personal, professional, and legal papers and photographs to the Archives, and people from throughout the world use the facility as a resource for academic and personal research. The Archives is a department of Butte-Silver Bow County and is generously supported in part by the Friends of the Butte Archives, a private nonprofit organization.

Butte and its sister city Anaconda have been designated a National Historic Landmark for their contributions to America's industrial and labor history. It is our hope that through this publication a greater appreciation of the role they played in America's history will be fostered.

The documentation accompanying the photographs within this volume is taken from the Archives' manuscript collections, some of the best books written about Butte, and the documentation of the National Historic Landmark Form. The photographs used are from the Archives' photograph collections unless otherwise noted. A bibliography and an index for this work are available upon request at the Archives.

The authors would like to thank Janet Finn for her thoughtful review and recommendations, and they extend a special thank you to John Poultney, editor at Arcadia Publishing.

INTRODUCTION

In the Christmas edition of the 1905 *Butte Evening News*, Thomas F. Rooney wrote an article titled "Butte, The Cosmopolitan, the Strenuous, the Unique, the Prosperous." He epitomized Butte as a city unlike any other, "Butte is not described; Butte defies analysis. One must see it to appreciate it; one must live in it to know it; for it has the face of an ogre and a heart of gold." This book provides insight into and expands on Rooney's views.

BUTTE THE COSMOPOLITAN

Butte, of course, did not begin as a cosmopolitan city. Its dependence on the extraction of natural resources provided only a tenuous existence for a time. Initially it was gold that brought miners to the hills of Montana, but there was little gold in what later would become Butte. Silver, though, was more plentiful, and by 1864, tents sprouted up in the valley that became home to the miners who scoured the earth for signs of the precious metal. By 1867, approximately 5,000 men were working mining claims, and the silver boom of 1875 enticed more and more interest in the area.

When the silver market crashed in 1893, the focus turned to copper, and it was the production and smelting of copper ore that put Butte on the map for many decades to come. Copper was not as easy to mine as gold and silver, however. The search for copper took the city to new heights and literally new depths as miners created shafts below the ground to ferret out the elusive copper ore. Large-scale headframes (called "gallows" or "gallus" frames) were erected to transport men and machinery in cages to underground levels that in some mines reached nearly a mile deep.

People came from throughout the world to work the mines and support the miners, making Butte uniquely cosmopolitan—a city like no other in Montana. It was the largest city within the Rocky Mountain Region, boasting nearly 100,000 residents shortly after the beginning of the 20th century—the most significant city between Minneapolis and Spokane. Butte led the state in political might and the country into the industrial age and the electrification of the world. Butte's zeal in the fight for workers' rights earned it the name "the Gibraltar of Unionism." People throughout the country endeavored to emulate Butte's fervor and resolution to ensure the safety of workers and to earn an equitable wage commensurate with the high degree of risk involved in underground mining.

Butte was a melting pot of ethnicities and cultures that shape it to this day. From all corners of the world, immigrants came to this tough mining town, created distinct neighborhoods, and brought with them the cultural heritage of their native countries of Ireland, Wales, China, Croatia, Italy, Serbia, Lebanon, England, Canada, and Finland, to name just a few.

Nothing defines cosmopolitan like great entertainment, literature, and food to a mix of people who are cultured and worldly. Butte offered much in this regard. A multitude of theaters offered first-class entertainment from opera to vaudeville. Every conceivable form of entertainment—from sports to card games—could be found, along with every conceivable form of music from jazz bands to classical symphonies. The restaurants were unmatched, receiving deliveries of imported goods and fresh fish daily. The menus were sophisticated and gourmet as well as hearty and filling. Grocers carried many specialty items such as kosher meat, and coffee brokers could be found in the warehouse district. In addition to great food, ladies' fashions were up to date and reflected the latest Parisian styles.

Butte the Strenuous

The men and women of Butte worked strenuously to establish the city, to bring it beyond the realm of a mere mining camp, and to survive during fluctuating economic times. Men endured back-breaking work to unearth the ore that lay beneath the surface of the steep terrain, and families learned to accept the fact that their loved ones risked their lives daily for the want of that ore. Women and children also worked to support their families, and they organized as the Newsboys' Club, the Women's Protective Union, the Retail Clerks' Union, and the Laundry Workers' Union. Some of these unions were the first of their kind in the nation and certainly in the West—an impressive example of Butte women and children making history and working to better the lives of others.

The demand for gold and then silver established Butte as a major mining area, but it was the labyrinth of copper ore veins coursing beneath the surface that would establish Butte as a significant force in the industrialization of America and the electrification of the world. Butte played host to immigrants who were content to make a modest living as well as to money mongers who were willing to gouge the land for the sake of a dollar—or preferably many dollars. Butte became the arena for the War of the Copper Kings that pitted William A. Clark, Marcus Daly, and F. Augustus Heinze against one another. The seven-year-long battle culminated when the Butte Coalition Mining Company was formed to successfully buy out the smaller companies and form the Anaconda Copper Mining Company (ACM), a mammoth company that controlled the mining, smelting, refining, timber, and newspaper industries in the state. For most of the 20th century, the ACM was the largest employer in the state. Its network was vast, and it influenced every political and financial decision made in Montana for decades.

The mining companies worked from dawn to dawn, exploring for every last ounce of ore. Their concern was production and profit, and at the end of the "shaft," so to speak, were the miners. Little attention was paid to their health and well-being, and when mining went deeper and deeper underground, conditions worsened. On a daily basis, workers were faced with perils that could take their lives in seconds or eat away at them for years. Such conditions generated unionism in the West, and Butte was hurled into the center of firestorms that would ignite the country and shape the lives of working men and women in the United States for decades.

Butte was passionate about fair wages and benefits and the safety of the working class. The first strike in Montana occurred in Butte in 1878 over wage discrimination. The strike began at the Lexington Mine and was fostered by the Butte Workingmen's Union, later to become the Butte Miners' Union. In the early 1900s, there was not a trade or shop in Butte that was not unionized and not a place in the country that did not try to imitate the success of Butte's unionization. Butte was a place made by the people, for the people, and the workers insisted that they be treated fairly.

Butte the Unique

The city is unique in the Rocky Mountain West in myriad ways, from its industrial landscape to its large mix of ethnicities. Butte's very placement near the crest of the Continental Divide is unique. The sheer elevation of nearly 6,000 feet makes the journey to the city a challenge. The terrain of the city is a dichotomy between "the flats," a stretch of even terrain that spreads south, and Uptown Butte, the face of the city that saw the majority of growth in the late 1800s and early 1900s.

Butte has always had a different perspective on social order and class distinction; class distinctions did not survive well and social order was nonexistent. Perhaps it was the fact that, from the earliest days, a man could be a millionaire one day and a pauper the next day, or perhaps it had to do with the settling of the West. The courage and fortitude required to make the trip to Montana, let alone to Butte, was impressive. Or maybe it just had to do with the fact that the climate and terrain were so strenuous that everyone needed to stand respectfully together to survive. Whether one or all of these factors combined, they created among the people of Butte a strong democracy, a rugged individualism, and unmatched tolerance for other people's rights, foibles, and beliefs.

Butte was a generous, democratic community. It did not make a difference who the person was, where he or she came from, or how much money he or she had.

As Michael Malone observed in *The Battle for Butte*, Butte was a town of personalities: a city that allowed the church and the brothel to coexist peacefully together. The sheer number of working-class citizens defined the city. Their penchant for drinking, prostitution, and gaming set the stage for the city itself and what appeared to the onlooker as a dark city, a city of despair, which in actuality was a glittering city, with its people bound together by common forces—the Catholic Church, the Democratic Party, and the incredible force of organized labor.

BUTTE THE PROSPEROUS

The wealth from the mining industry was only one measure of Butte's success. From 1890 to World War I, Butte enjoyed a boisterous adolescence. Its impressive mineral wealth appeared limitless. The city was thriving, the business district was booming, and the miners fed saloons, restaurants, gaming halls, and a notorious red-light district. Mary Murphy, in *Mining Cultures*, stated, "Butte's population was overwhelmingly young, single, and predominantly male." Most of the young single males were under the age of 40 and working, living, and playing as if each day was their last. The city was young and offered a wealth of opportunities as well as entertainment.

When women came to the town, they improved themselves and their community by establishing clubs around literature, social needs, art, civic beautification, churches, and schools. Among these were the Homer Club, St. John's Episcopal Sewing Club, Mountain View Methodist Ladies' Aide Society, and Junior League. Many women's groups met community needs by establishing food and clothing programs for the poor and by forming classes in civics and English for new immigrants. Civic clubs reached beyond the neighborhood and into every level of society, making Butte a richer community.

The past has been kept alive in Uptown Butte in many ways, and it has merged with the present, particularly in relation to the cosmopolitan feel of the community, the built environment, and the citizens' endeavors to preserve and revitalize the historic portion of the city. Butte certainly has strip malls, chain stores, fast-food restaurants, and coffee kiosks like any place else. However, it also has old-style men's apparel stores where owners know their customers' sizes, furniture stores that have been operated by the same families for a century, welcoming bookstores where clerks can recommend a book that is a perfect fit, and cafés where the coffee is on the table before the patron sits down.

Dorothy Kilgallen made an interesting observation in a 1953 *Good Housekeeping* article, "Butte is a place with a rough past, a sedate present, and probably a genteel future." And that is where it is now—a city that has become genteel, where education is held dear and preservation of local history is a priority, where a democratic philosophy is honored and practiced, where tolerance of others' beliefs and lifestyles is the norm, and where people enjoy the fruits of a garden with family and friends. Butte is a community that cherishes its past, including its ethnic diversity, and it comes together at every opportunity: Chinese New Year, St. Patrick's Day, the Fourth of July, Evel Knievel Days, Irish and Celtic festivals, and Eastern Orthodox holidays, not to mention more traditional times like Christmas, Easter, Thanksgiving, and New Year's Day.

Today Butte's face tells a story without words. The city is much brighter than it was in the past: greenery gives it a healthy look, and mining plays a lesser role than it once did. However, one can still see the scars inflicted upon it by decades of mining and visualize the struggle necessary to ascend the hill and lay claim to its riches. Residential and industrial structures commingle to this day. The massive headframes stand testament to the sheer determination that was required to erect them, let alone descend a mile deep into the ground. These headframes are symbolic of Butte's fortitude, of people whose "can do" attitude has never failed to meet a major challenge head on. Butte has experienced remarkable prosperity and has found comfort in the richness of its heritage and the strength of its citizens.

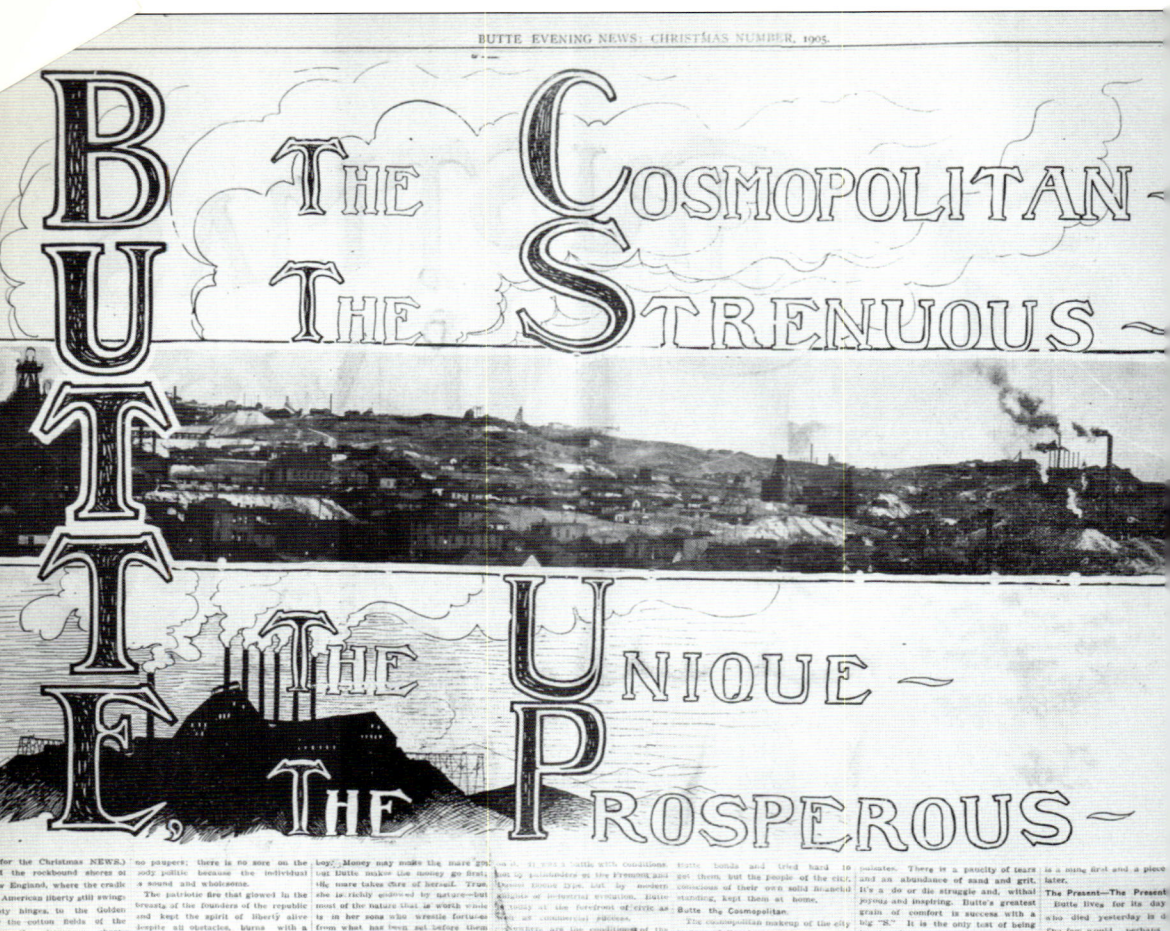

This is the actual image used as the title for Thomas F. Rooney's article in the 1905 *Butte Evening News*. The heading and the article, which covered the entire page, inspired the themes presented in this book.

One

Butte the Cosmopolitan

The cosmopolitan makeup of the city is one of its strangest features. For a town of its size it has as big a representation of citizens from every corner of the earth as the big city of New York. There are Irish, English, French, Scottish, Finns, Norwegians, Swedes, Danes, Germans, Poles, Manx, Canadian, Mexican, Indians, Persians, Welsh, Jews, Spanish, Swiss, Huns Belgians, Dutch, Turks, Romanians, Italians, Greeks, Serbians, Russians, Assyrians, Afghans, Negroes, Chinese, Icelanders, and fifty-one varieties of Austrians.

—Thomas F. Rooney, *Butte Evening News*

Immigrants brought with them a wealth of cultural heritage from their native countries. Old World flavor permeated the neighborhoods and influenced all elements of Butte's many ethnic communities: schools, churches, stores, restaurants, saloons, and boardinghouses. Ethnic groups were impassioned to preserve their culinary favorites the way their ancestors prepared them and to practice the customs and traditions they knew so well. They also brought with them deep loyalty and the biases they grew up with. Ethnic solidarity was renowned. The Irish did not cotton to the English who did not cotton to the French who did not cotton to the Germans. And yet, despite their pronounced ethnic differences, the people of Butte knew that to succeed in ways other mining communities did not, they had to stick together, put aside biases, find common ground, and work to make this new home a successful one. The cosmopolitan essence of Butte did not come easily, but the significant rise of Butte from a struggling mining camp to a metropolitan city made for developments that last to this day. Most notable are the sturdy buildings that still define Uptown Butte as the largest Historic Landmark District in the country. As other cities tear down the old to erect the new, Butte has retained many of its historic structures that today are seeing new life. Through battles that were waged among those who became its loyal residents and those who would exploit its resources, Butte the Cosmopolitan survives and sits proudly in a valley of the Rocky Mountains.

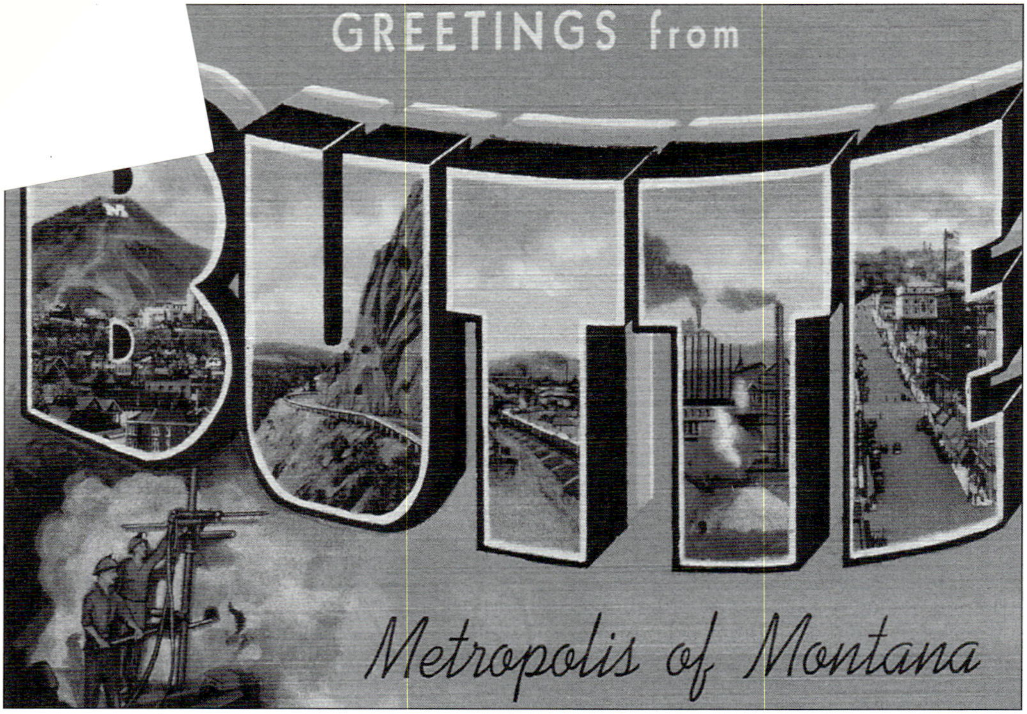

GREETINGS from BUTTE *Metropolis of Montana*

Butte was a melting pot, a delicious mix of immigrants from every corner of the world. Immigrants brought with them their own customs and idiosyncrasies, and they usually resided in very distinct, ethnic neighborhoods that were like little countries in and of themselves. The Irish resided mainly in the Dublin Gulch and Corktown. On the East Side was Finntown. McQueen was home to Slovenians, Austrians, and Croatians. The Cornish lived in Walkerville. The Welsh, Scandinavians, and African Americans lived below the center of town, and the Lebanese neighborhood was called Syrian Colony. Nearly every nationality in the world was represented.

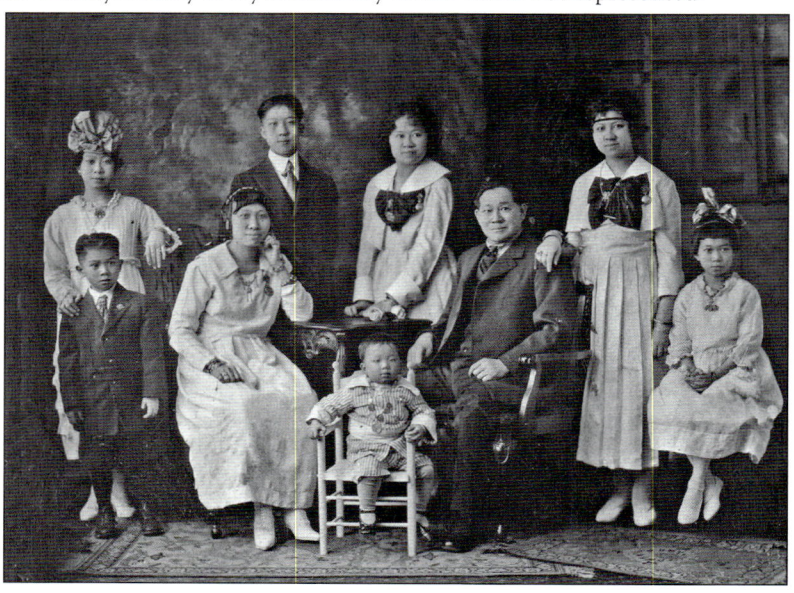

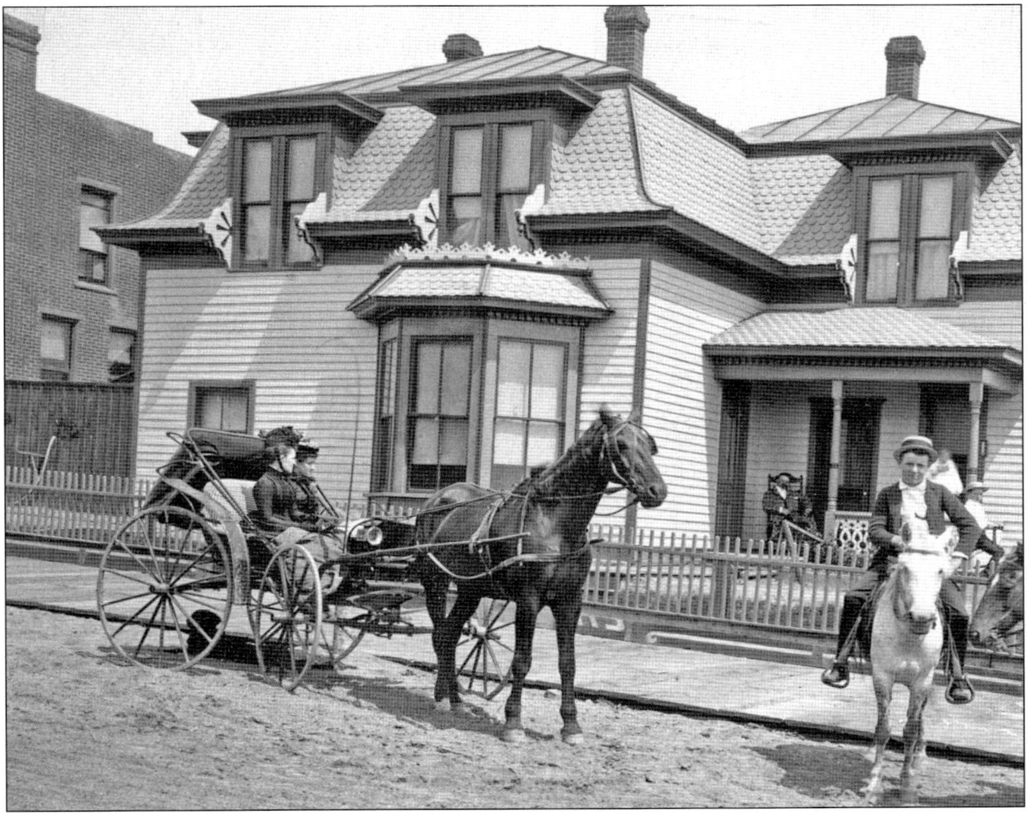

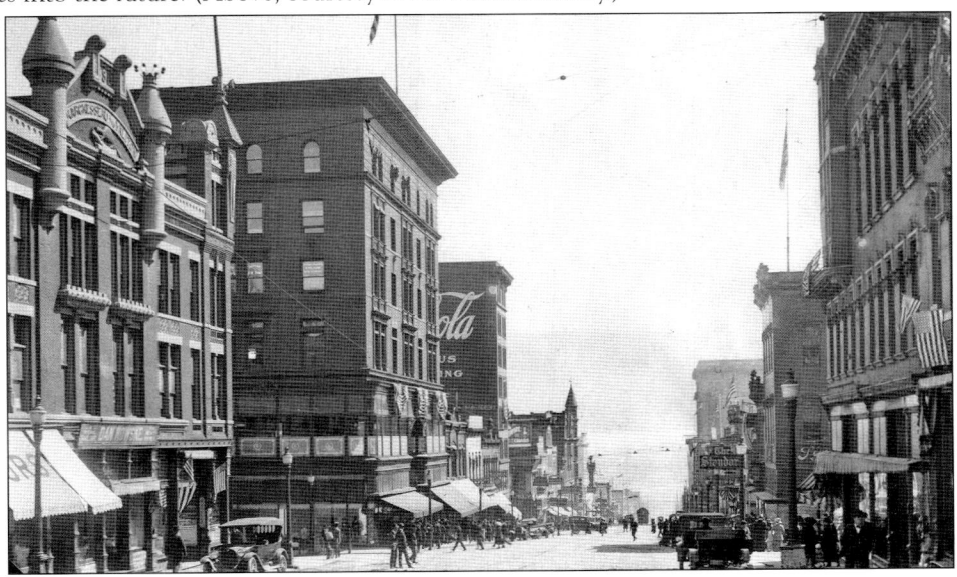

The Corette family home shown above is an example of Butte's ascent from mining camp to metropolitan city. Many homes were furnished with the latest technology: electric lights, range, and clothes washer. Such appliances and advances were harbingers of big changes in women's lives into the future. (Above, courtesy of the Corette family.)

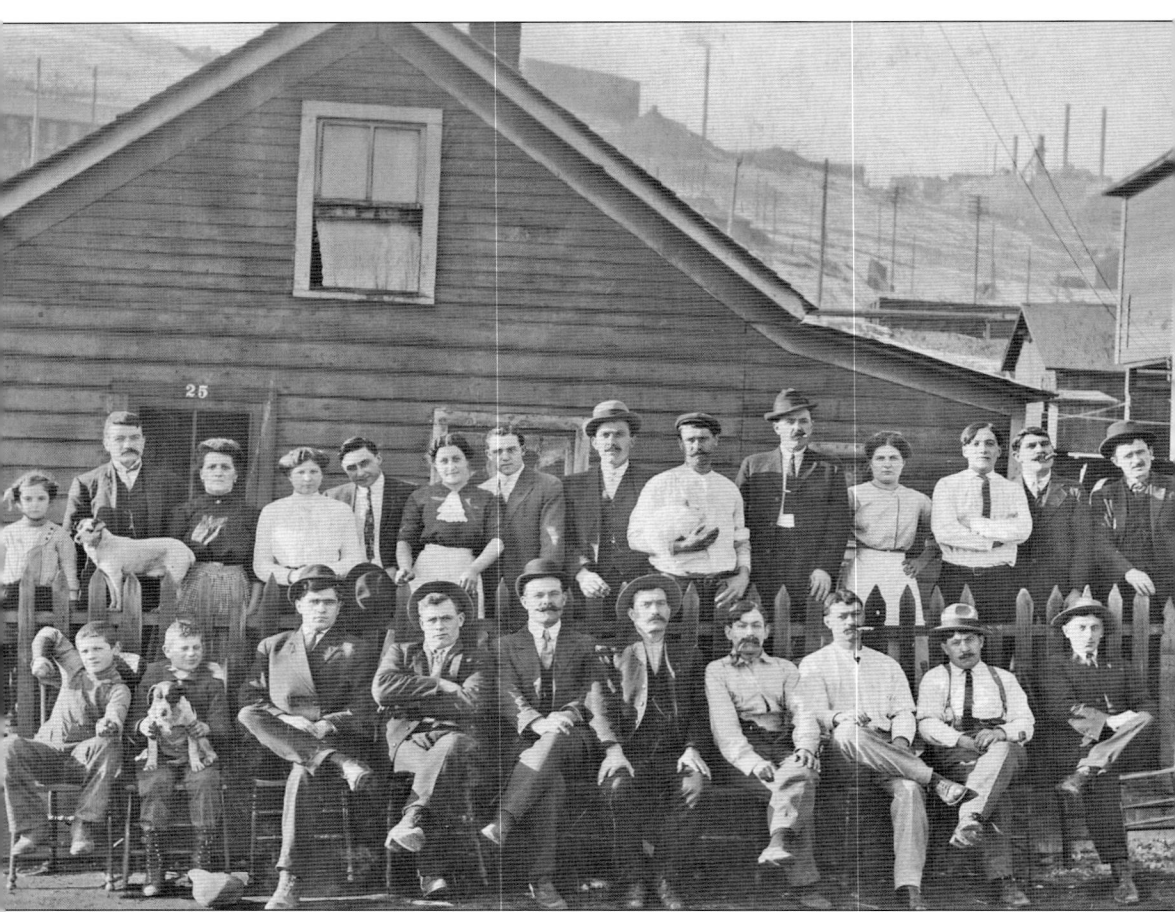

The Irish in Butte held the record for sheer volume. David Emnons, in *The Butte Irish: Class and Ethnicity in an American Mining Town, 1875–1925*, noted, "Nowhere do all of the factors involved in the development of an Irish working class in the West converge as they do in the copper-mining center of Butte. In population, production, and size of workforce, Butte had no rivals among mining cities anywhere in the world, and it was one of the most overwhelmingly Irish cities in the United States. Twenty-five percent of the residents of Silver Bow County were either Irish-born or the children of Irish-born—a higher percentage of Irish than in any other American city at the turn of the century." Irish Catholic families tended to be large and close-knit. Grandparents had almost as much influence as parents did on children's lives.

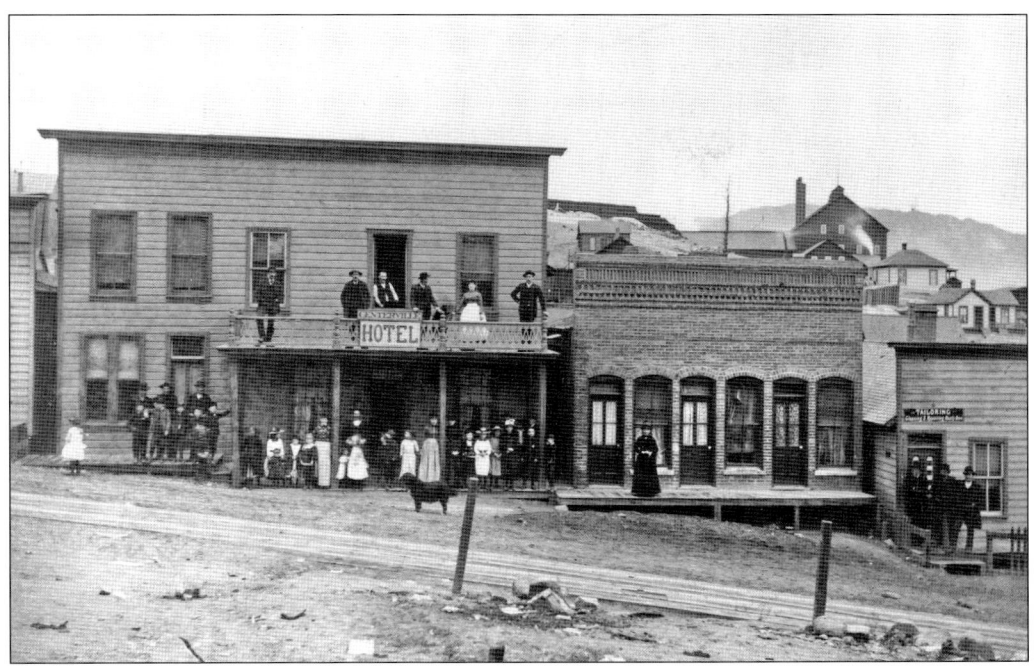

The majority of the Irish lived on the face of the Hill, close to where they worked. They soon adapted to their new country and became political and economic leaders. The flair for drama and passion won the Irish their place in both local and state politics, and they held tight to the reins of political power for decades. Considering the vast population of Irishmen, there was little doubt that come Election Day an Irish candidate would succeed. The Irish also dominated occupations in firefighting and law enforcement. The firehouse in the photograph below has been home to the Butte-Silver Bow Archives for 28 years.

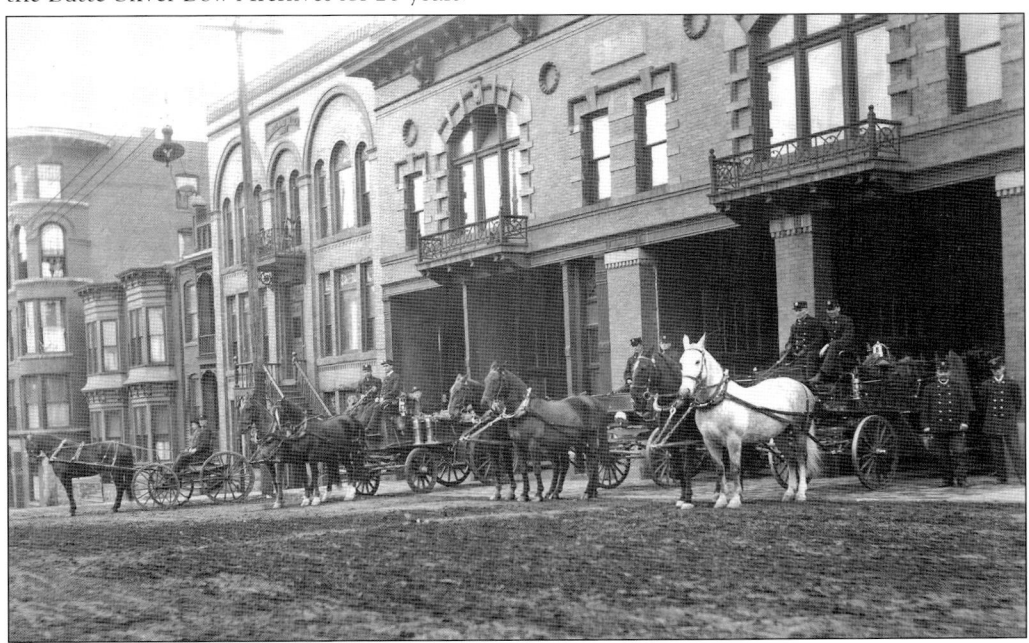

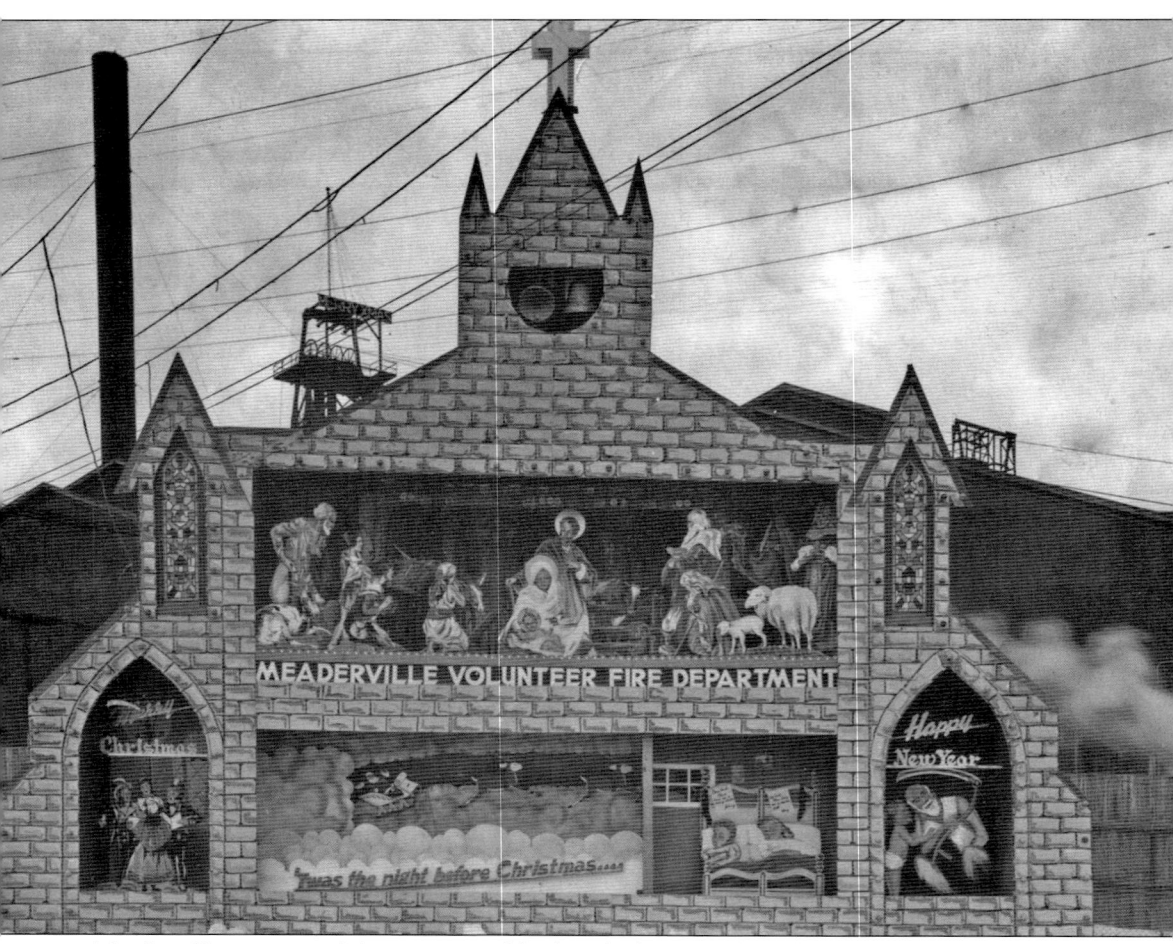

Meaderville was one of the many neighborhoods that were heavily populated with mainly one nationality—in this case, Italian. Located on the East Side, Meaderville was known for its restaurants whose cuisine spanned the globe, exciting nightlife, and grappo, a homemade Italian wine. Meaderville boasted beautiful Christmas displays that were constructed by members of the Meaderville Volunteer Fire Department. The life-size displays are legendary, and today they are seeing a resurgence through the efforts of area high school students. Although the neighborhood no longer exists, having succumbed to open-pit mining in 1955, former residents of Meaderville are faithful to their legacy and hold an annual reunion to share memories, laughter, and food. (Courtesy of the World Museum of Mining.)

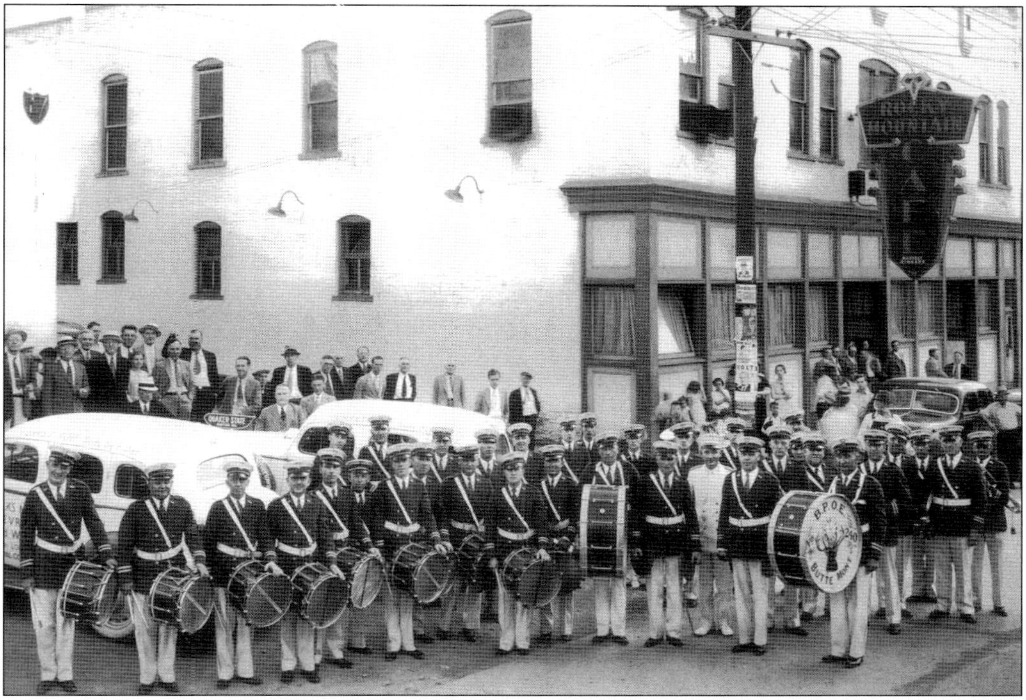

One of the most famous restaurants was the Rocky Mountain Café in Meaderville, owned by Teddy Traparish. The Butte Mines' Band is seen standing in front of the café. A local favorite, Traparish became a world-renowned restaurateur who prided himself on knowing all aspects of his trade, from selecting the meat and produce that was served to personally training his waitstaff. The café was the subject of numerous national publications throughout the years. Traparish was well known for his love of Cadillacs; he purchased his 51st Cadillac shortly before he died in 1971.

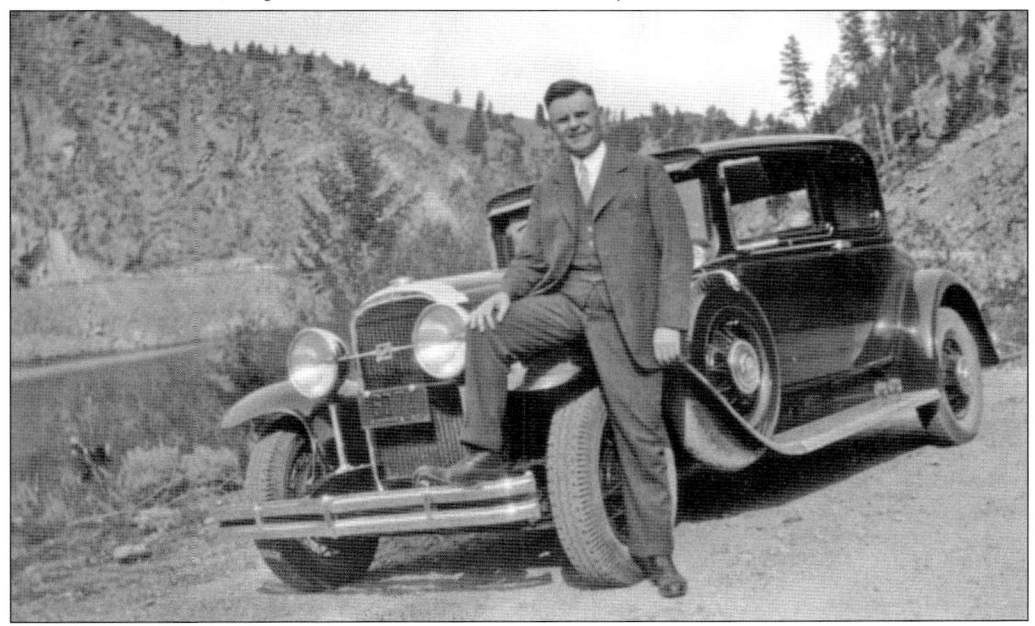

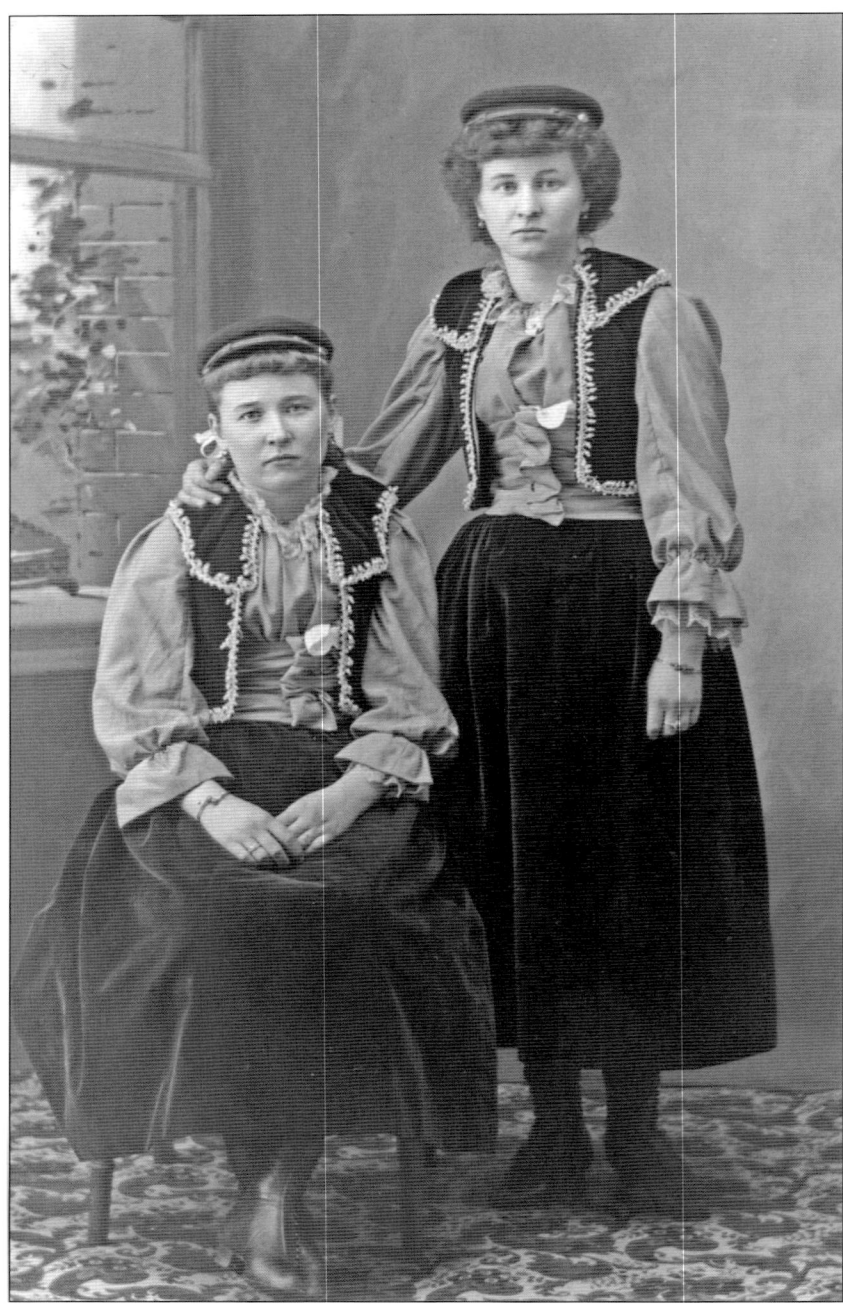

Scandinavian residents at one time boasted a total of 6,000 people. They lived mainly in South Butte and Finntown, which were on the East Side. The logging, rigging, and iron shipbuilding expertise of the Scandinavians was much needed to frame and bolster the mine shafts, rig the ropes to hoist the men and ore, and build the steel gallus frames. They also worked in various other capacities throughout the city. The Scandinavians supported five fraternal lodges to keep alive their language, heritage, literature, and music, but they also learned quickly to adapt to the quirks of other nationalities.

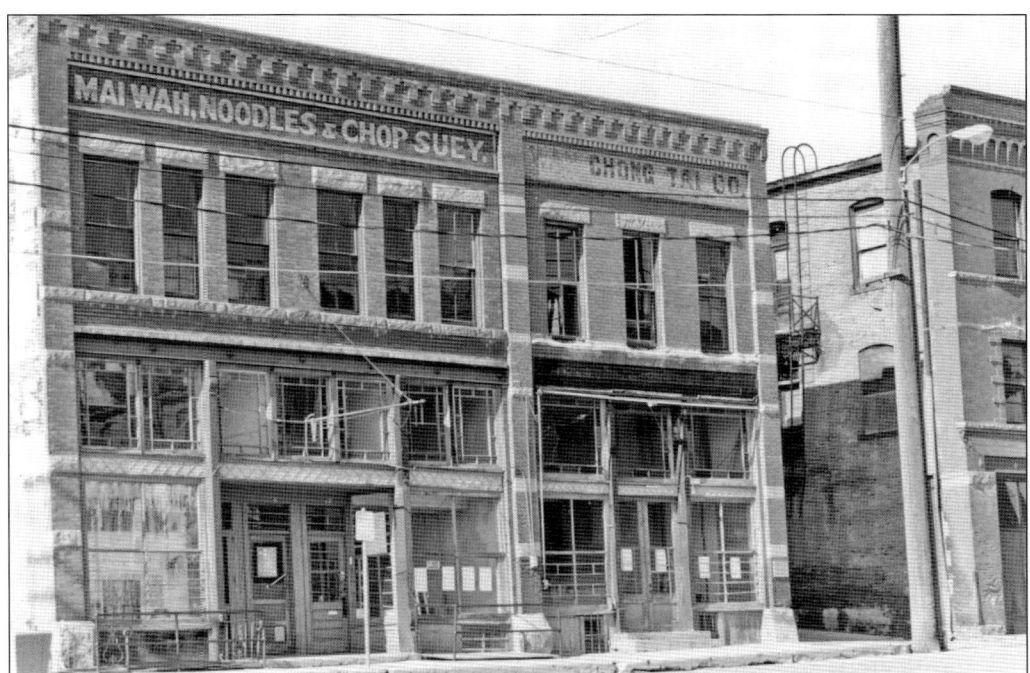

Butte's Chinese settled in the central business district, where an active Chinatown thrived in the early 1890s. Chinatown was home to herb shops, noodle parlors, and laundries. Underground opium dens that could be reached via tunnels were rumored to be plentiful under the alleys. Although the early buildings that made up Chinatown no longer exist, the Mai Wah Noodle Parlor, the Wah Chong Tai Company, and the Pekin Noodle Parlor all reflect the importance of the Chinese population in Butte. The Mai Wah Society has put a crisper look on the face of the noodle parlor, and the building is now a museum of Chinese artifacts.

Butte received a black eye in the 1890s when the unions placed a general boycott on Chinese and Japanese residents. Facing fears that by working for lower wages they would steal jobs from others, Chinese and Japanese residents were relentlessly discriminated against. They were taxed higher than people of other ethnic groups were; they experienced intimidation, physical assault, and sometimes death; and they faced national exclusion laws that were enacted to try to entice them into leaving the country. Despite the discrimination, approximately 1,000 Chinese lived in Butte in the early 1900s. (Courtesy of the National Archives of the United States.)

BOYCOTT

A General Boycott has been declared upon all CHINESE and JAPANESE Restaurants, Tailor Shops and Wash Houses by the

Silver Bow Trades and Labor Assembly

All Friends and Sympathizers of Organized Labor will assist us in this fight against the lowering Asiatic standards of living and of morals.

AMERICA vs. ASIA
Progress vs. Retrogression

Are the considerations involved.

BY ORDER OF
Silver Bow Trades and Labor Assembly.

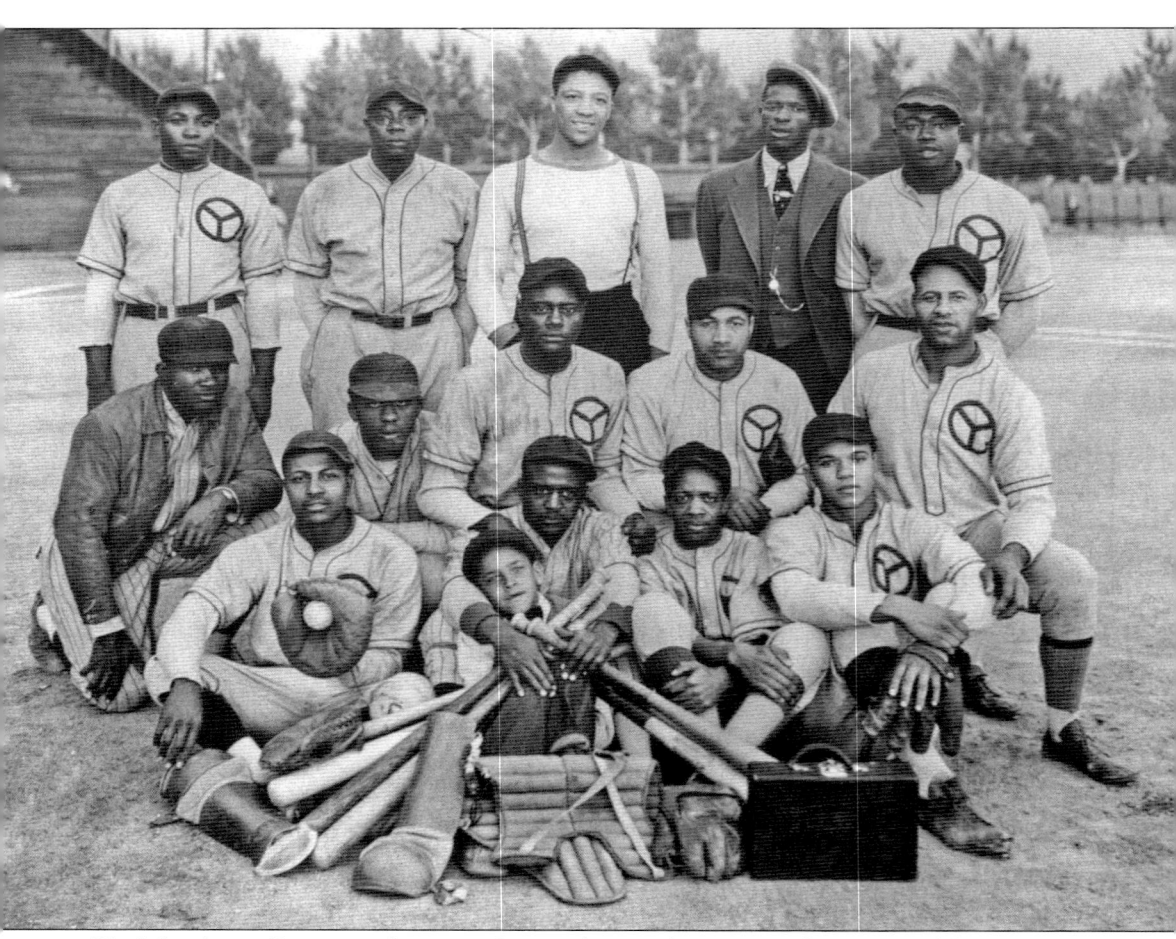

Black families in Butte were from very diverse places such as New York, Boston, Alabama, Georgia, and Mississippi. The highly educated Duncan family provided podiatry and medical care and education to many Butte families. The black families from Camp Carolyn just east of the crest of the Continental Divide provided timber to the underground mines. The black community also organized a baseball team called the Colored Giants that played in the Butte Mines League.

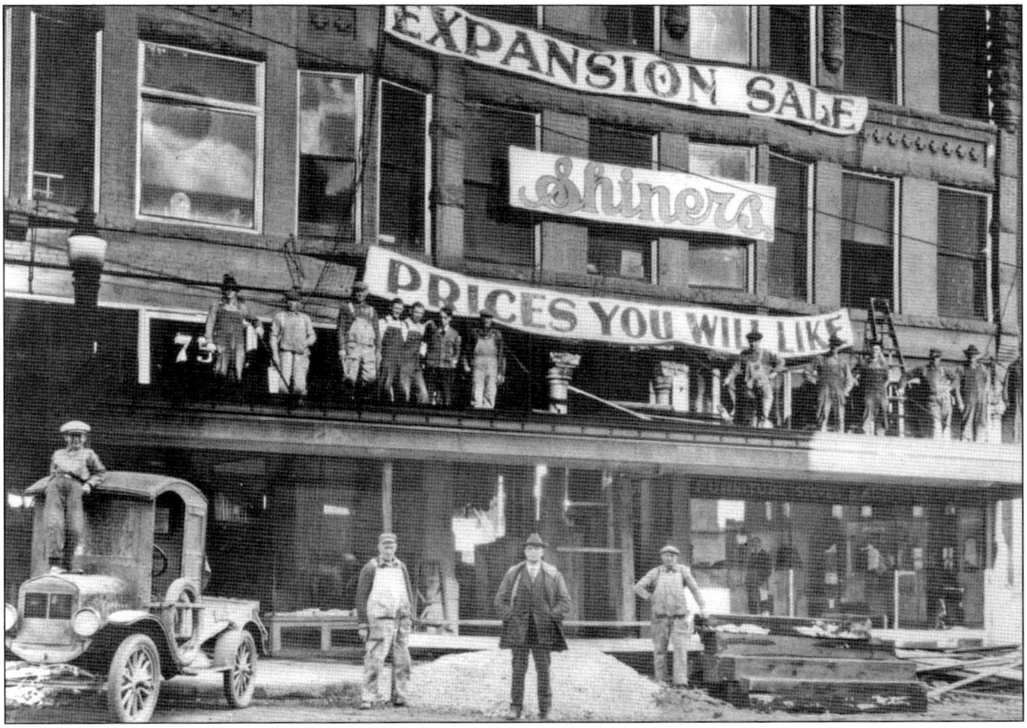

Butte's Jewish community generally worked in the service industries that supported the throngs of miners. Many of these businesses, such as Wein's Men's Store and Rudolph's Furniture Store, still exist today and proudly provide the same services their ancestors espoused. Another of those businesses, Shiner's Furniture, opened its doors in 1915 and would become the largest furniture business between the Twin Cities and Spokane. The building is currently undergoing renovation.

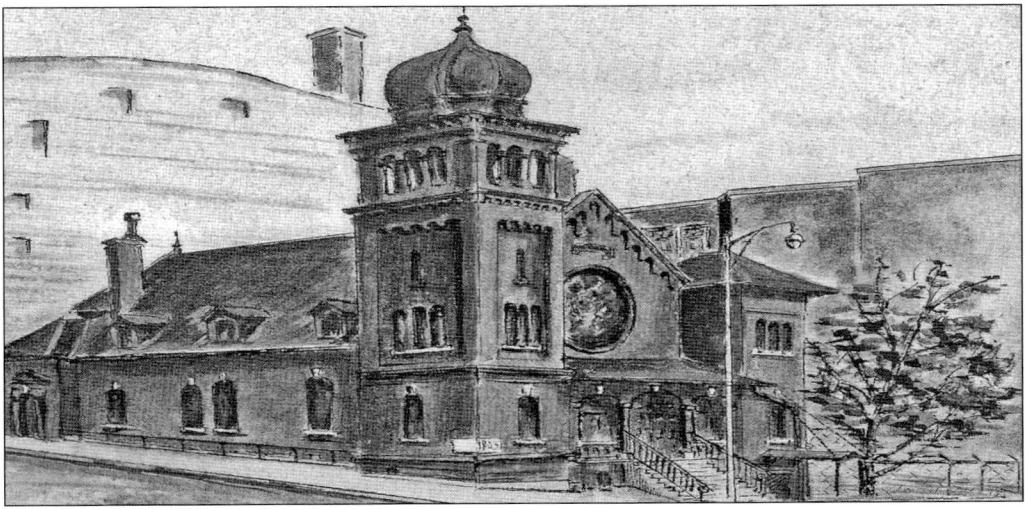

The Jewish community built the B'nai Israel Synagogue, located at the corner of Washington and Galena Streets, in 1903. The beautiful facility with its onion dome roof, square corner bell tower, ornately corbelled front gable end, and rosette windows remains the home of the Jewish community today. (Courtesy of B'nai Israel Congregation.)

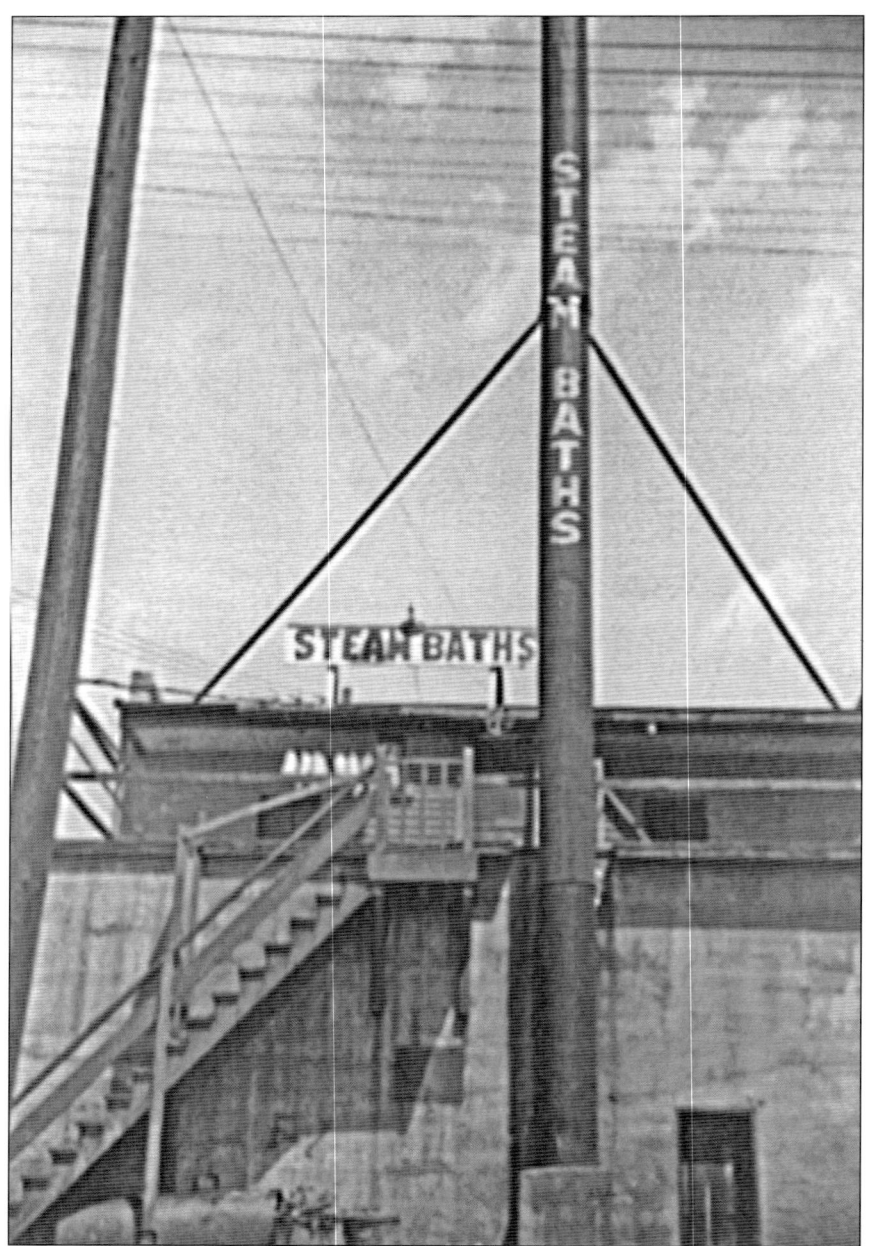

Finlanders formed a strong, long-lived enclave on Butte's East Side. The Finns were powerful labor people. They built a Finnish Lutheran church and an ethnic hall to hold meetings and social functions. The last ethnic institution associated with the Finns is the Helsinki Bar and Sauna. Still standing and in use, the building was constructed between 1890 and 1898. As early as 1915, the proprietors offered Finnish steam baths, a luxury that many people, regardless of ethnicity, enjoyed. Friday night would find as many English and Chinese in the saunas as there were Finns. Finnish or not, the place to be on St. Urho's Day (March 16) is at this location, now humorously called the Helsinki Yacht Club. (Courtesy of the Library of Congress; photograph by Arthur Rosenstein.)

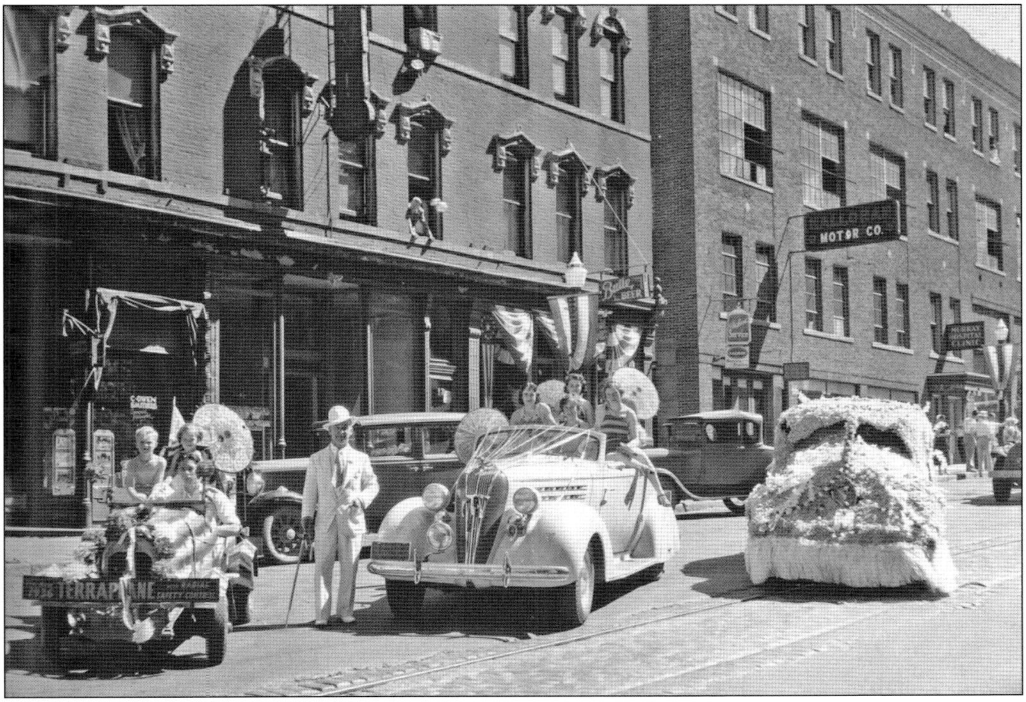

Celebrations were divided among nationalities, although most groups took part in one another's festivities. St. Patrick's Day is still celebrated with great fervor. Even for the non-Irish, on St. Patrick's Day everyone plays the part. An annual Chinese New Year parade celebrated in early February is called the Shortest and Loudest Parade in the World. The parade is led by a beautiful 50-foot dragon that was a gift to the people of Montana from the people of Taipei. Although not a major event by Butte standards, Norwegian Independence Day is still acknowledged on May 5 with the raising of the Norwegian flag at the courthouse, where camaraderie is apparent and Norwegian women pass out delectable cookies.

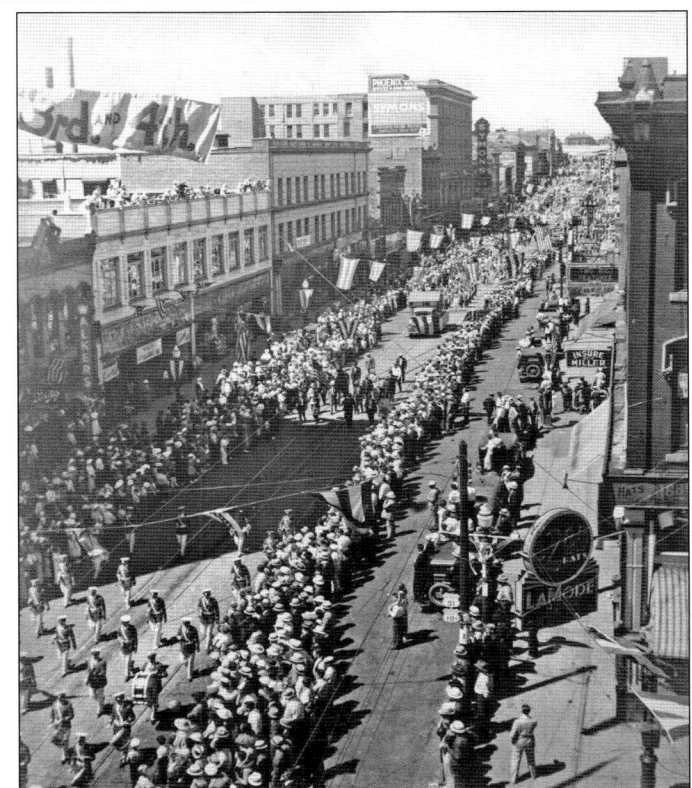

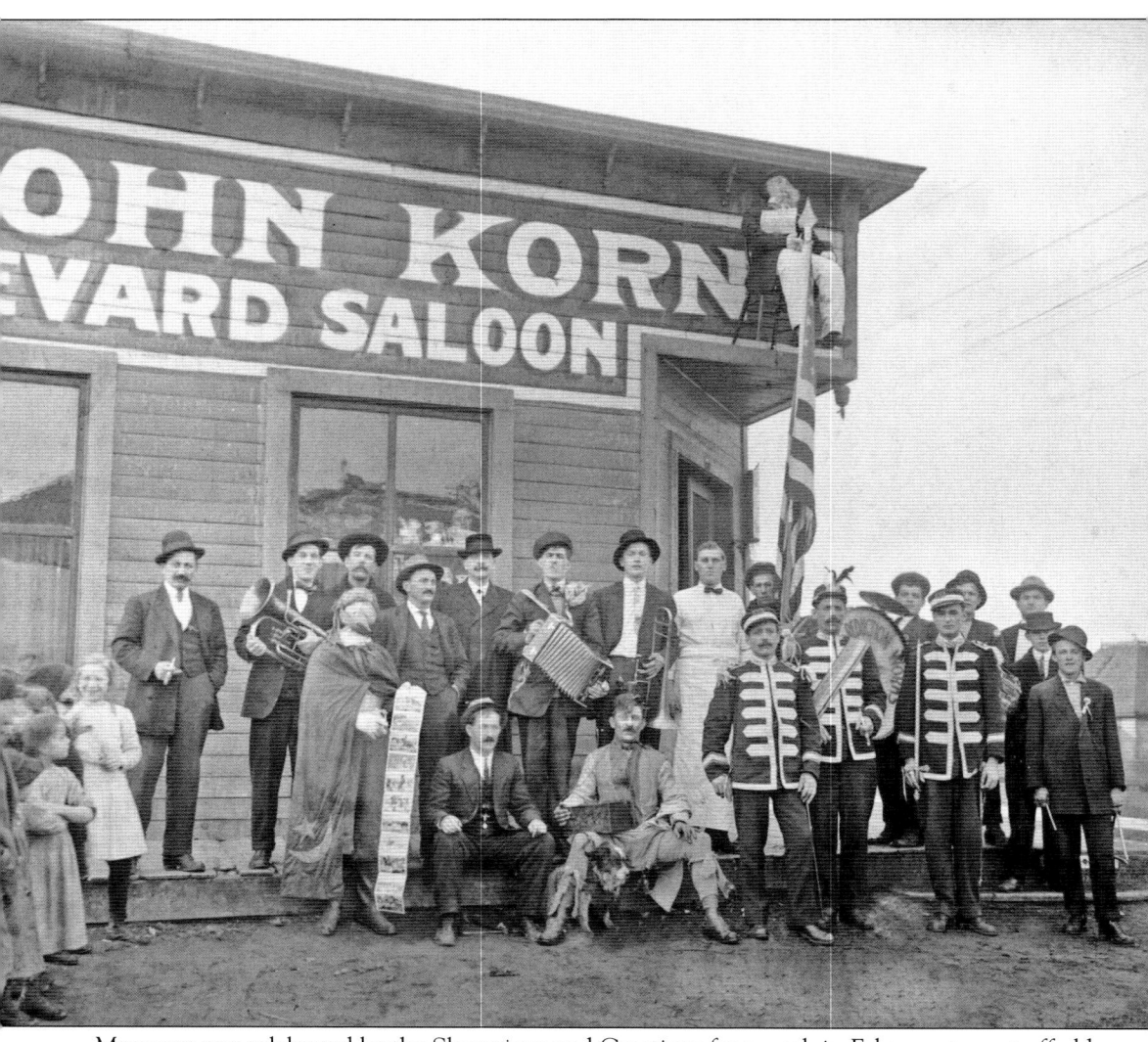

Mesopust was celebrated by the Slovenians and Croatians for a week in February to cast off old fears, grudges, and misunderstandings. It was a time for socializing, storytelling, eating sarma and kielbasa sausage, dancing, and singing. Non-Slavic people joined the celebration, making it another all-Butte event. The week's festivities culminated with a trial of the Mesopust, a straw-filled effigy that was the evil embodiment of hard luck and hard times. At the trial, the Mesopust would be found guilty, and a joyous parade would lead to the burning of the effigy, a harbinger of a good fortune for the coming year.

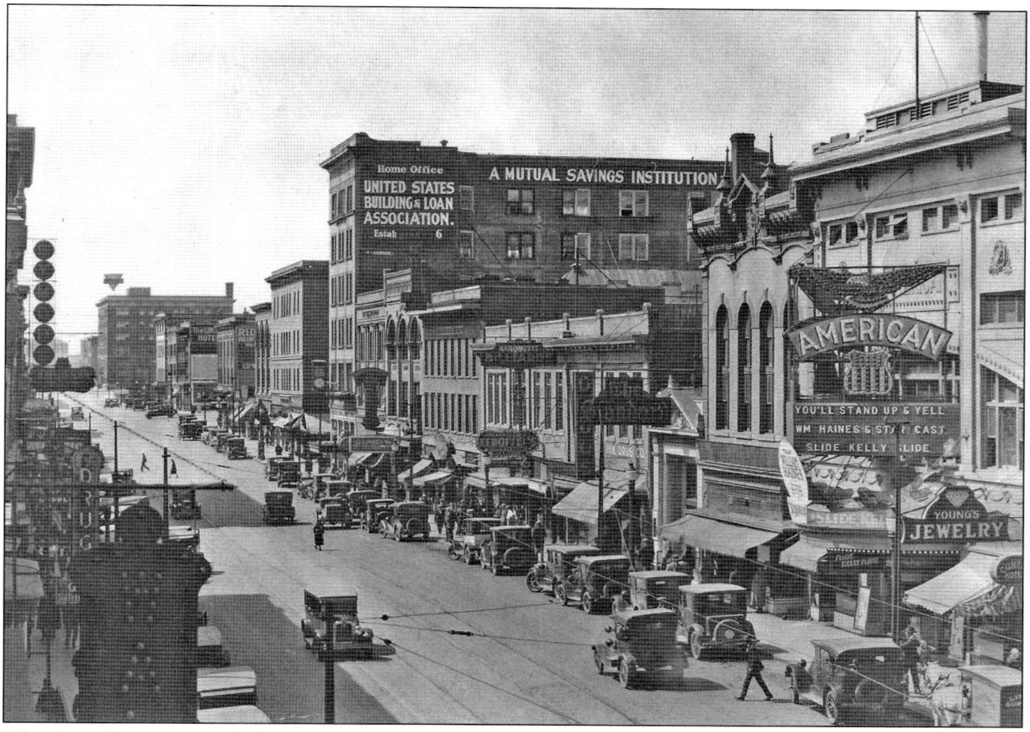

The last four years of the 19th century contributed significantly to the cosmopolitan aura of Uptown Butte. When Butte became the world's premier copper producer, the city endeavored to create architecture to match its status. With an eye to the larger world and inspired by the architectural grandeur of larger cities, Butte shed its mining-camp image and metamorphosed into a metropolis. As other places find their pasts shrouded among strip malls and modern edifices, Butte has been able to hold onto much of its turn-of-the-century cosmopolitan appearance: beautiful architecture and intact historic neighborhoods.

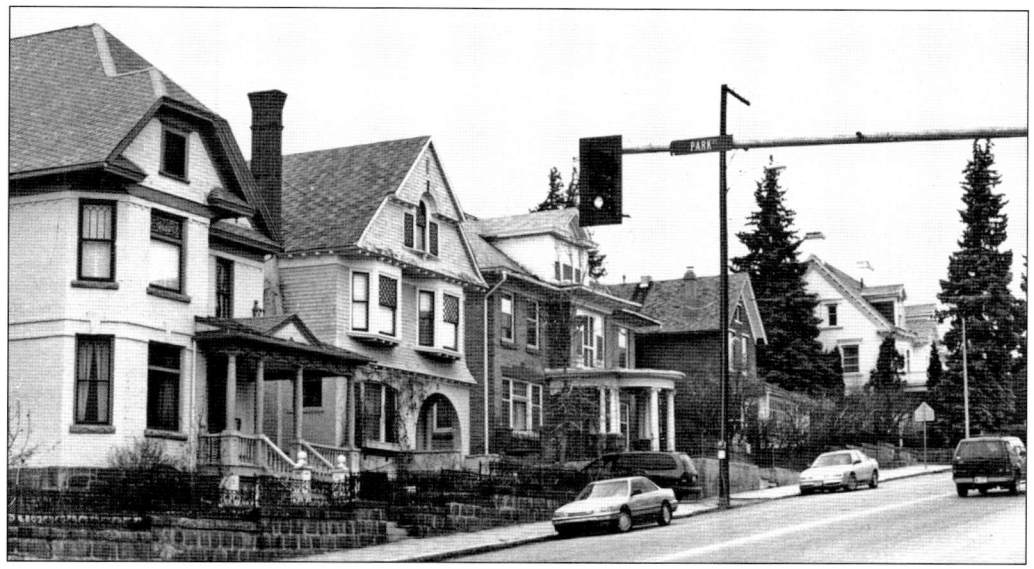

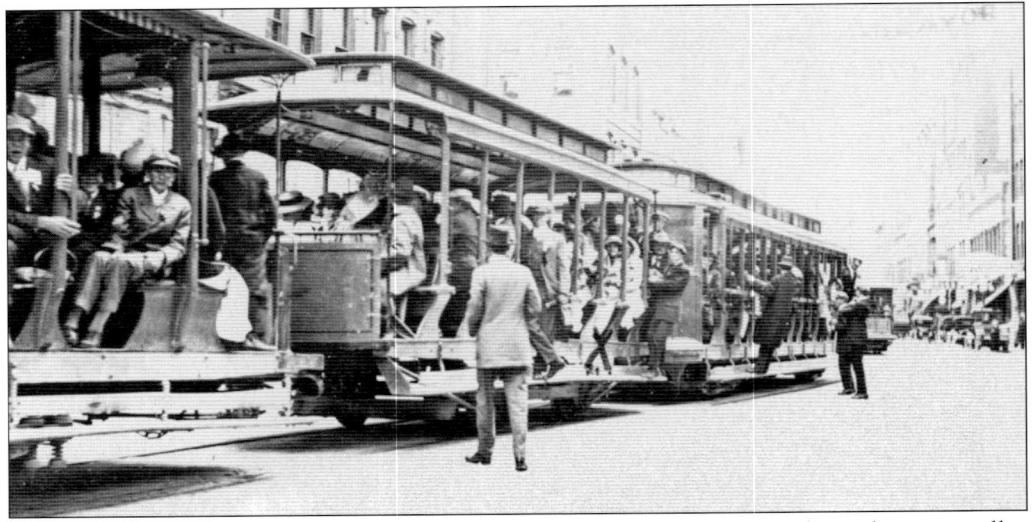

Butte was a symphony of the hustle of urban life and the boisterousness of industrialization: trolley cars rumbling, bells ringing, mine cars banging, and trains roaring and whistling. Smells seeped through the walls and open doorways from restaurants and up through the hollow sidewalks under which were accesses to restaurant and saloon basements where products were stored. Restaurants served every imaginable type of food—Italian pastas and raviolis, Irish stews, English pasties, Chinese wontons, German strudel, and Mexican chilies and tamales. All of these smells were combined with odors emanating from breweries and taverns, automobile exhaust, and industrial pollution to assault the senses. The cacophony of noises and profusion of odors found in New York City today are reminiscent of Butte at the beginning of the 20th century.

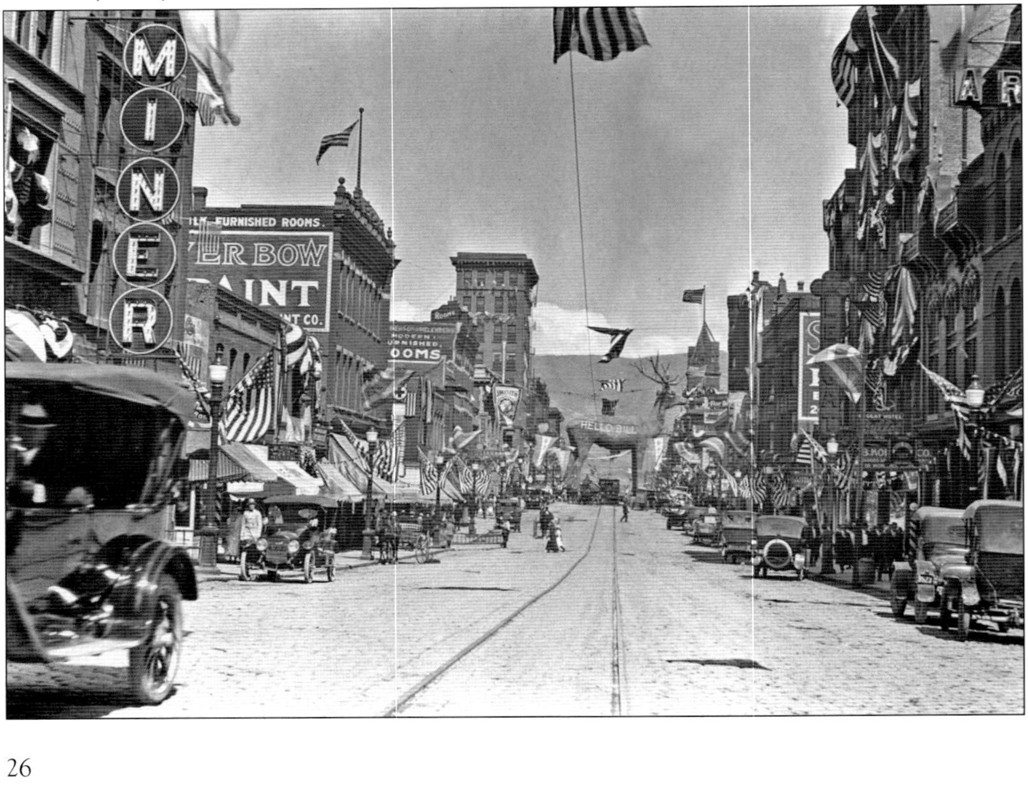

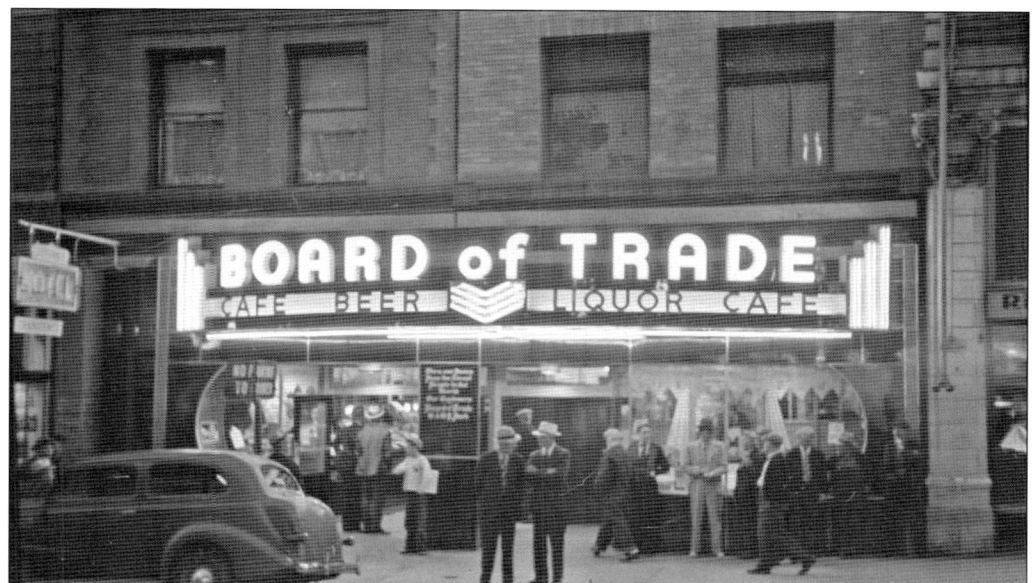

Everyday life was big, bright, bold, exciting, and dangerous. Many businesses in the late 1800s and early 1900s operated 24 hours a day, providing every convenience and vice imaginable. Life for the nearly 100,000 residents of this rough-and-tumble community was not the dream they had imagined, but it was a life they embraced daily with pride and dignity. And they knew how to have fun. After days spent underground with only hard hat lights for illumination, the boys were ready to party. The partying went on all day and all night to accommodate the various work shifts. (Courtesy of the Library of Congress; photograph by Arthur Rosenstein.)

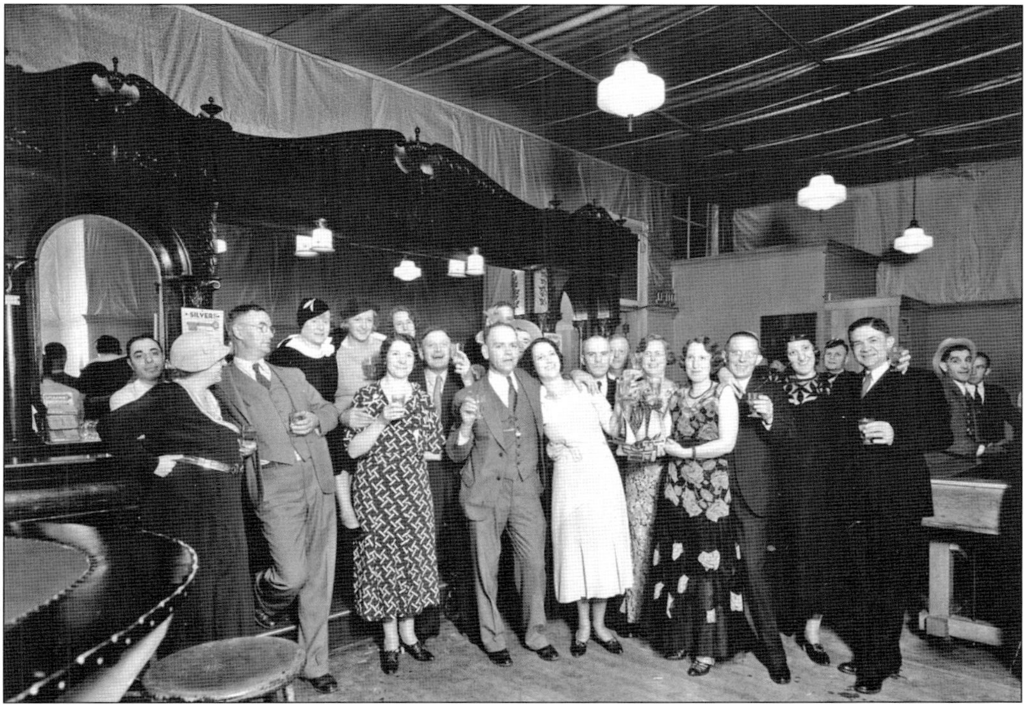

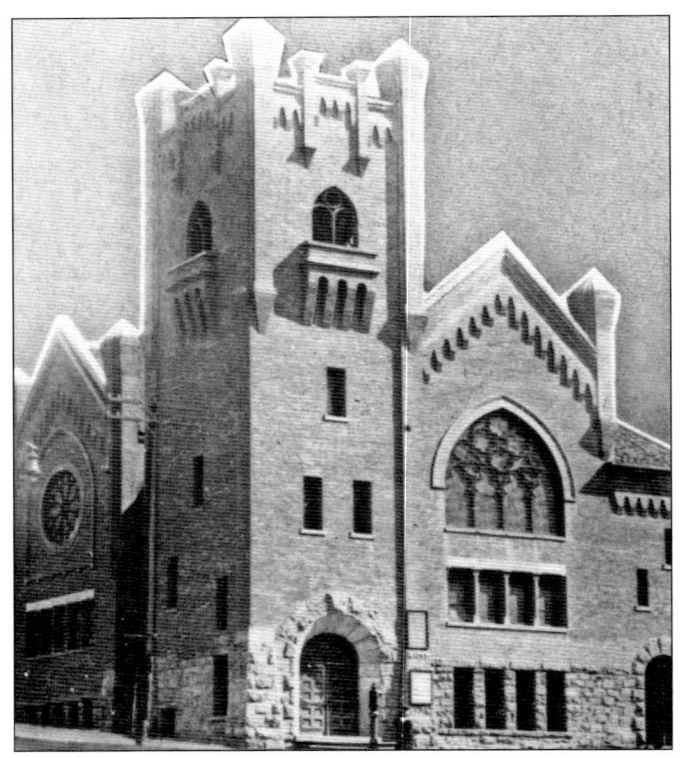

Butte's Uptown commercial area acquired a decidedly late Victorian flavor by the close of the 19th century. H. M. Patterson was Butte's most prominent 19th-century architect, and his work incorporated elements of many late-19th-century revival styles. Patterson set the pace for commercial architecture in Butte, designing at least nine substantial Uptown buildings. The Gothic Revival First Presbyterian Church on West Broadway and the Thornton Hotel on East Broadway are two examples.

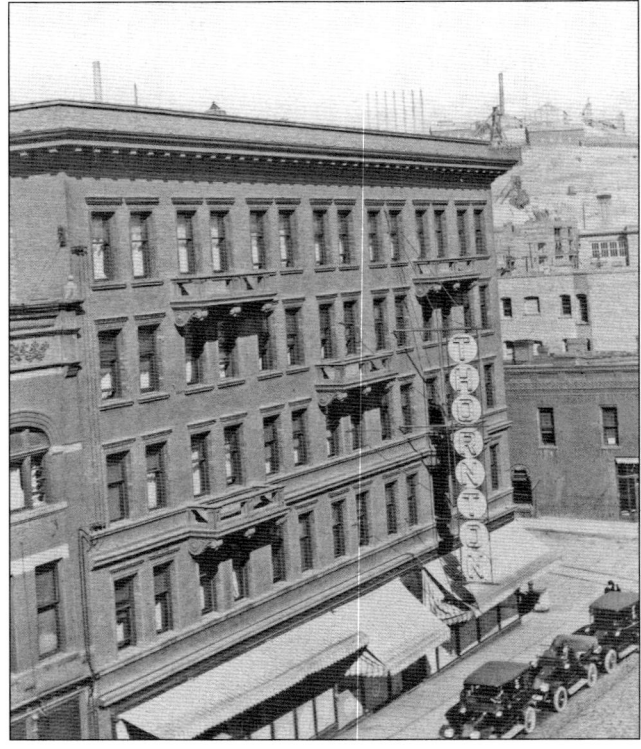

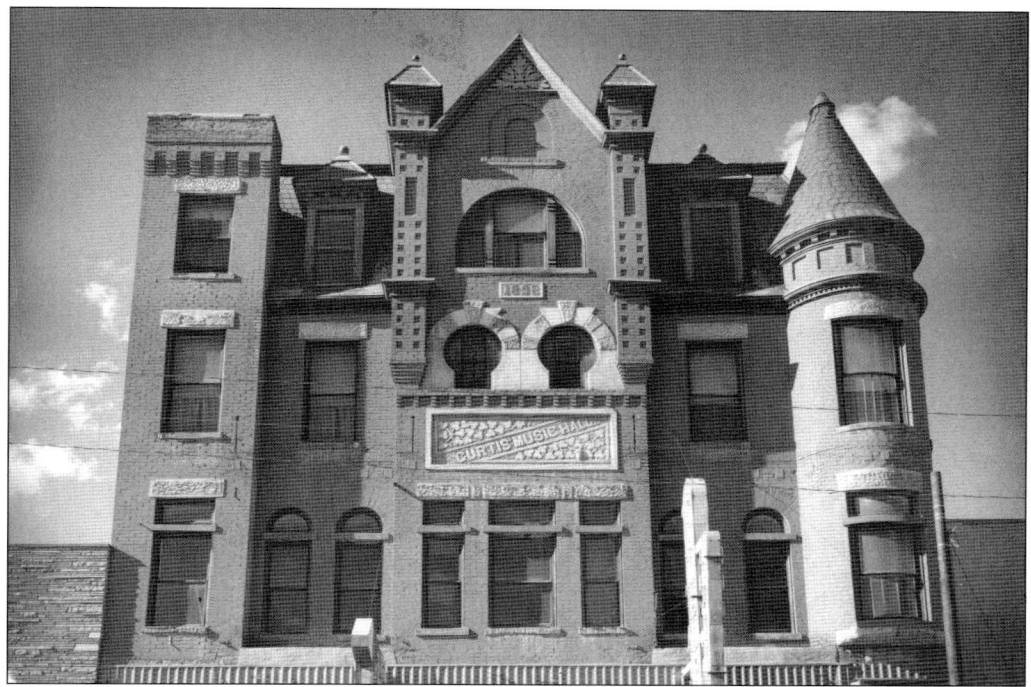

A building permit was issued to Irish-born lawyer and businessman John H. Curtis to erect the Curtis Music Hall in 1892. The design of the building combines gables, turrets, arched and keyhole-shaped windows, carved stone, and decorative metal—one of Butte's most treasured landmarks. It has operated as a music hall, theater, saloon, rooming house, and restaurant. The upper floors of the building are shown above. The first level is shown below.

Carl Rowan operated Gamer's Confectionery from 1944 until 1993 in the Curtis Music Hall. Rowan, a natural entertainer, welcomed everyone with a heartiness and warmth that was legendary. Rowan knew everyone who walked into his establishment, whether he did or not, and he never took payment in hand for his food and services. Rather he had people ring up their own costs and put their money in the cash register. The building today is home of Gamer's Café.

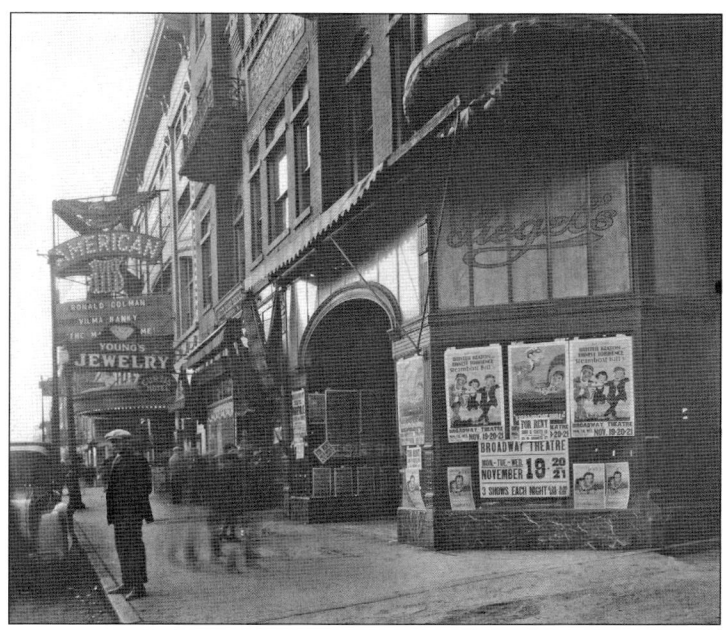

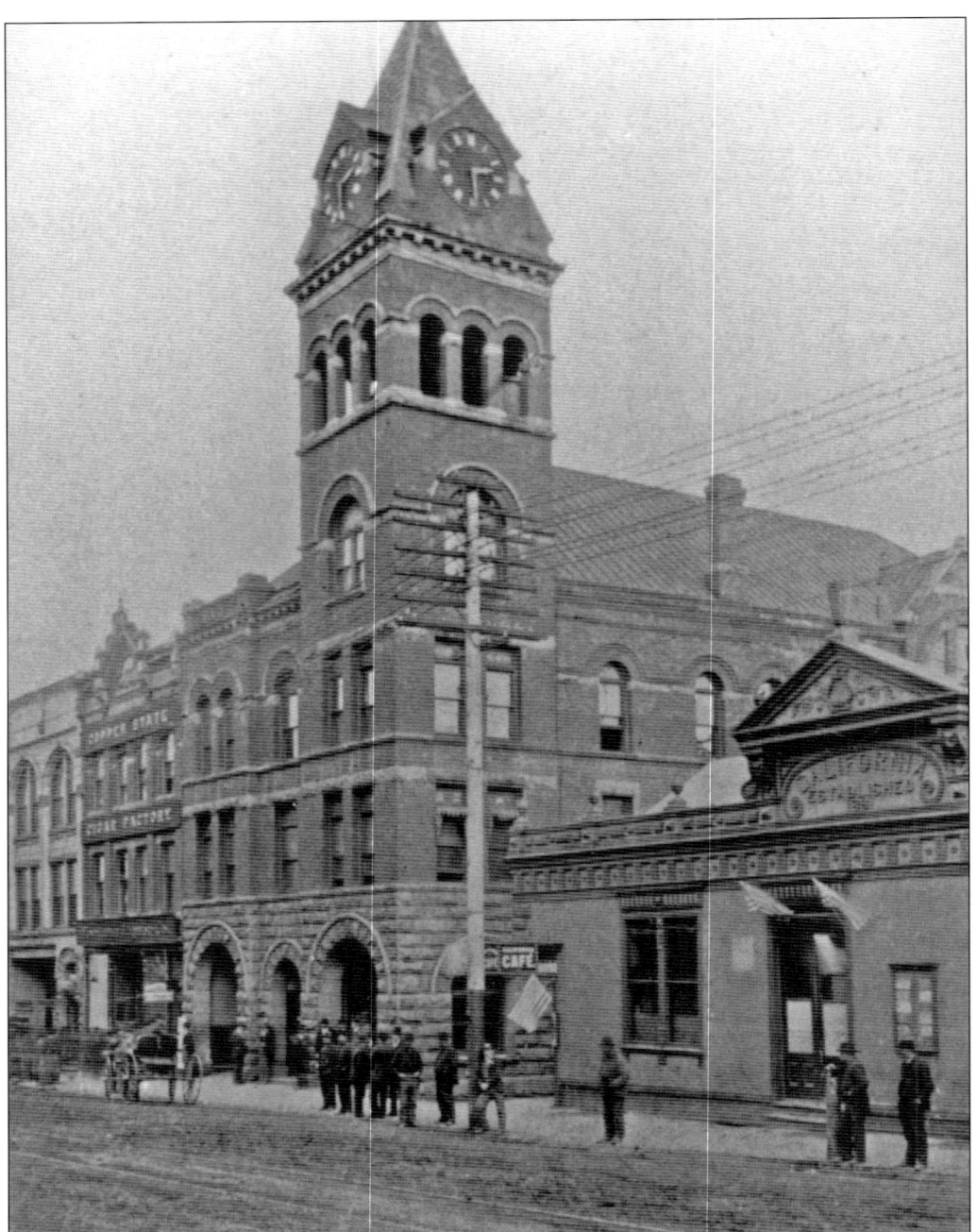

Three late-19th-century buildings that reflect the city's concerted effort to remake its image from a dirty mining camp were the Hennessy Building, the Owsley Block, and Sutton's Broadway Theater. Another impressive Victorian building is Butte's Romanesque-influenced city hall. This three-and-a-half-story building combines a first story of rusticated stone with upper floors of brick, round arches, and a square clock tower. The city government operated from the building from 1891 until 1977, when the city and the county were consolidated. The building now houses medical and legal offices.

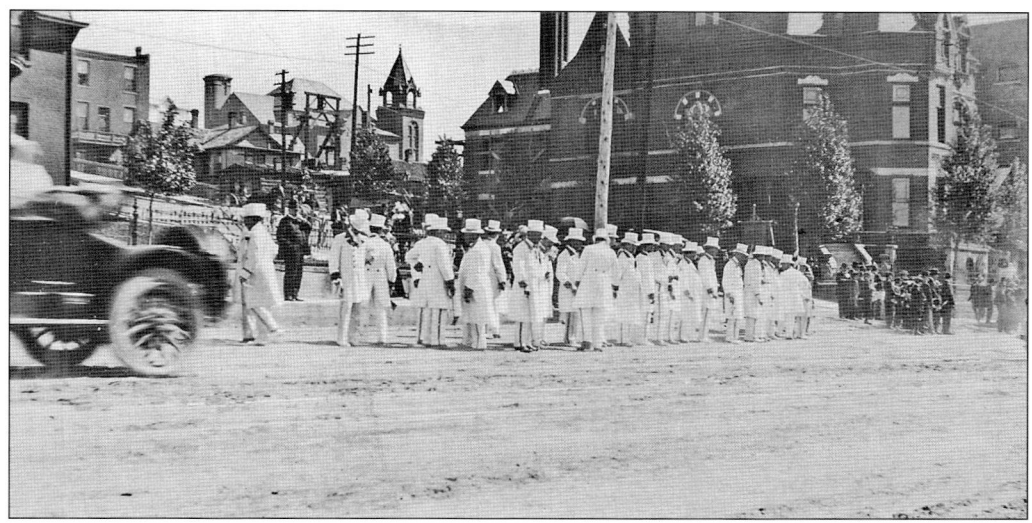

The Copper King Mansion, once the home of William A. Clark, is an example of a Butte neighborhood. It is surrounded by a commercial building to the east, smaller but stately homes to the west, and miners' cottages and a church to the north. The mansion today is a museum and popular bed-and-breakfast. Jerry Calvert in *The Gibraltar* notes, "The copper mines attracted large numbers of workers, making Butte a uniquely cosmopolitan city, an enclave of urban culture and ethnic diversity in an essentially, rural, agricultural state."

The Charles W. Clark Mansion was erected in 1898 by William A. Clark for his son. Reflecting a French chateau, the building was designed by architect Will Aldrich. It is a beautiful two-and-a-half-story mansion that contains 26 rooms and numerous bathrooms. The floors and moldings are hardwood, and there is mahogany paneling on the main floor. The building still stands and is now a public cultural center dedicated to providing arts education and local, regional, and national artist exhibitions.

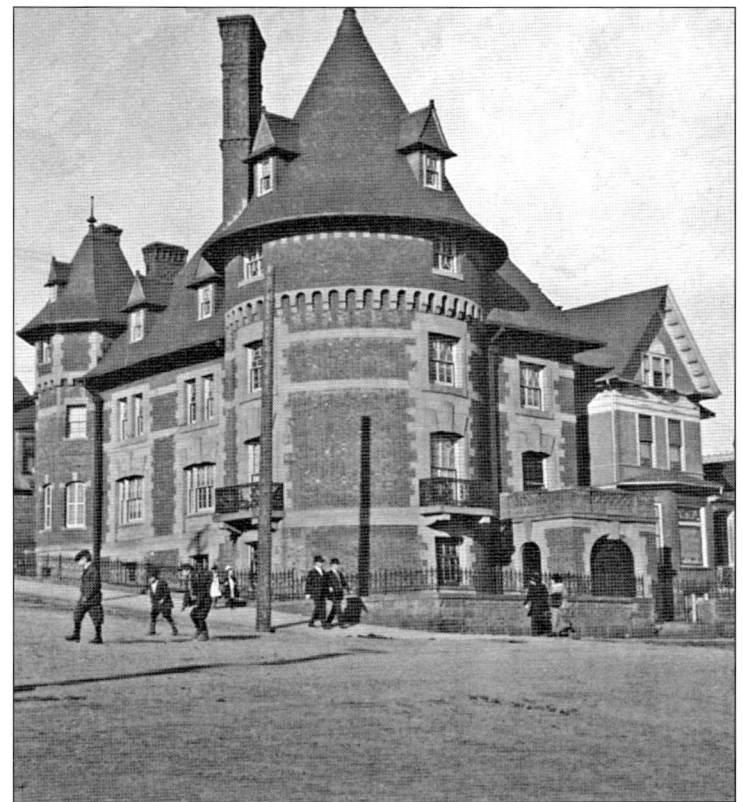

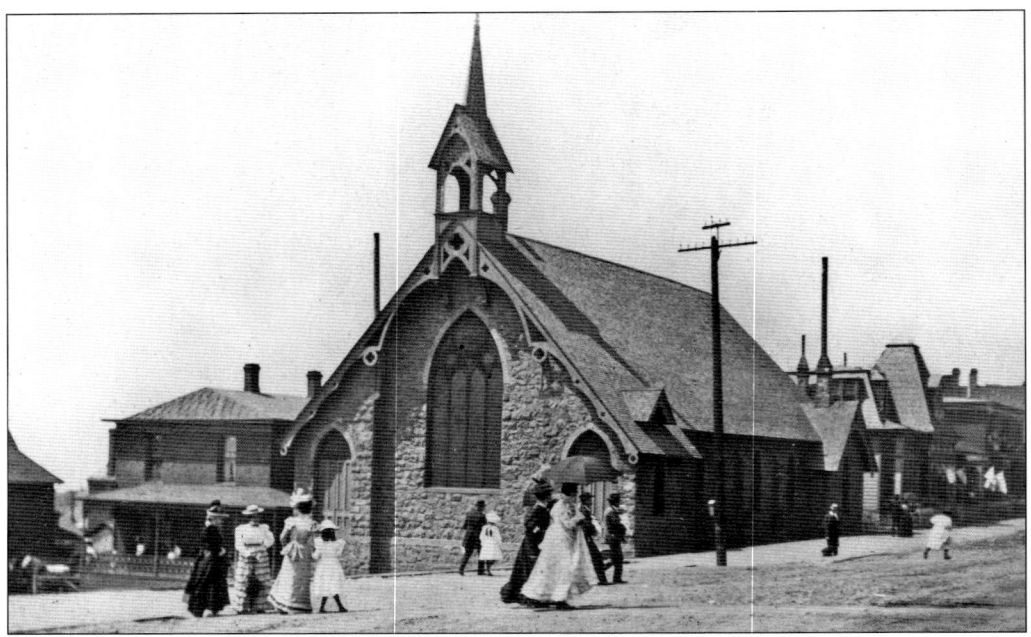

St. John's Episcopal Church is an example of the Norman style of architecture characterized by rounded arches over windows and doorways. The stone church was built in June 1881, but a fire in 1918 completely destroyed the interior. Renovation true to the original design was completed by 1921. St. John's Church today, although altered somewhat during its renovation and expansions, is much as it appears in the above photograph. The photograph below is that of a 1900 Episcopalian confirmation class.

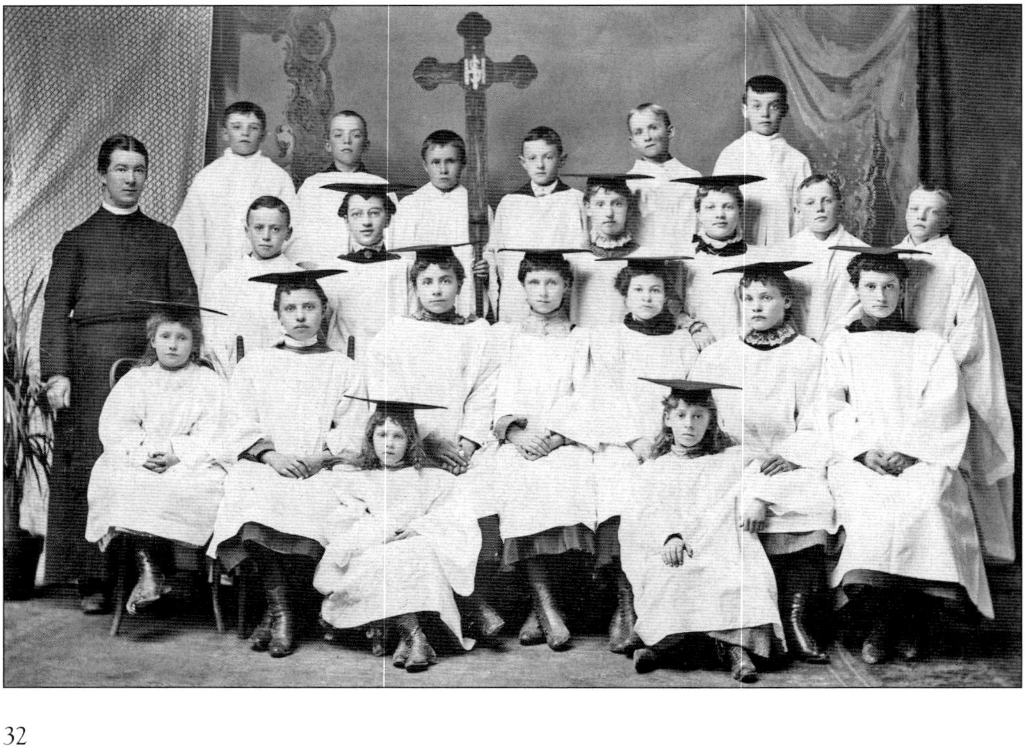

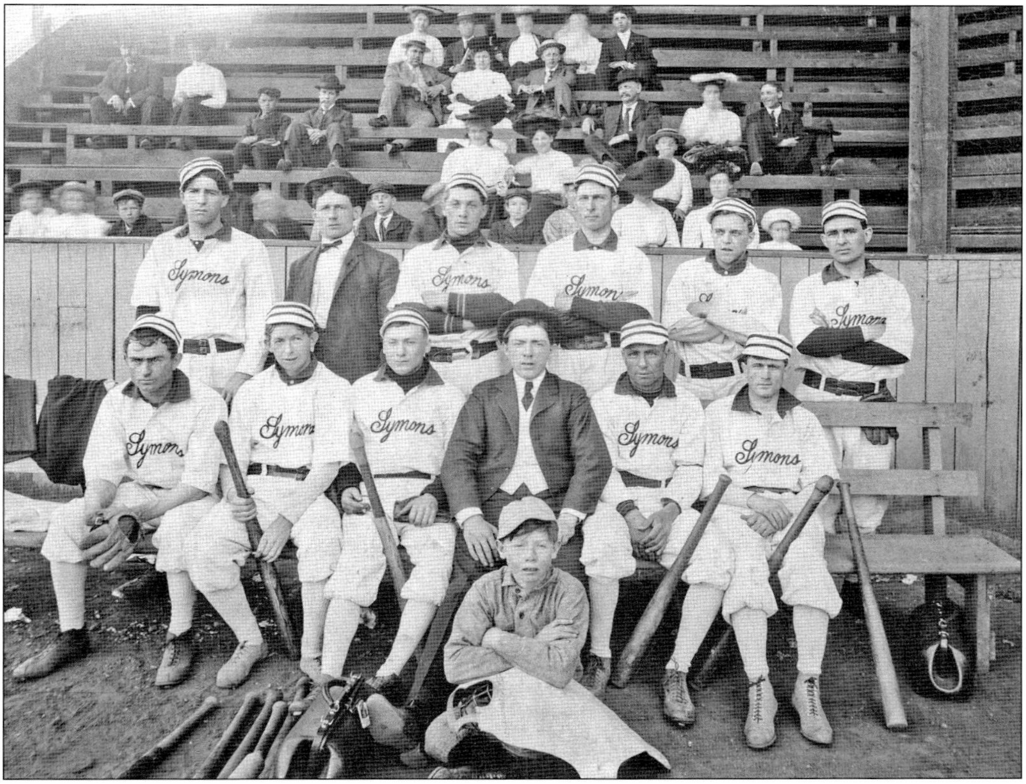

Entertainment was extremely important in a boomtown that beckoned mostly young, single miners. Saloons, pool houses, and gambling parlors were plentiful, but more physical exertion was needed to calm the nervous energy and testosterone. Not content to sit in their small rooms, which often had space for only a bed and a dresser, the workers organized neighborhood sports teams and events: baseball, football, rugby, handball, curling, boxing, coursing, hockey, and motorcycle racing.

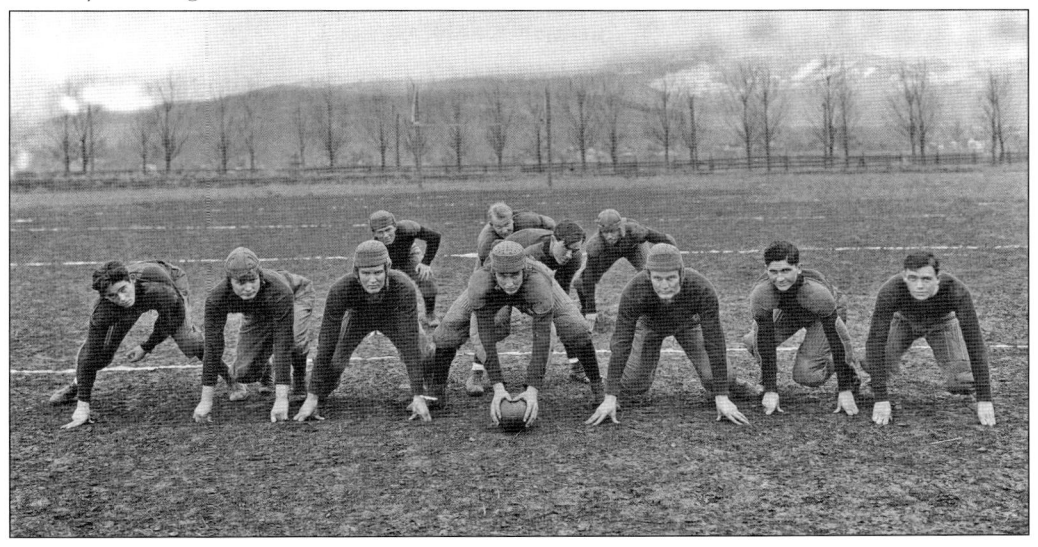

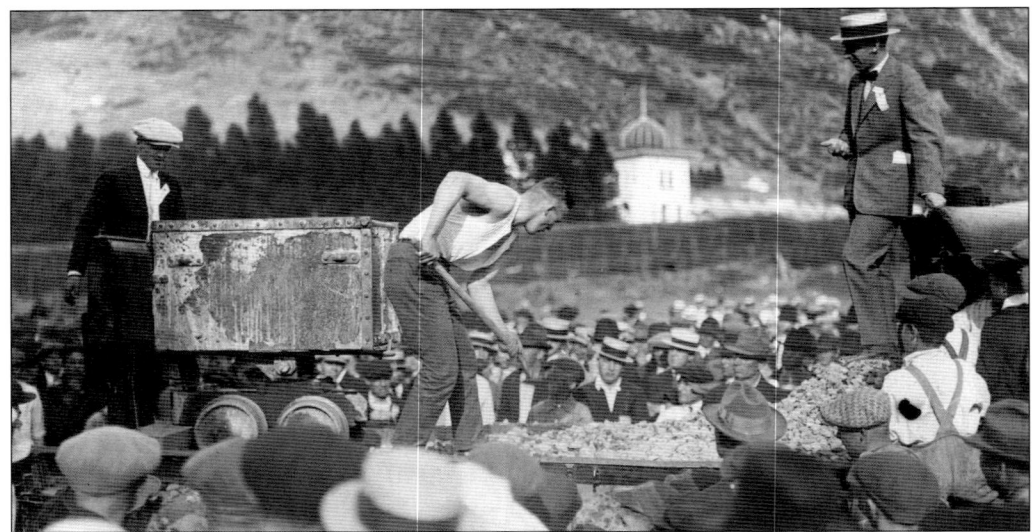

The miners themselves would enter into local and national mining competitions. The mining competitions are still impressive demonstrations of men's skills in mucking, single and double jack drilling, and timber setting. Today state mining colleges host the competitions.

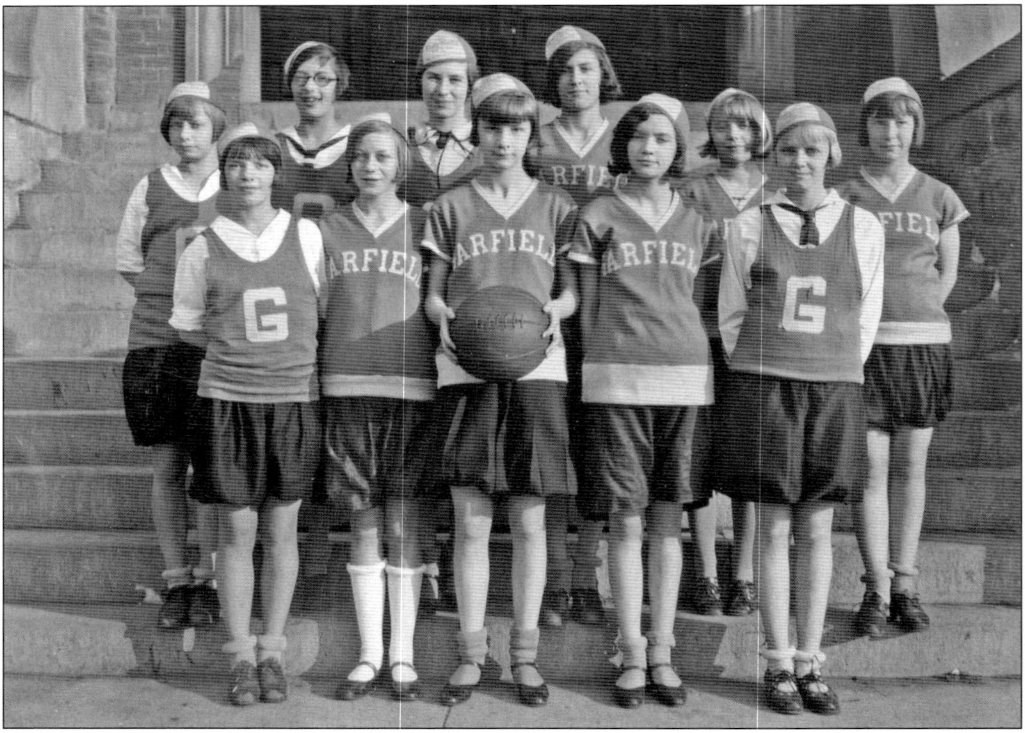

Sports played a large role in Butte—everything from bocce in Meaderville to Gaelic football in the Dublin Gulch and croquette on the West Side. At first, informally organized teams pitted neighborhood against neighborhood, ethnic group against ethnic group. Eventually leagues were established, and teams drew members from throughout the city. Schools also formed teams, and girls' sports grew in popularity.

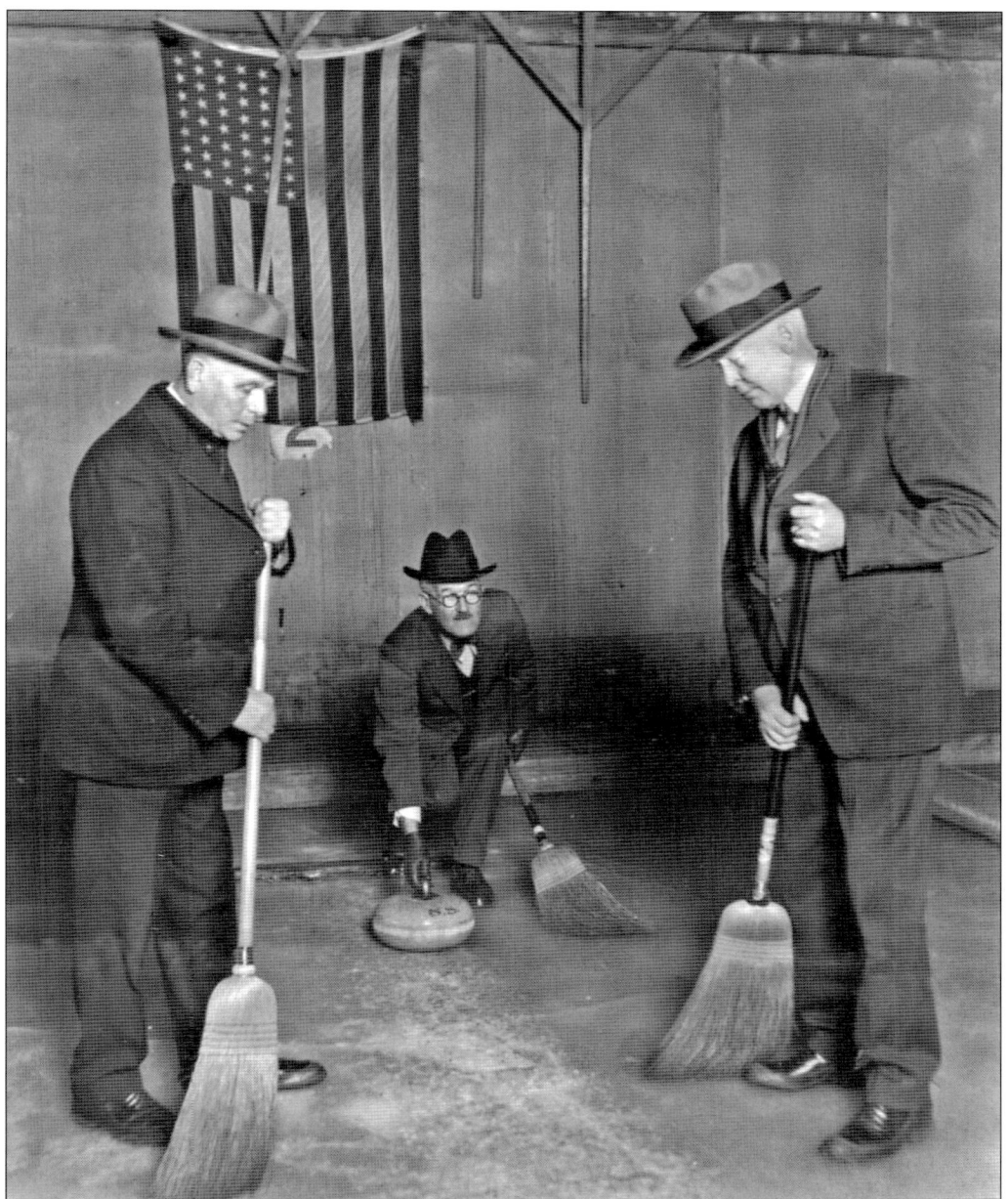

Curling was obviously a gentlemen's sport based on this photograph of the men in their suits. Curling had its roots in Scotland and grew to be a favorite sport in Butte. Initially it was difficult to round up enough players to fill two teams, as a key asset for selection was being of Scotch ancestry. As time passed, however, other nationalities were encouraged to join, and names like Murphy, Batali, and Kovacich were common in the sport. In 1923, the Curling Club boasted 120 members, representing nearly every nationality in the world. The Butte teams traveled throughout the United States and Canada to play in matches.

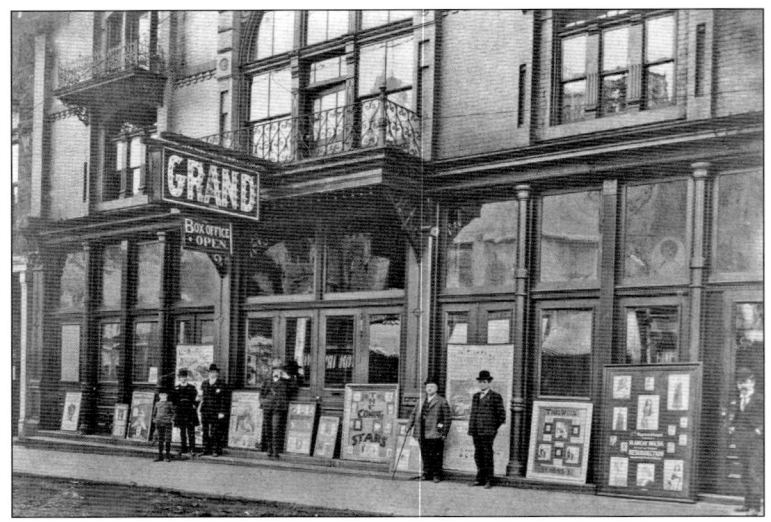

Live entertainment enjoyed a long and energetic presence in Butte. Theater came to town early, with performances on makeshift stages in various buildings. There soon was a bevy of plush theaters and opera houses that lured professional entertainment from both coasts. Wonderful music from all genres could be heard any night of the week.

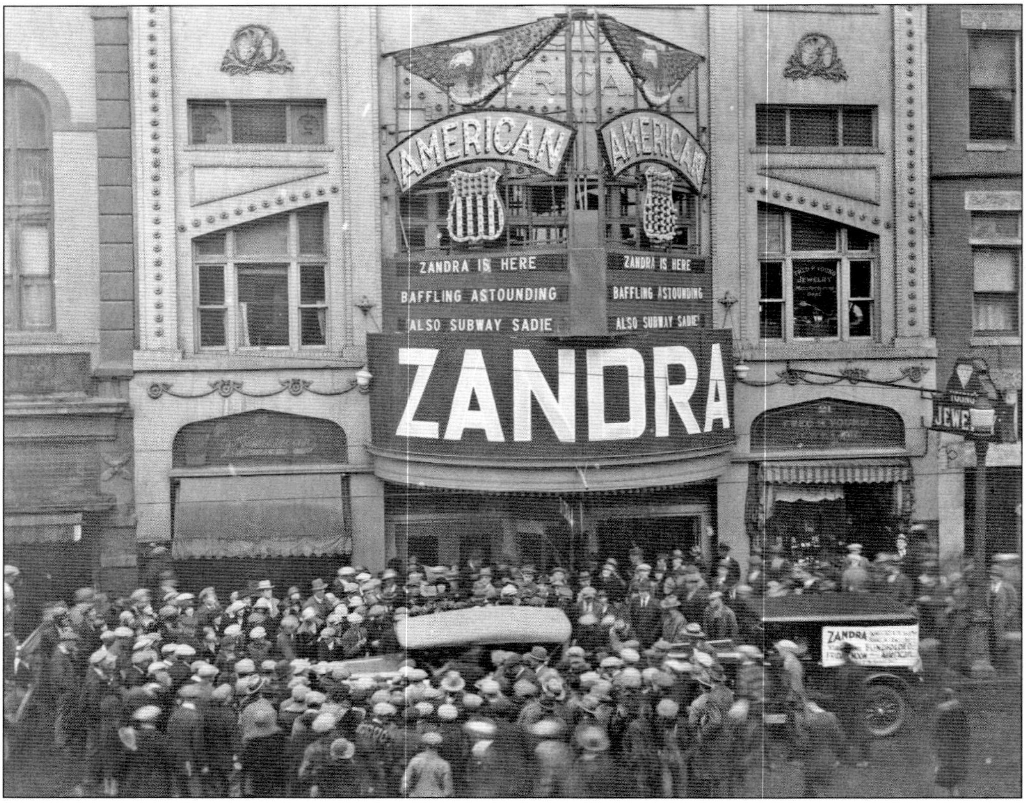

The first formal theater, the Maguire Grand Opera House, was built in 1885 by John Maguire and James Murray. It was the first of many theaters in Butte during the glory days of theater that spanned over two decades. In 1910, Butte boasted 10 theaters, many of which were opulent buildings that could seat 1,500 to 2,000 patrons, and 20 dance halls that provided live music on weekends. The theaters and sports arenas were generally filled to capacity.

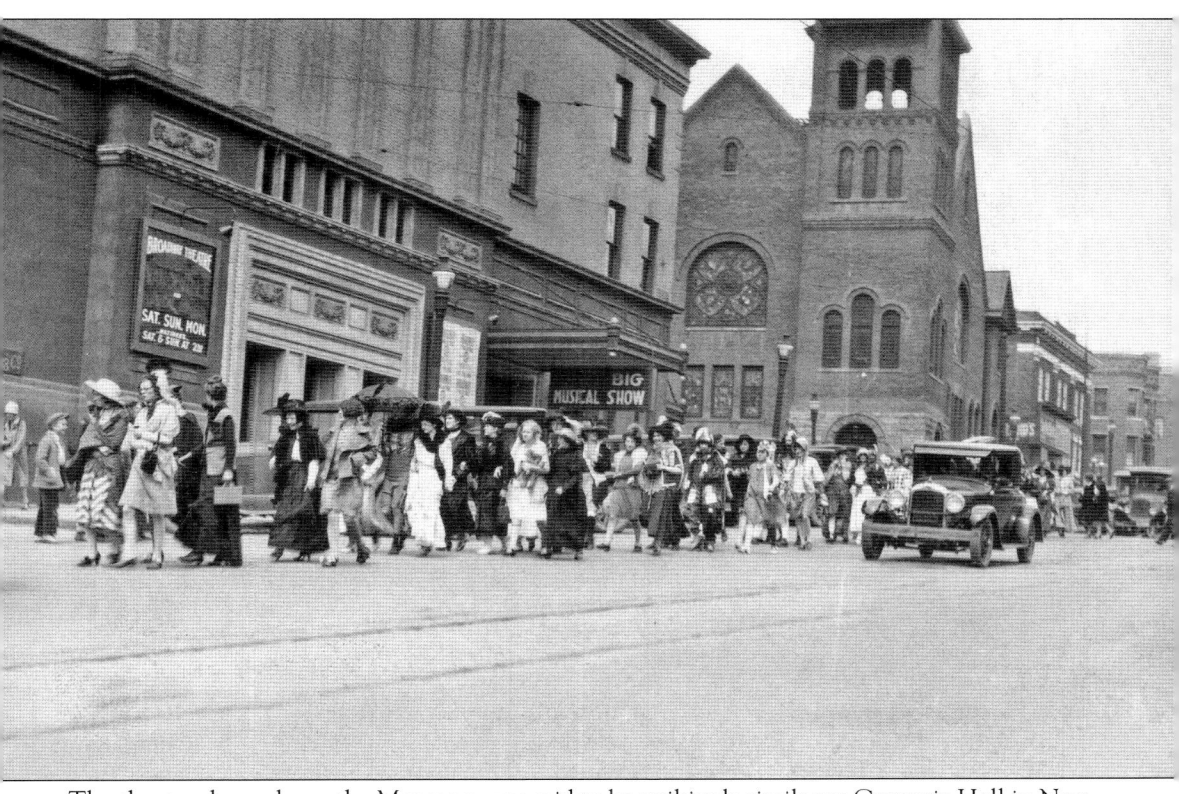

The theater shown here, the Montana, was said to be strikingly similar to Carnegie Hall in New York City, and it once hosted the delicate dancing of Pavlova, the Russian ballerina, and the unmistakable voice of Al Jolson. Among the many other entertainers who regaled Butte audiences were Charlie Chaplin, Sarah Bernhardt, Eddie Foy, Ethel Barrymore, and Mark Twain. Sarah Bernhardt performed *Theodora* in French, and even though most people other than the French Canadians could not understand a word, the Butte audience was enthralled. Other performances included *Macbeth*, *Henry VIII*, *Lend Me Your Wife*, and *As You Like It*, presented by touring companies from throughout the country.

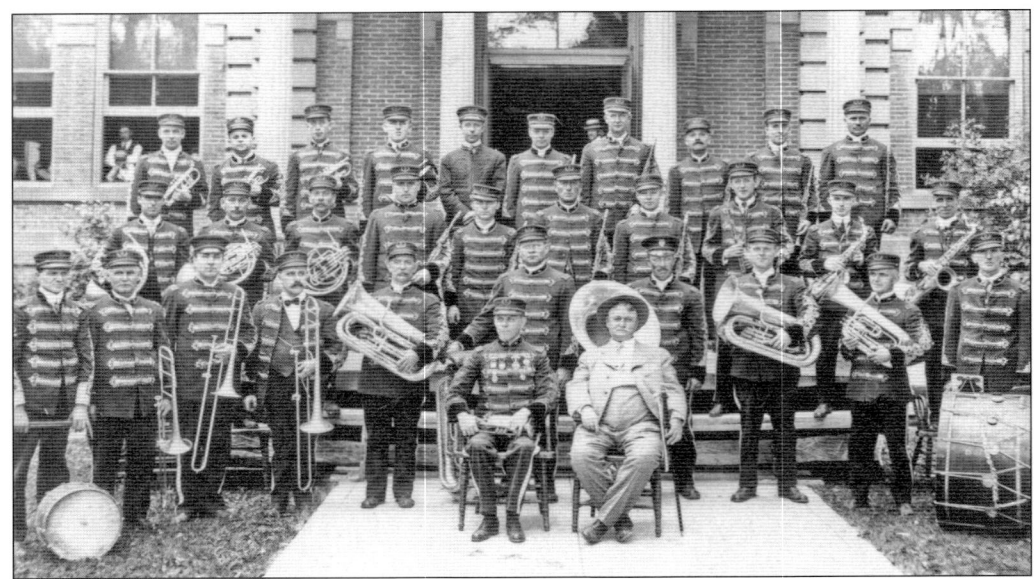

One of the most notable local band ensembles for many years was the Butte Mines Band, which was formed in the late 1800s by nationally acclaimed bandleader Sam Treloar, who worked as a miner for a number of years but was passionate about music. In 1887, he requested permission to put together a band consisting of mine employees and asked that the members, in return for performances for the mine owners and employees, be placed in the coveted day-shift positions. Permission was granted, and the band was formed. Many bands found their niches in local dance halls and other establishments and earned reputations throughout the state. There was a time when any band worth its salt could find a gig in Butte on any night of the week. (Above, courtesy of the World Museum of Mining.)

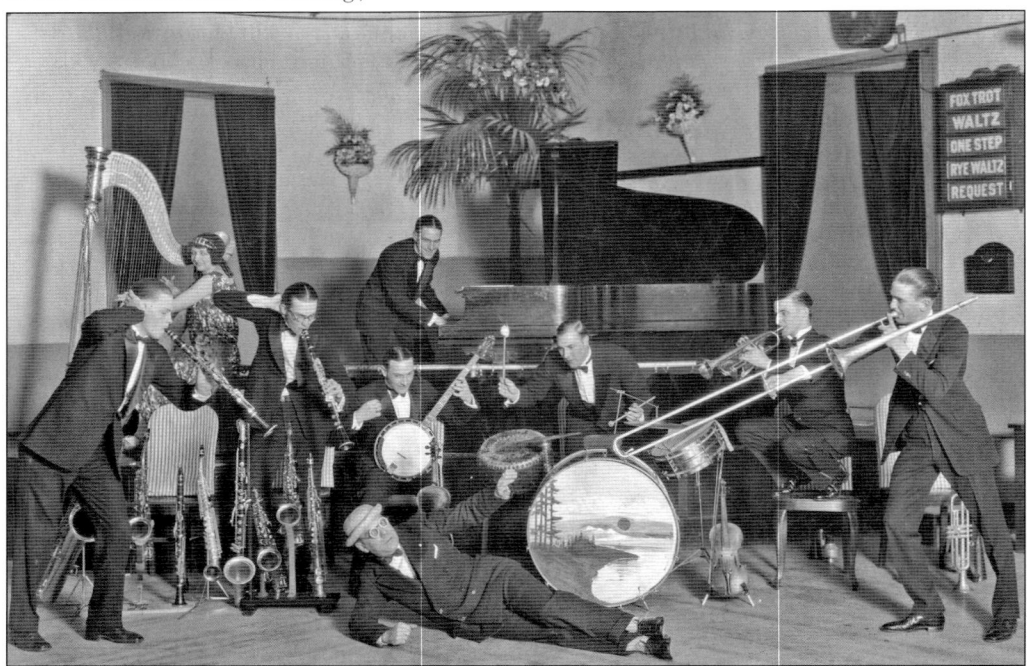

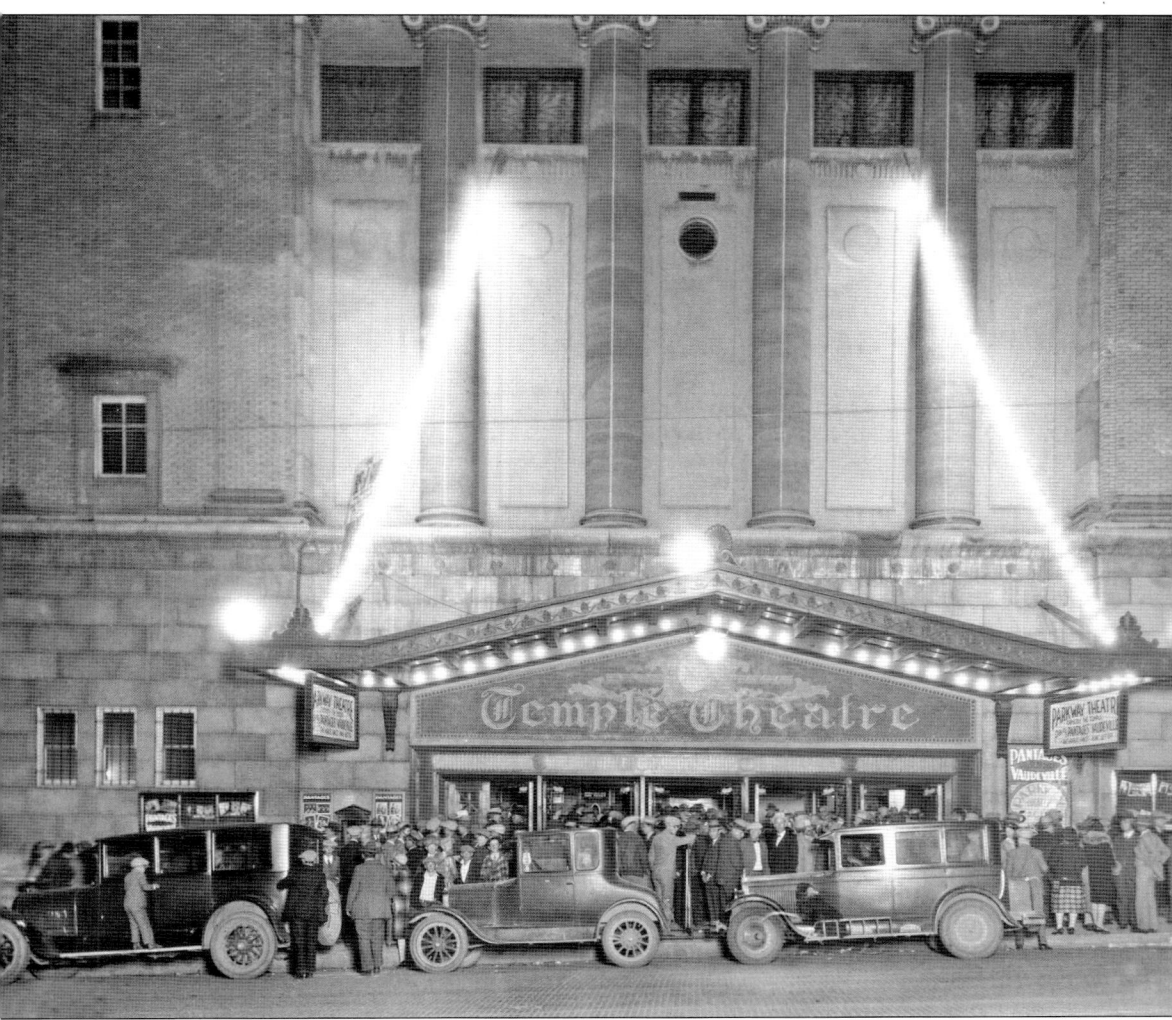

Built in 1923 by the Masonic bodies alongside a six-story temple, the Temple Theater was used for ceremonial services. During the Great Depression in the 1930s, the building was leased as a theater for live performances. Butte is still graced with the building today, now known as the Mother Lode Theater, a marvelous edifice that has been refurbished to its original glory with a hand-painted ceiling; rich, lush carpet and upholstery; and technically sophisticated stage and sound systems. The Mother Lode is host to national touring companies, the local symphony orchestra, international performances, and local theater. It also houses a children's theater called the Orphan Girl.

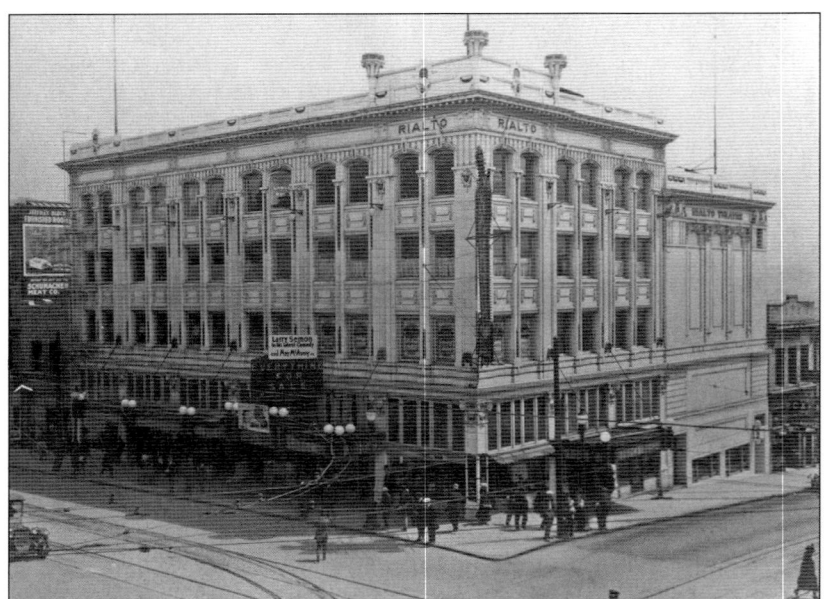

The Rialto building was erected in 1916, and the famed 1,600-seat Rialto Theater hosted stage shows, silent films, vaudeville, and, later, talkies. It was equipped with an organ that was reputed to be one of the finest in the entire West.

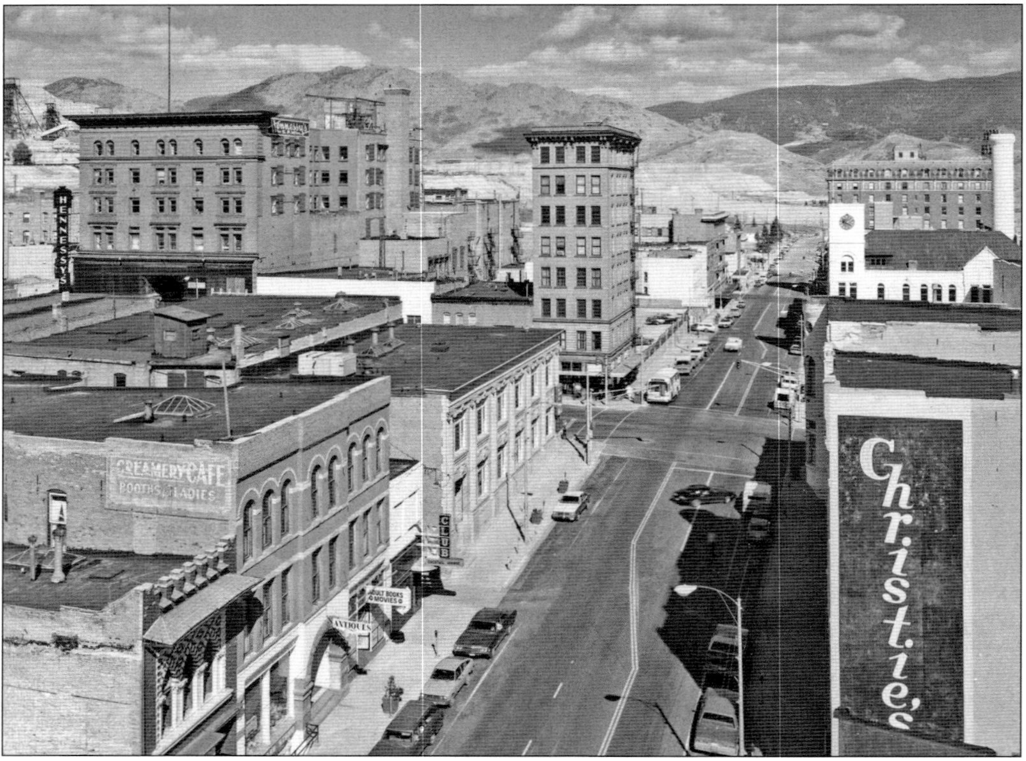

The Hirbour Block (center) is one of the high-rise buildings that were commonplace throughout the city center. Even though it is only six stories tall, it is considered a skyscraper because, like the Empire State Building, it has skeleton steelwork that supports all of the floor systems and extension brick walls.

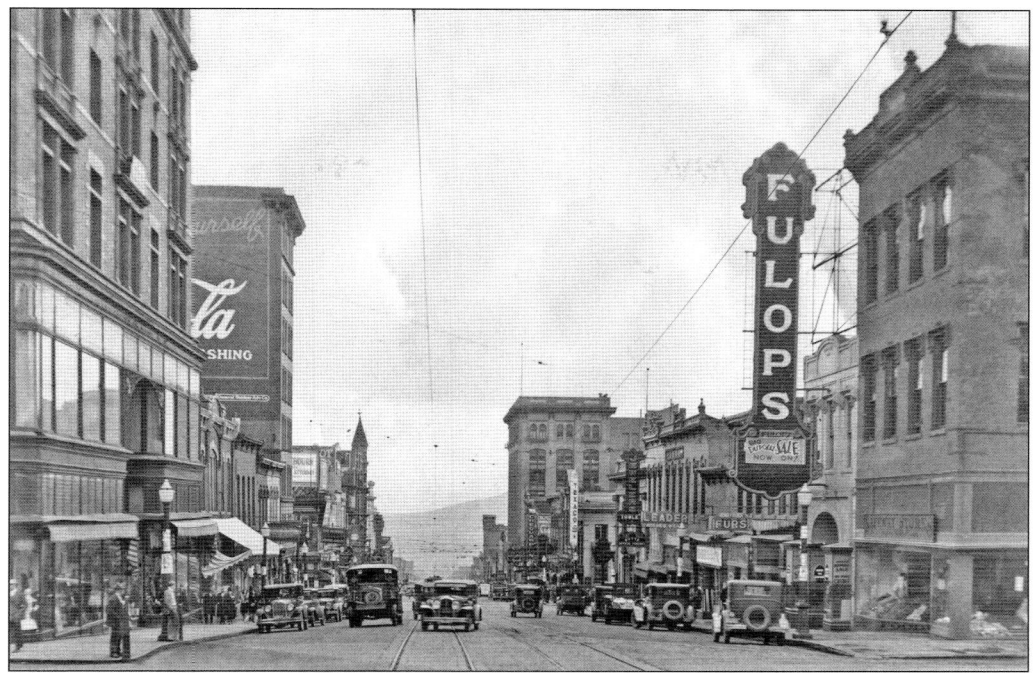

Butte maintains its cosmopolitan aura through its historic district. Despite numerous fires that destroyed almost full blocks and efforts in the 1970s to clean up the town by razing its older, historic structures, the city has retained sections of intact business and residential neighborhoods. It is magical to walk down the street and be welcomed by similar lighting that nearly a century ago illuminated the Temple Theater, to admire the view of the city from the seventh floor of the Metals Bank Building (below), or to sit on a grassy knoll listening to folk music being played under a towering headframe with the Highland Mountains as the backdrop.

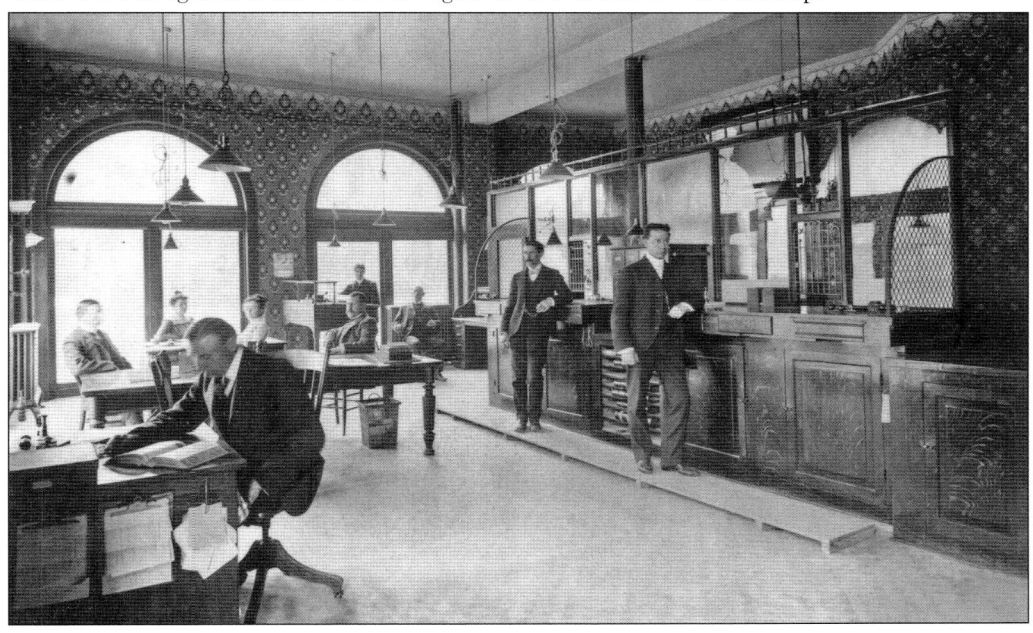

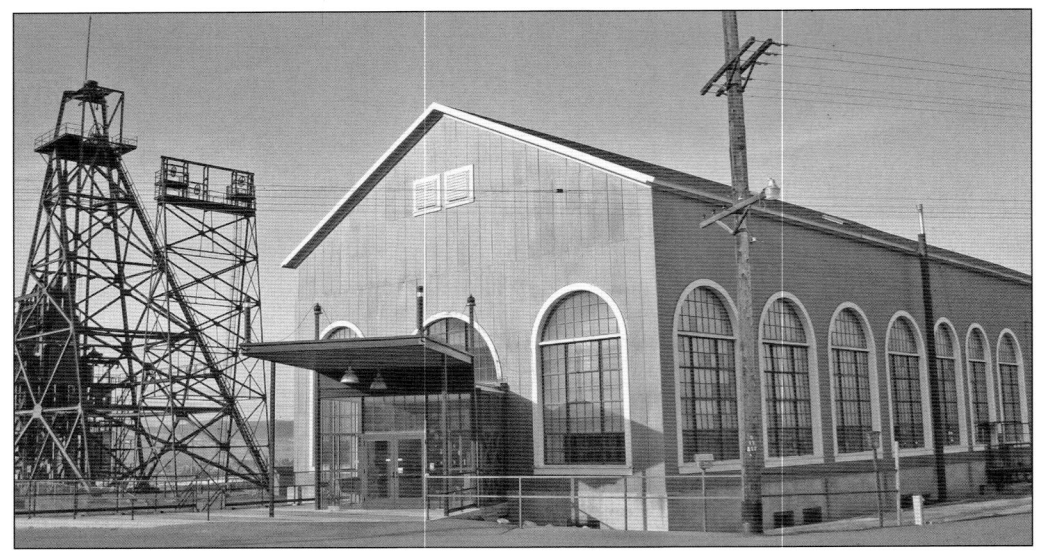

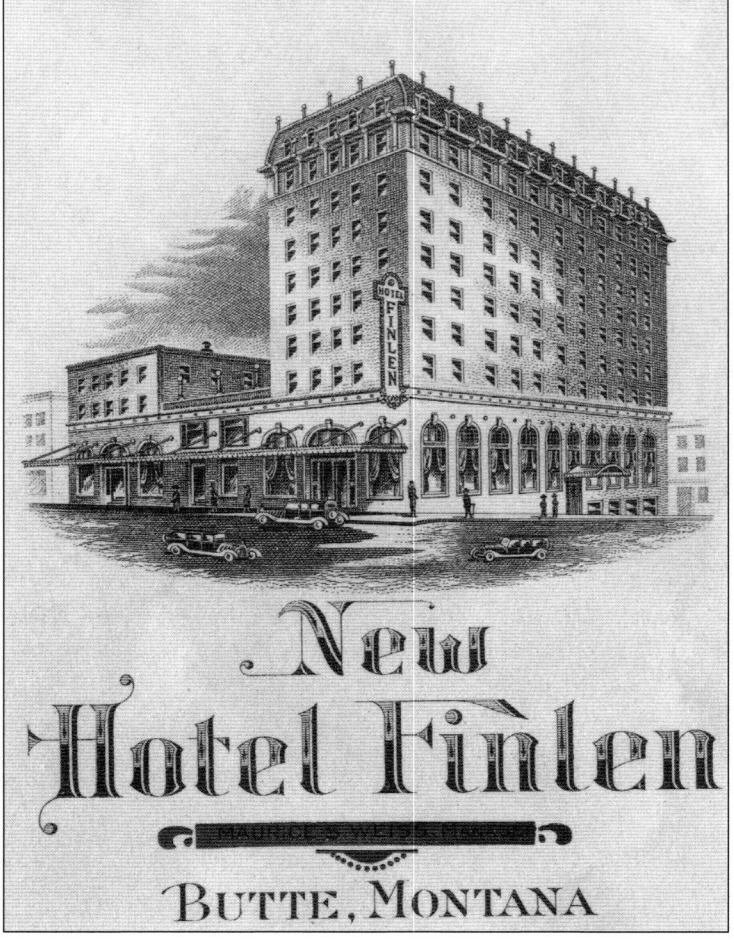

The last three decades have seen a growing interest in maintaining the flavor of the historic district and adaptively reusing the structures and beautiful architecture. Upper floors of buildings have been converted to apartments, condominiums, and New York–style lofts, while main levels have been converted into restaurants, offices, and art galleries. It is a slow process but one in which the citizens of Butte take great pride. Pictured here are the Belmont Senior Citizens' Center (above), once a hoist house, and the Finlen Hotel, a replica of the Hotel Astor in New York City, where the lobby and other public areas have been restored to their original 1923 grandeur. (At left, courtesy of the Taras family.)

Two

Butte the Strenuous

From the rockbound shores of New England, where the cradle of American liberty still swings on its rusty hinges, to the Golden Gate . . . through this broad land, from coast to coast, there is but one Butte. Butte, the exemplification of American grit, of American push and American accomplishment! Butte! The pool of individual strength! There are no parasites in its make-up; everyone stands on his own feet, without a resting place. It is a city of men, of blood and sinew, and not a pack of sheep.

— Thomas F. Rooney, *Butte Evening News*

In many ways, Butte was like any other boomtown throughout the American West in the late 1800s. It grew to be unlike them, however, in that Butte did not bust. There were times when it faltered, times when it struggled, times when it was concerned about its future, but it did not bust. It rolled with the punches, some of them well placed and nearly incapacitating. It refused to give in to the concept that it was "just a boomtown." Metal prices surged and dropped. Investors won and lost. Men worked and sat idle. Women worked continuously regardless of the impacts of the inexplicable and often unexpected changes in the economy. Through it all, decade after decade, Butte the Strenuous parlayed its resources against the odds and rose above the chatter of doom and gloom. The very landscape of Butte is strenuous, located 6,000 feet above sea level and surrounded on three sides by the high, steep ridges of the Continental Divide. The climate is just as demanding—displaying dramatic temperature swings from negative 40 degrees in January to 80 degrees in late July. Winter comes early and stays late, spring rushes into summer, and summer becomes fall in what seems like moments. Through it all, however, the people of Butte, tough and formidable like their climate and terrain, endure and flourish.

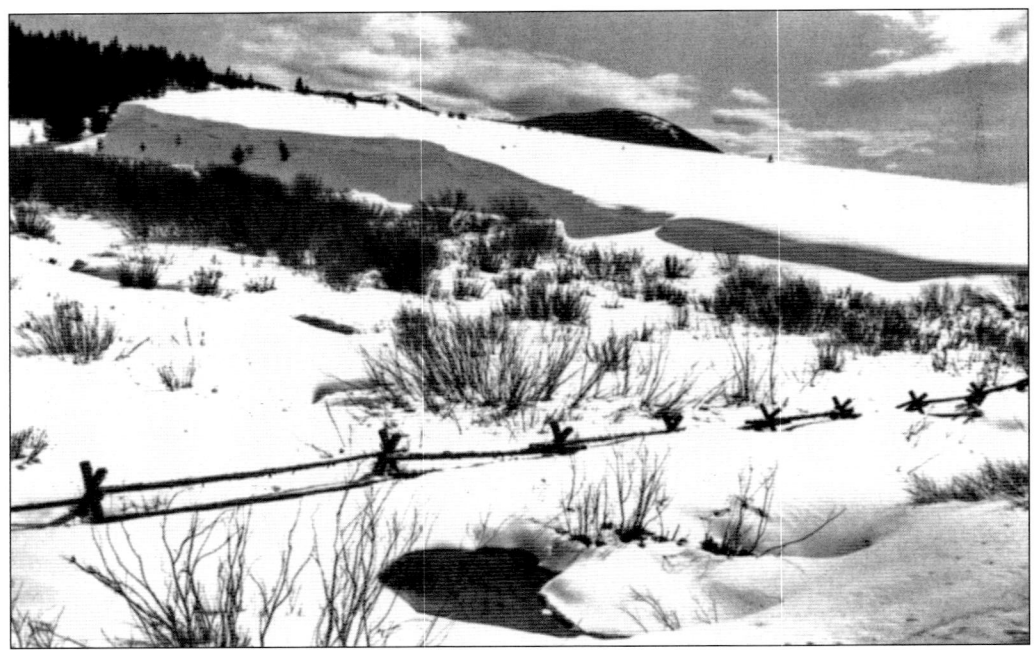

Butte presents awe-inspiring vistas of high mountain peaks and intense blue sky. Crossing the Continental Divide was not for the weak at heart. Huge outcroppings of boulders awaited the shift of time to loosen their grip on a hill's wall and obstruct a path. Rivers of dirt roads flowed for miles through the mountainous terrain. Ice and snow in winter made the steep inclines even more precarious. Springtime brought mud and rain. The view from the mountaintop, however, is magical.

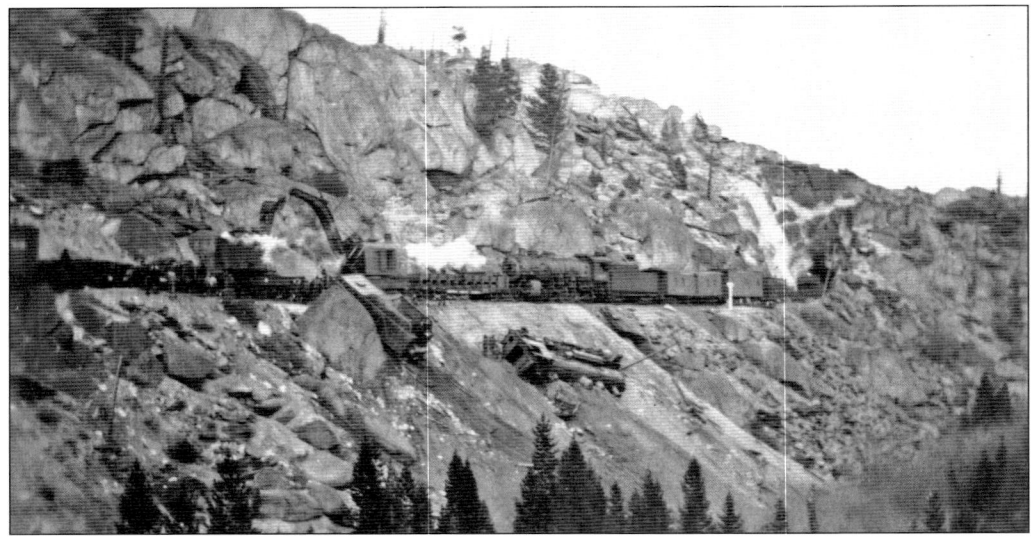

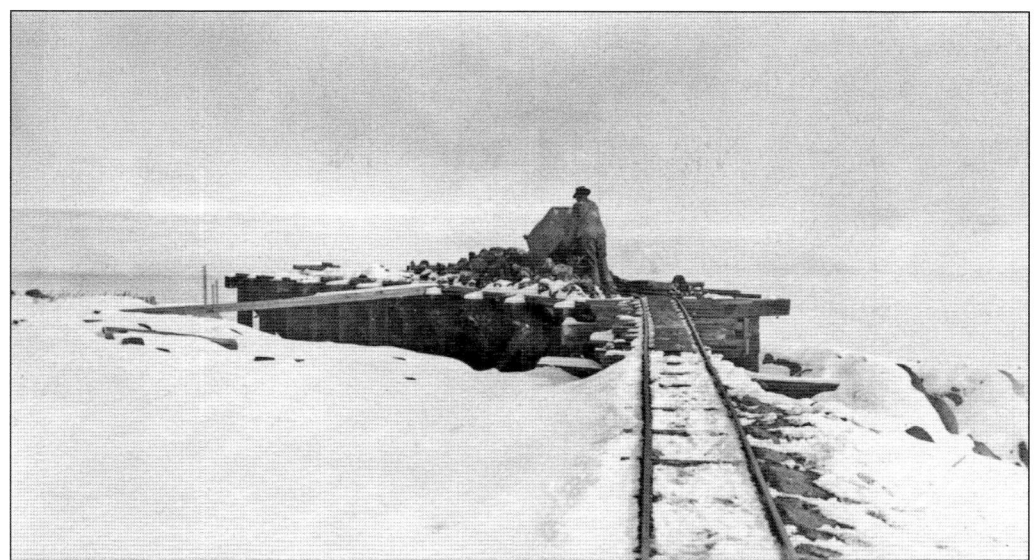

The sheer force of man's determination to do his work is demonstrated in this photograph of a man in the dead of winter dumping an ore car into a skip. Deep snows and cold temperatures contributed to the high death rate among miners in the early part of the last century. Miners had to be hardy to survive. They not only had to endure the ruggedness of the land and mountains but also the extreme weather conditions that chilled them to the bone and the hazardous conditions associated with mining.

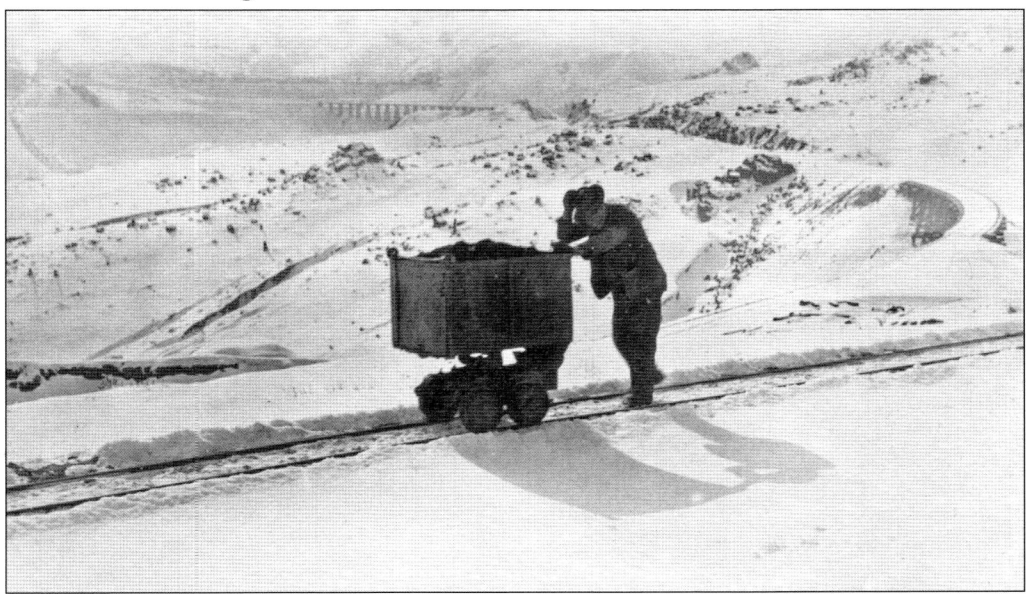

Butte was not a city for the weak, and it is still not a city for the weak today. Although free from the torments of hurricanes, ice storms, and floods that beleaguer other parts of the country, Butte endures cold and harsh winds that can bring the thermometer to 40 degrees below zero. A warm day in winter in Montana is when the sun is shining and the temperature reaches a "high" of 30 degrees. Despite what the thermometer states, the brilliant sun makes the temperature bearable. (Courtesy of the World Museum of Mining.)

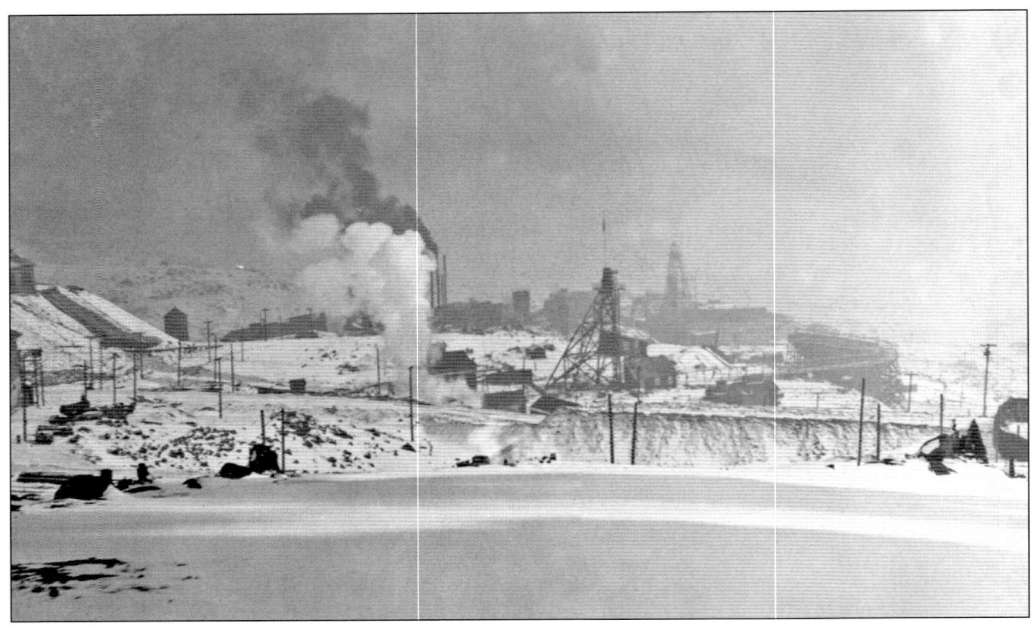

The dramatic weather experienced in Butte can be measured visually by the high columns of steam rising from the underground shafts' air vents. Steam rose straight into the sky before billowing out when the temperature dropped below freezing. The higher the column, the deeper into negative numbers the temperature was. There are many days when the temperature falls to negative 20 degrees and then warms up to only negative 10 degrees. (Below, courtesy of Chris Fisk.)

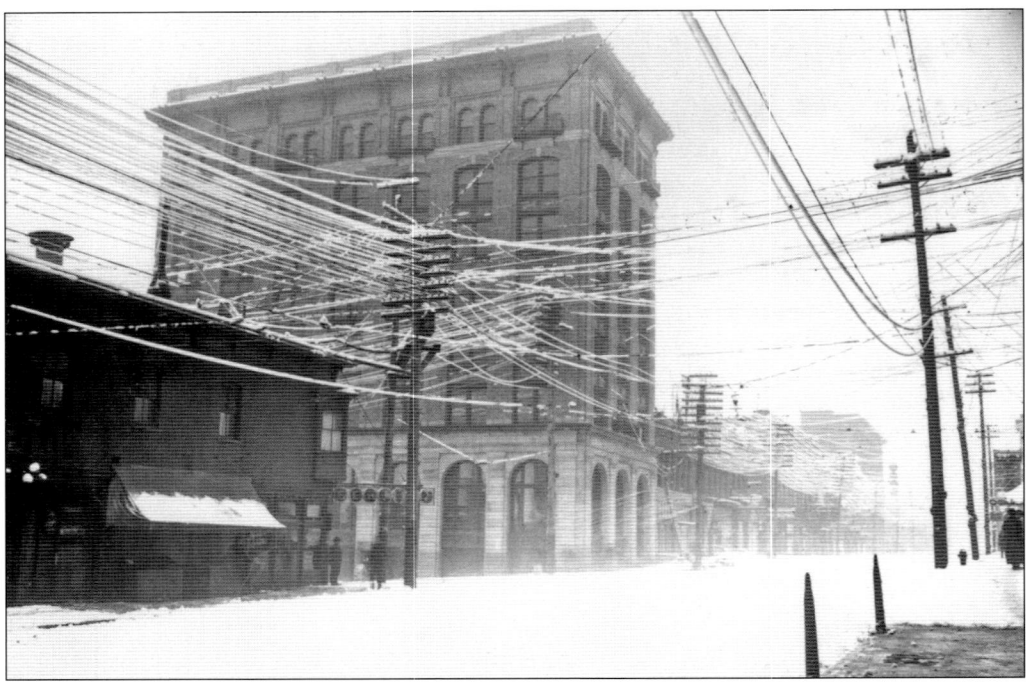

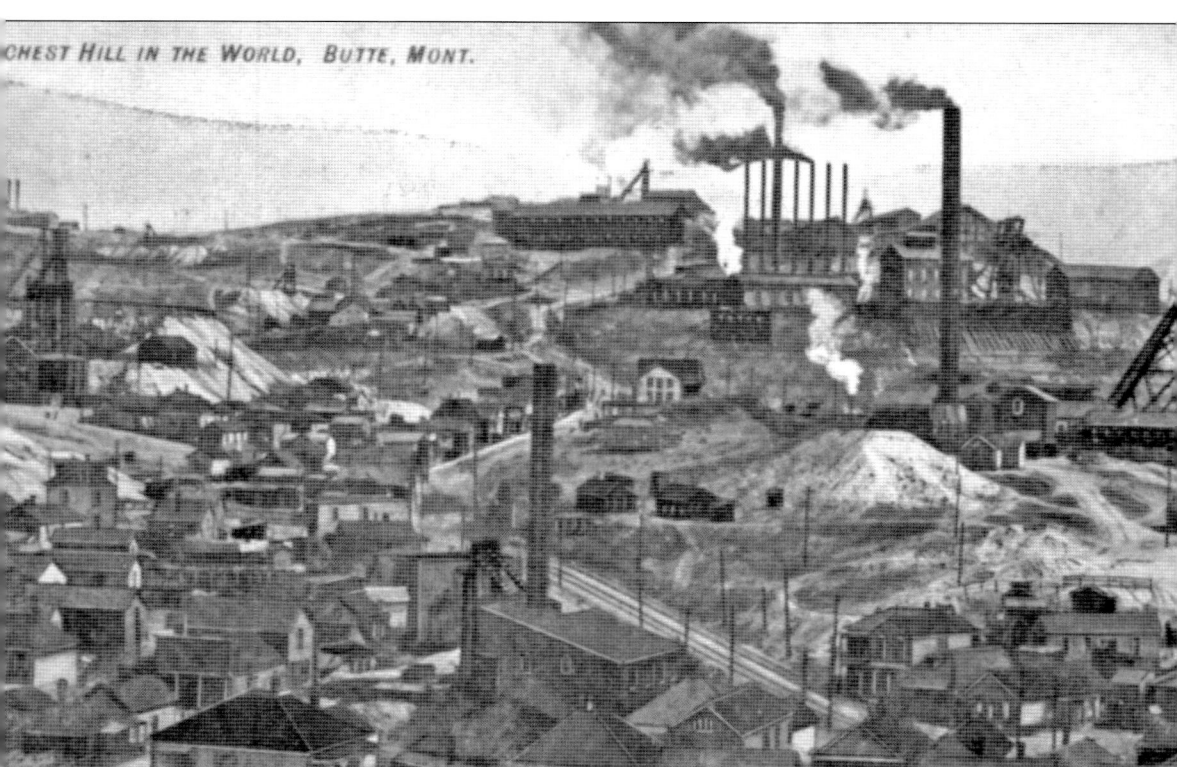

From the very earliest days, miners traversed the mountains, following streams and drainages, until they reached the headwaters at the Continental Divide. Miners in the late 1860s followed Silver Bow Creek to its source and found some gold but mostly rocks containing silver and copper. Other men followed to toil in the underground in order to release the riches held in the hard rock. The city was built on a foundation of granite that holds gold, silver, copper, molybdenum, zinc, and many lesser metals. These were the metals that fueled the second industrial revolution in America. Butte provided the copper ore that would electrify America and change the way the country would work, produce, and live for the next two centuries.

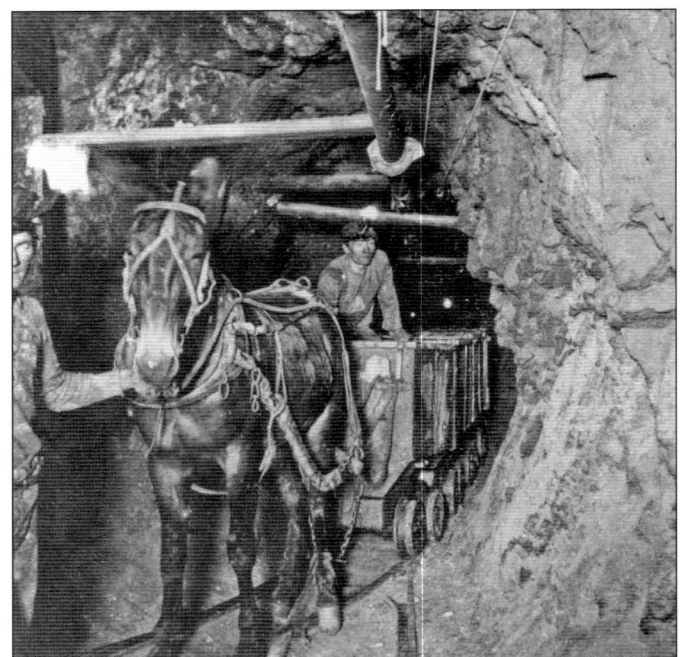

In the early days of Butte, work was literally backbreaking—man against rock. The use of primitive tools and beasts to move man and materials is visible in these photographs. Mules were sent down the shafts in leather slings and hitched to ore cars. They moved ore and supplies from the shaft to the stopes and raises underground. Mules often became blind within weeks if not days of working underground. Mules were retired to good pastures and were well cared for once they came topside. By 1930, the mules were totally replaced with electric motors.

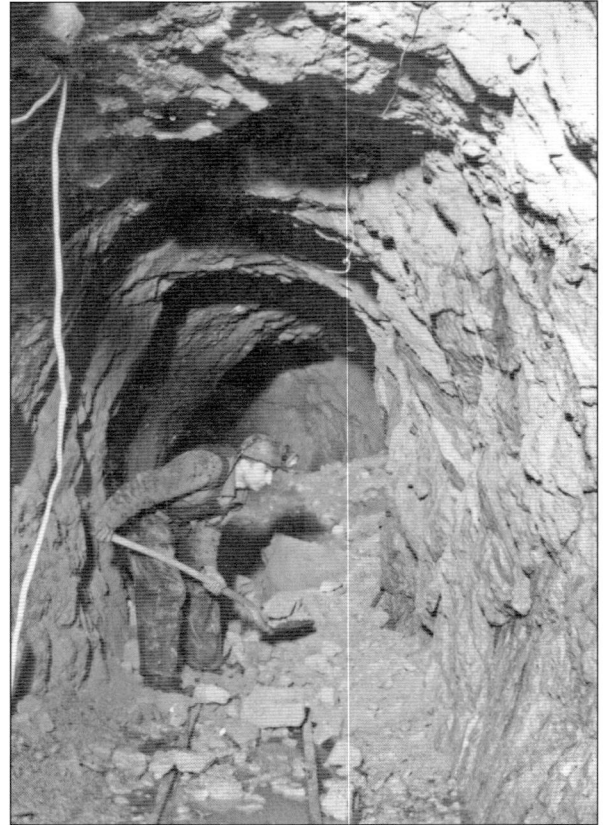

The fact that early mining required sheer muscle is most notable with the man shoveling ore in a drift. Early miners drilled holes in the wall face with a hammer and hand-drilled and loaded ore cars with shovels. Driving drifts was exhausting work. It involved breaking rock with dynamite at the face of walls underground and then shoveling or mucking the rock for disposal. The temperatures underground were as dramatic as they were above ground: from a cool 60 degrees to a high of greater than 140 degrees. There are places underground in the Steward Mine that the miners affectionately referred to as the "Chinese Laundry." The high temperatures underground and the subzero temperatures above ground were often deadly to miners.

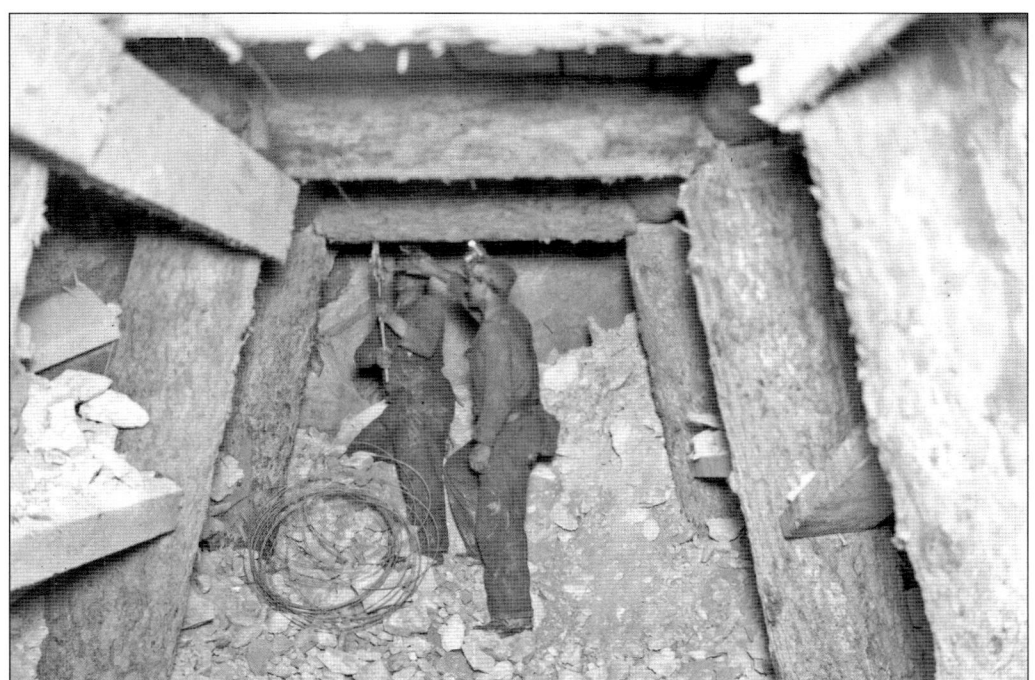

Men are shown here setting timber in a drift using an ax and sheer muscle. Timbering was done in shafts to prevent the ground from caving in. At one time, the Butte mines used 40,000 board feet of lumber a day, especially for the big square-set braces, which filled its deep stopes. Timber is a big industry in Montana, and the need for this raw material by the mines was immense. From the earliest days, French Canadian timber cutters were well paid and in high demand. The French settled on the flats in Butte, and they provided timber and dairy products to the miners. The French also ran the roadhouses at various locations from Butte to the top of the Rocky Mountains. (At right, courtesy of the Montana Historical Society.)

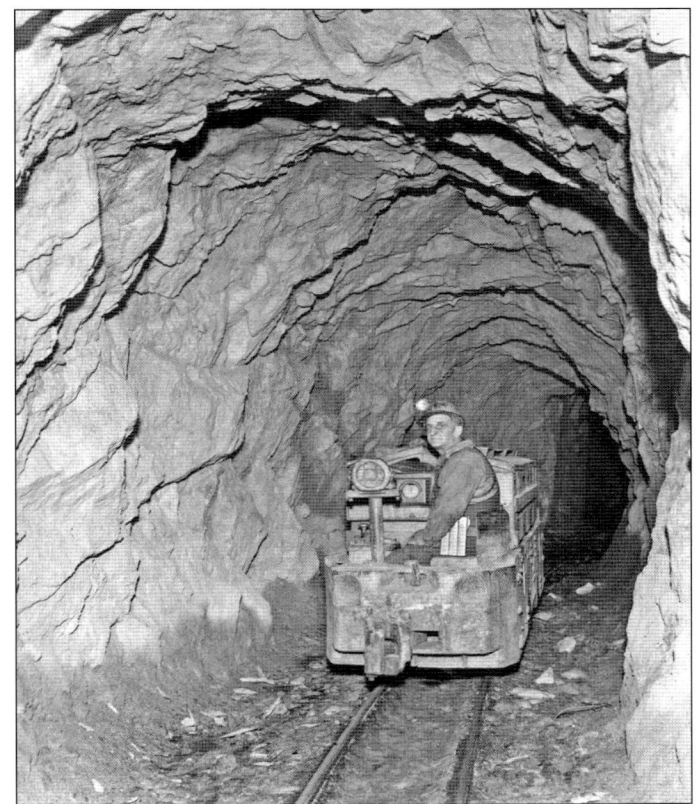

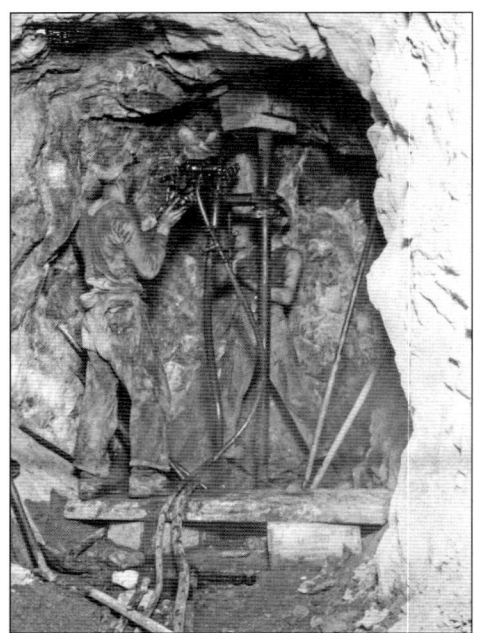

In Butte, the granite is complex, holding the ore hostage in its geology. The work to free the ore starts with setting dynamite to release the rock from the ground. Technology was developed to improve mining production, such as the compressed-air drilling machine shown here. It took two men to set the equipment and drill the holes in the rock face to place the dynamite. There would often be a round of 6 to 12 pieces of dynamite, and the safety call would go out—"Fire in the hole!"—to warn all men underground that a blast was taking place. Drills like this were referred to as "widow makers" because the dust settled in the miners' lungs and often caused early death. This image reveals that these were the days before hard hats and lighted helmets. (Courtesy of the Montana Historical Society.)

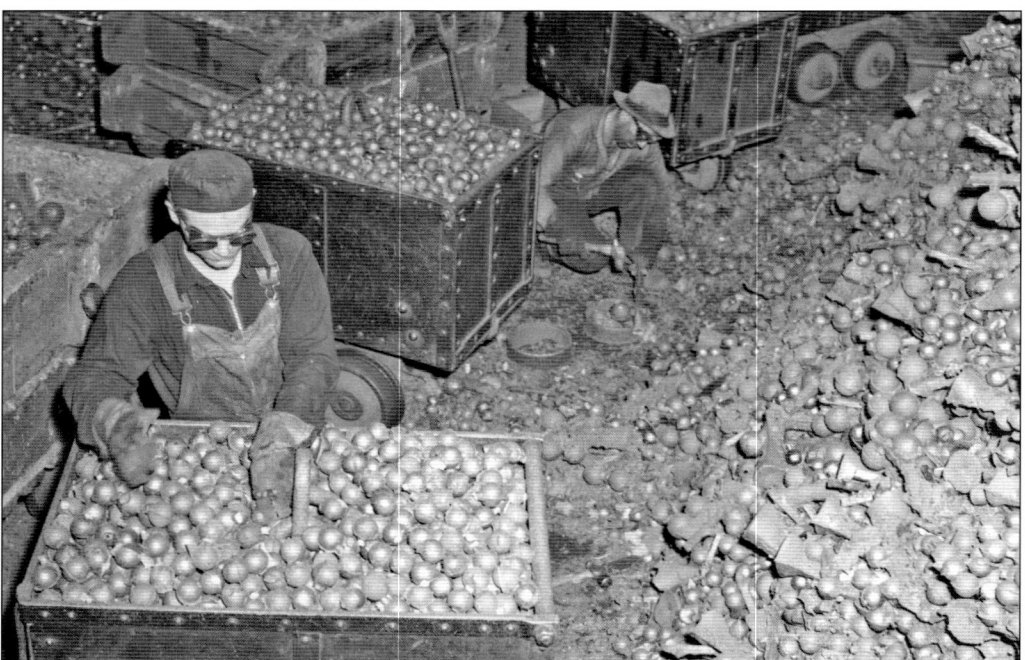

Once the rock was loosened from the ground and taken to the surface, it was sent by rail to the mill. Ball mills were the most widely used method of crushing ore. Ore and steel mill balls were placed inside a rotating hopper. The ore and the balls tumbled together with a mixture of chemicals to easily attract the metals together and assist the ore moving through the flotation process. The crushed ore was then sent through a series of processes to extract the metals for smelting and refining. These two men are sorting milling balls that were used from the early to mid-1900s. (Courtesy of the Montana Historical Society.)

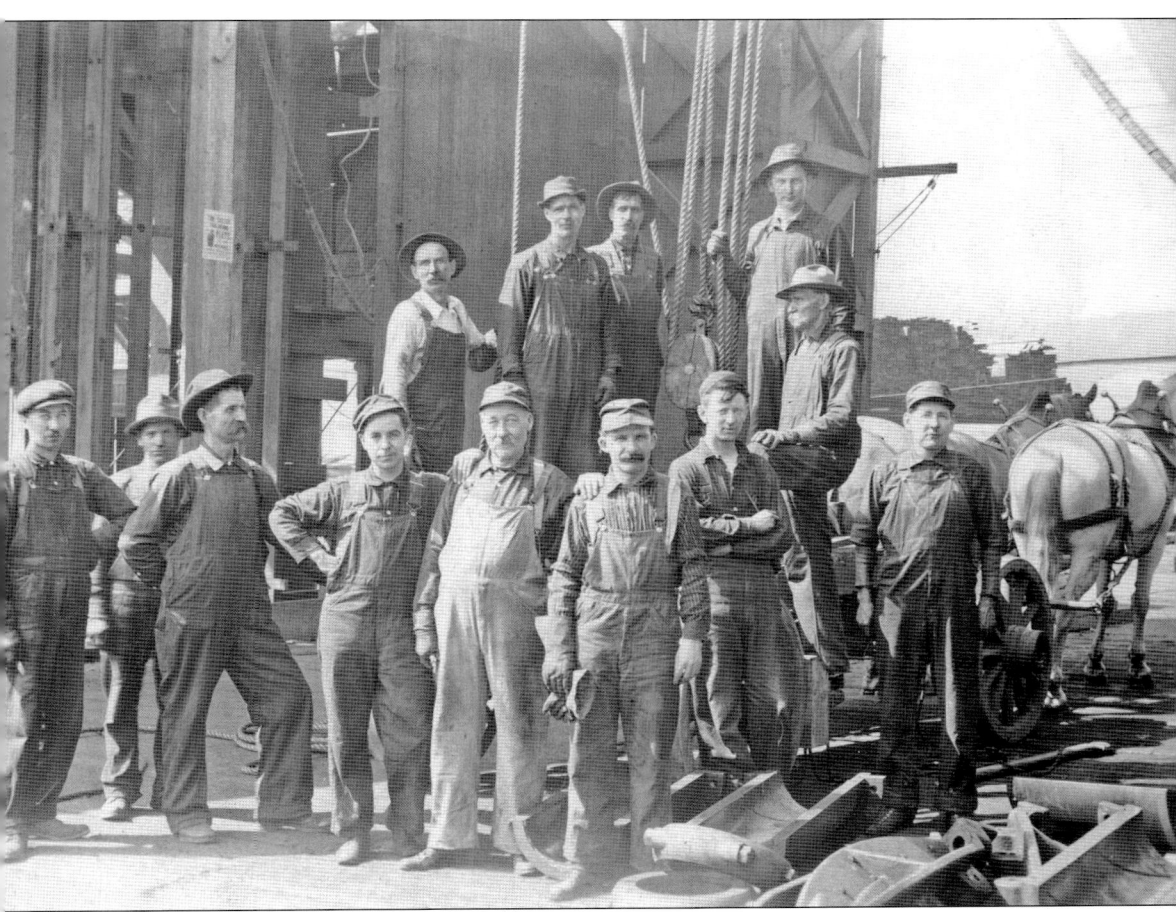

Before electric power became available, an entire mining operation was handled by beast and man. However, the need to move massive amounts of ore required better equipment and men with greater skills. By the late 1880s, mining required a plethora of craftsmen, tradesmen, and professional engineers. This 1890s photograph of an engineering group was taken at the West Colusa Mine. Engineers ran the hoisting equipment, which raised and lowered men and metals. The hoisting engineers required oilers to keep the riggings and machinery well lubricated and ropemen to ensure the rigging was correct and able to handle the weight of the ore and man cars. Other workers in demand included boilermakers, ironworkers, electricians, motormen, teamsters, blacksmiths, muckers, nippers, machinists, and pumpmen.

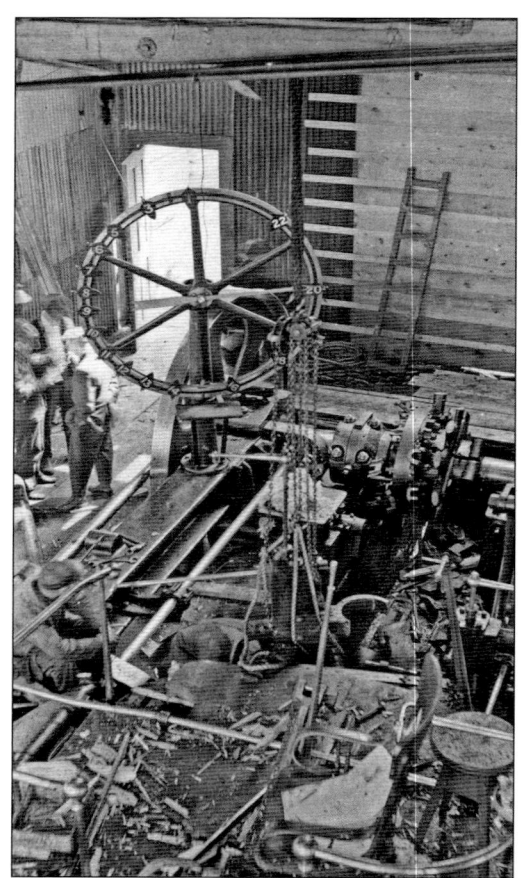

Mining was very dangerous. According to the Butte Health Department Reports from 1900–1910, one man per day died of mining-related diseases such as silicosis, and one man per week died in industrial accidents. This photograph of an engine explosion at the Leonard mine on April 23, 1913, illustrates the strenuous working conditions and inherent danger underground. The headline in the *Montana Standard* read, "Four miners crushed to death in mine depths and another killed by flying steel when a cable disintegrates. The engineer stays at his post." William Peters, the engineer, is quoted as saying, "All I know is that the engine went to pieces."

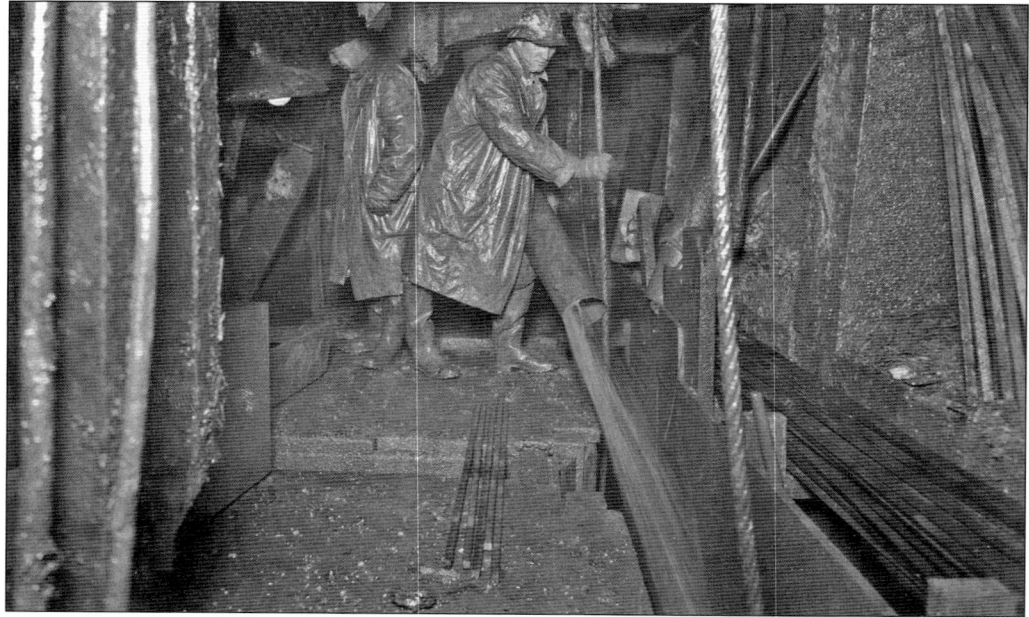

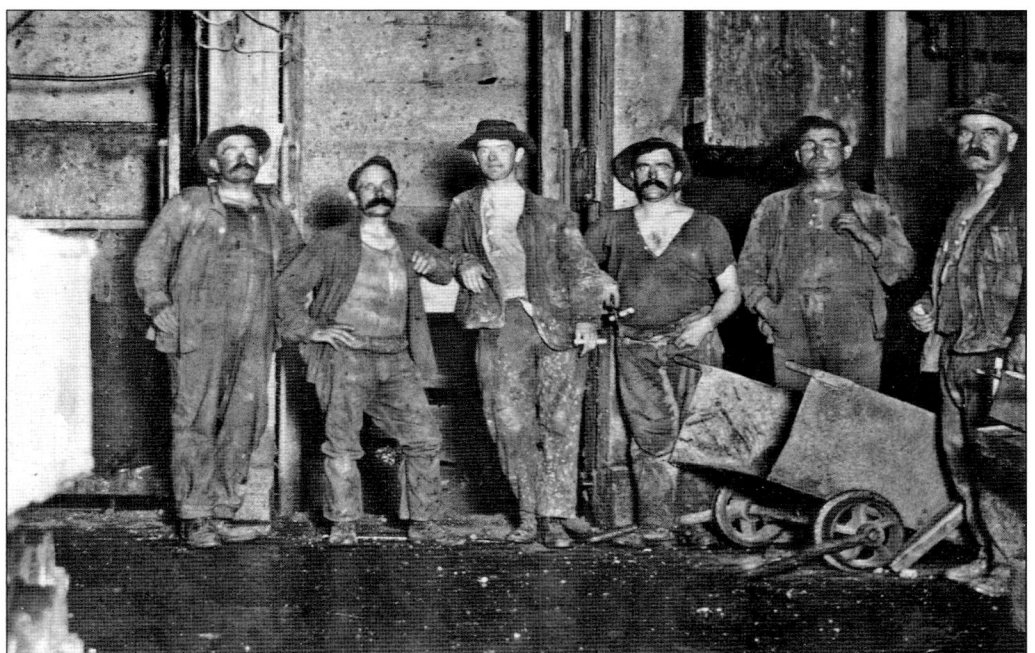

Conditions underground in the mines could be atrocious. In this photograph, miners stand on wet ground near a car that was used to transport minerals. Miners seldom came to the surface to eat their meals, instead finding a dry, safe spot to lean against or sit upon in order to relax for a few minutes before resuming work. Some of the most interesting mining terms define the activity of miners underground: miners often caught a nap on a laggin—a 2- to 3-foot-long board; miners drank boilermakers—a shot and a beer; they rustled a job; and they sent the nipper for supplies and used the chippy hoist to move equipment to and from the surface.

Copper is somewhat of a magical metal. It can multiply itself if attached to another metal. In this photograph, the men are sweeping the liquid in a precipitation pond to hasten the process in which copper attaches itself to junk metals and turns the metal to copper.

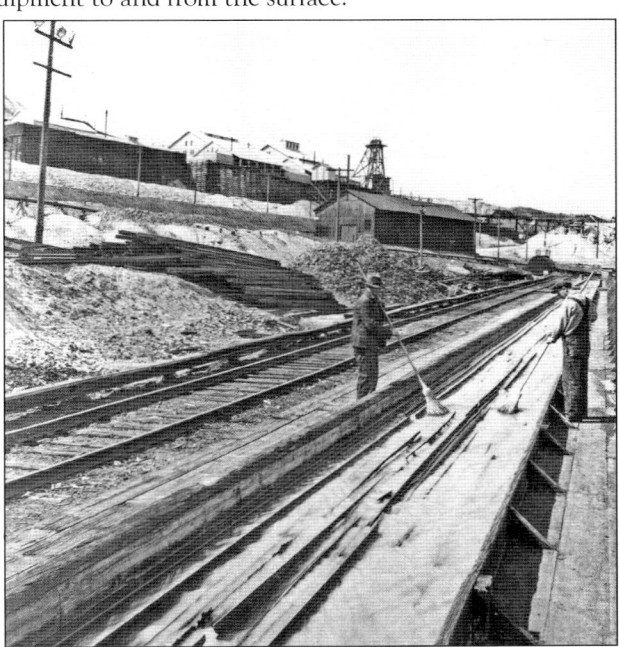

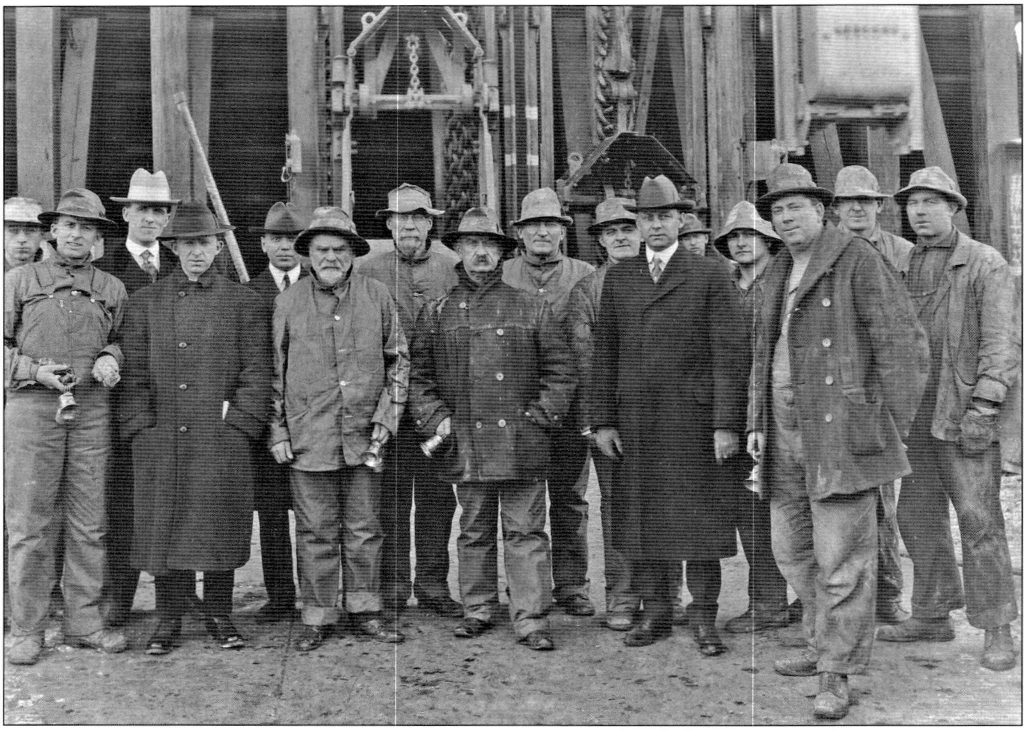

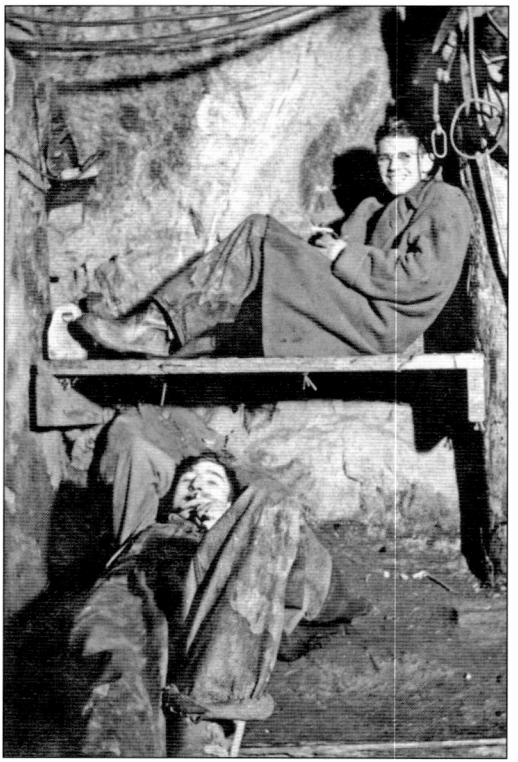

There was a strong camaraderie among the miners who bravely descended underground each day. The serious looks on the faces of these miners belie the fact that, despite the risks they took, the men enjoyed their time together, laughing, telling stories, and pulling pranks on one another. After work they would leave their posts for the nearest saloon or gambling parlor, and on the weekends they would enjoy playing or watching one of the many sporting events so popular throughout the area.

Miners worked as partners. Often it was a business relationship in which two men acquired a contract with the ACM together. This business partnership could make them fairly wealthy if they worked well together. The partnerships almost always crossed the line from business to friendship and beyond. The loss of a partner to a mine accident could be devastating—financially as well as personally. The reliance on a good partnership was not just good business, it was good sense, and it provided an element of safety.

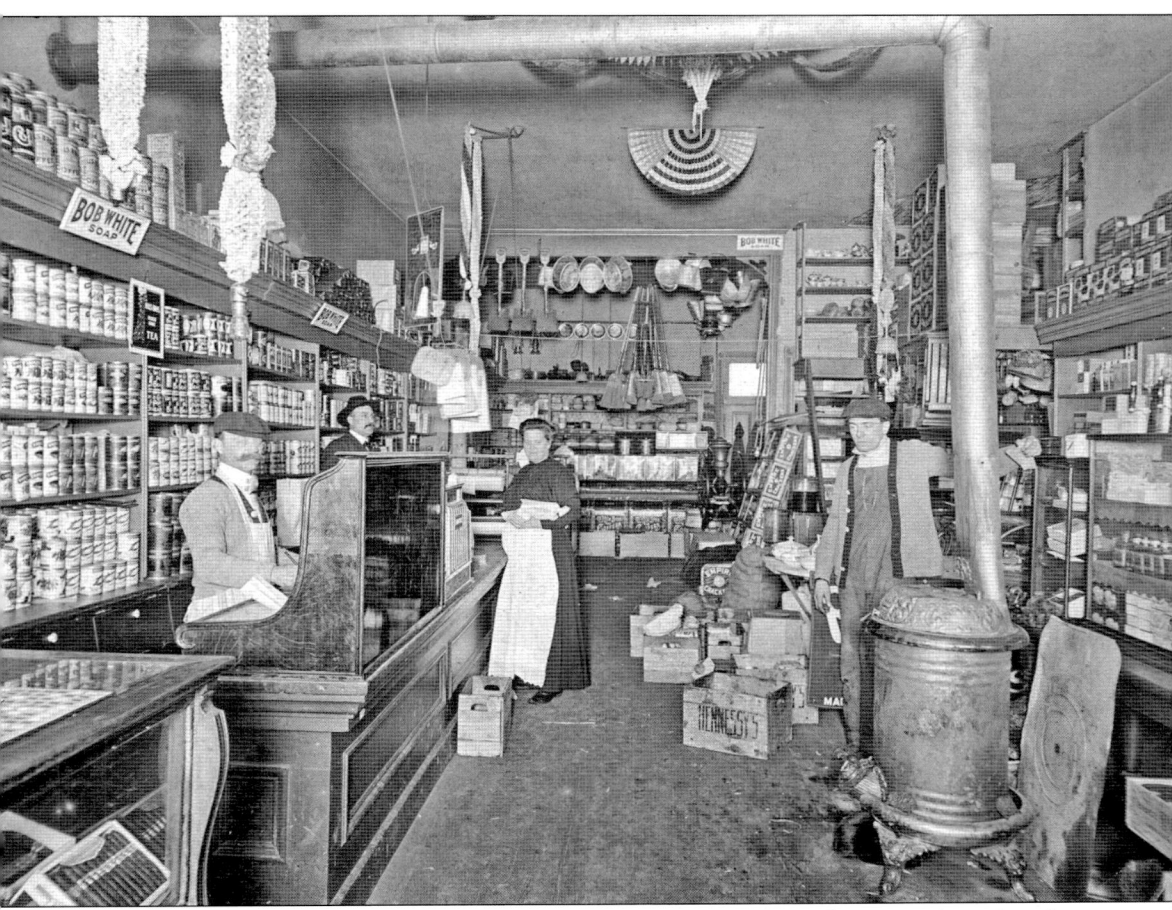

Occupations open to women were limited to service industries in the early 1900s: clerical work, selling chickens and eggs, taking in laundry, and housekeeping. Options for employment were particularly scarce for women with children. Because the mining industry was fraught with danger, there was a high death rate among miners, and many women became widows at young ages. Often the mining companies paid them stipends when their husbands were killed underground, which they could use to pay off their mortgages. Although not a lot, this money allowed them the opportunity to take in boarders to help support their families. Widows also put their daughters to work delivering lunch buckets to the miners and their sons to work selling papers, shining shoes, or delivering telegrams.

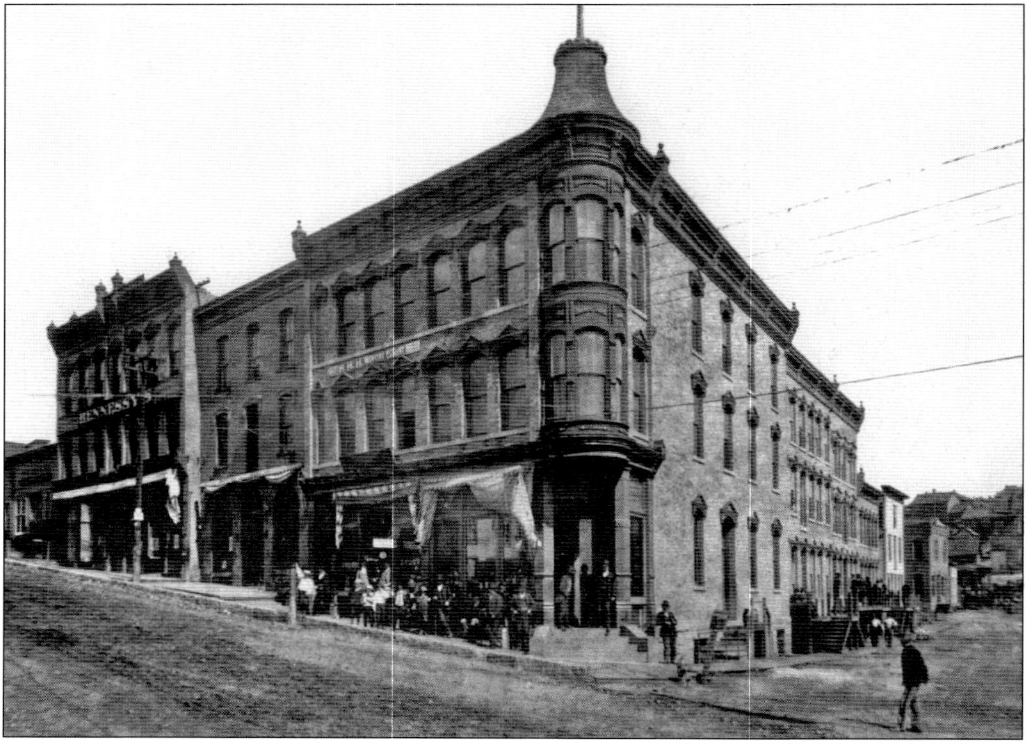

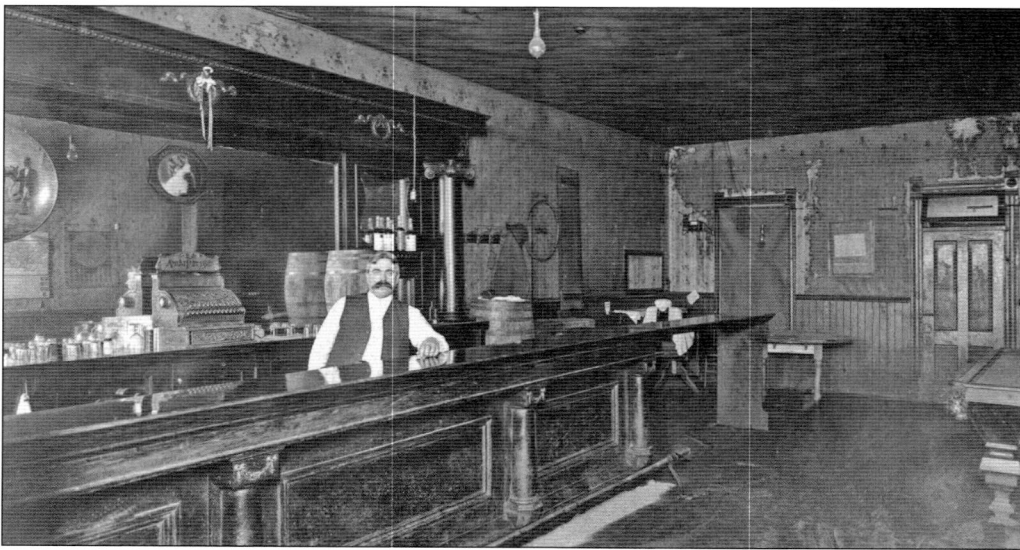

The conditions in the underground mines were characterized by narrow tunnels, jam-packed elevator cars, tight, musty quarters, and a metallic smell and taste that was difficult to erase from the nostrils and tongue. On the surface, many mine workers returned home to boardinghouses with rooms that had barely enough space for a bed and a small table or dresser. The Mullin House in Centerville, shown above, was one of those places that housed hundreds of miners in tight quarters. It is not surprising then that they spent most of their time away. The corner bar became a haven for men seeking space, a clean palate, and an odor that did not remind them of their day's labor.

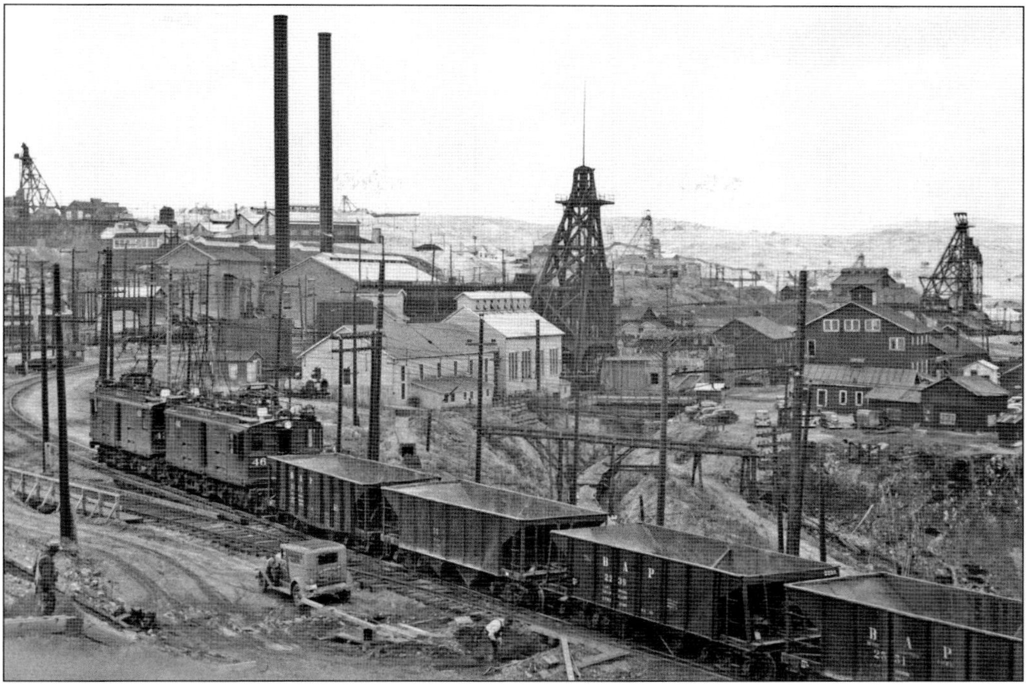

Cleave Bishop took this 1942 photograph looking north from the Mountain View Mine. The built environment of Butte reveals an intimate relationship between the industry and the people. The headframes stand gracefully above workers' cottages, schools, and churches all over the Hill. The Butte Anaconda and Pacific Railway (BA&P) was an interurban railway that provided transportation of the ore from the mine to the Anaconda Smelter some 30 miles to the west. The tracks and its right-of-way also provided an easier grade for foot travel through city neighborhoods for schoolchildren and housewives traveling to and from the grocer, church, school, and other of life's missions. This relationship among house, the school yard, and the mine yard creates a landscape that is like no other in the country.

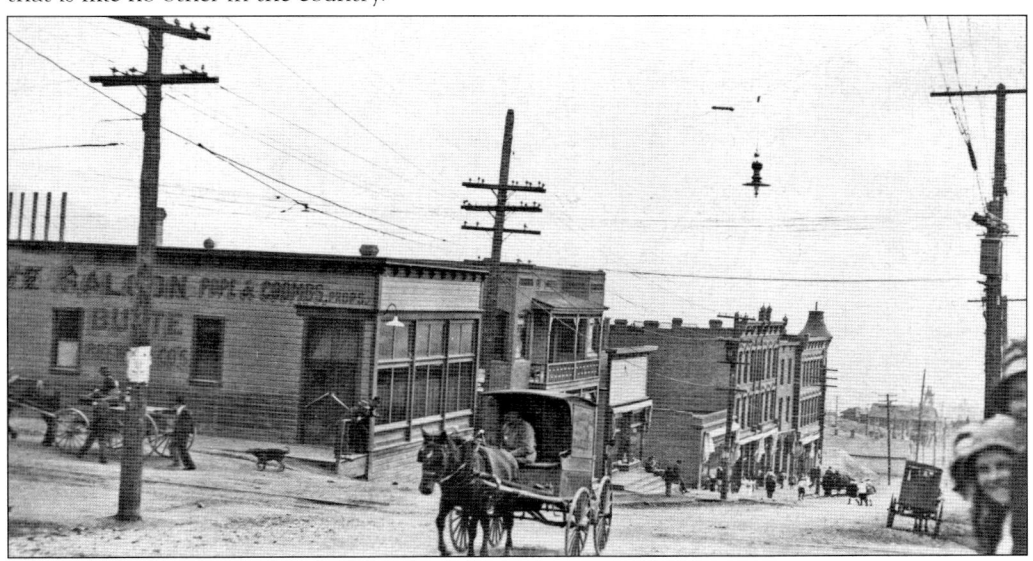

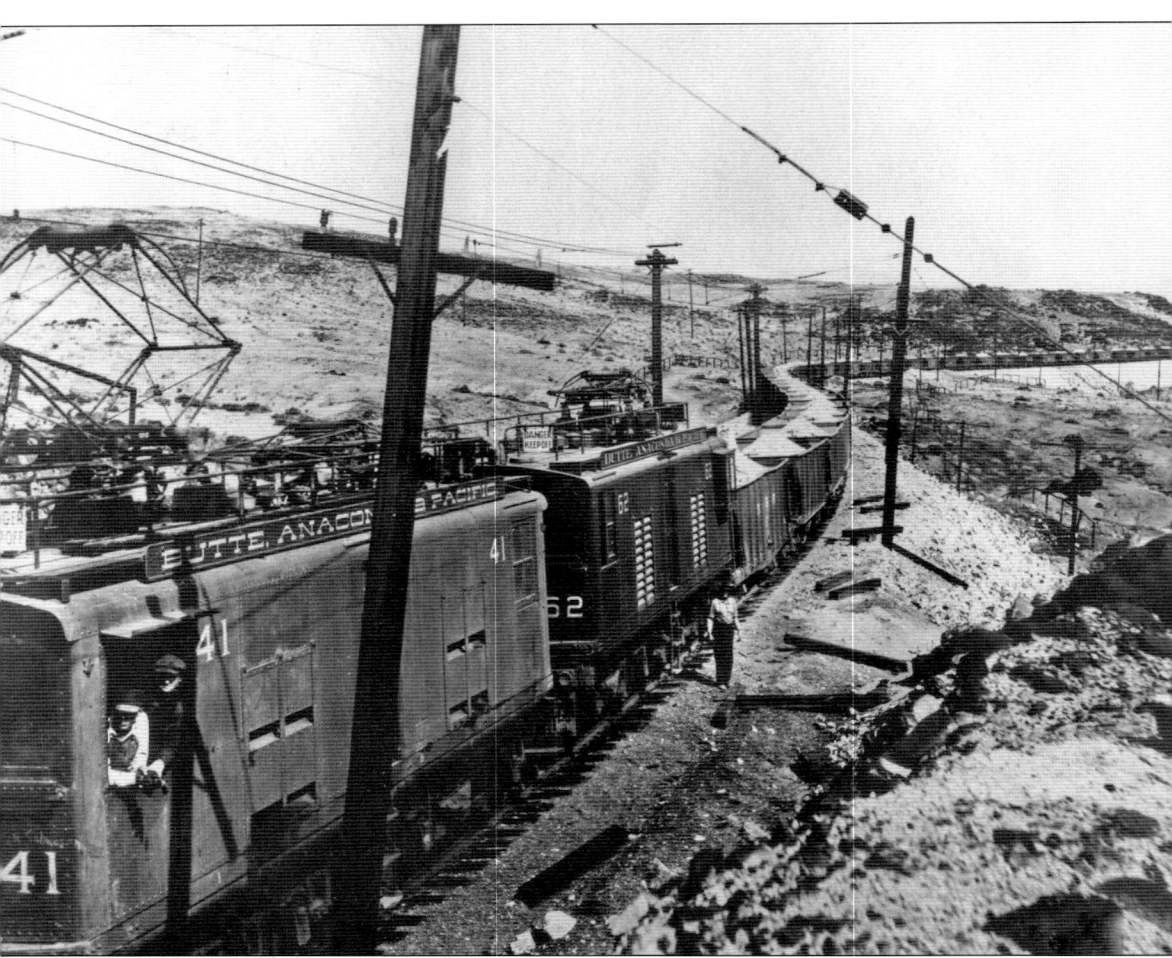

The BA&P was called the "Biggest Little Railroad in the World" because of the tremendous tonnage of ore that moved over the line. In its glory days, it ran approximately 1,000 cars per day from Butte to Anaconda, which translates to 48,731 tons of ore per day. The BA&P, an electrification pioneer, converted from coal-fired steam engines to electric engines in 1913 and was the first freight railroad in the world to electrify.

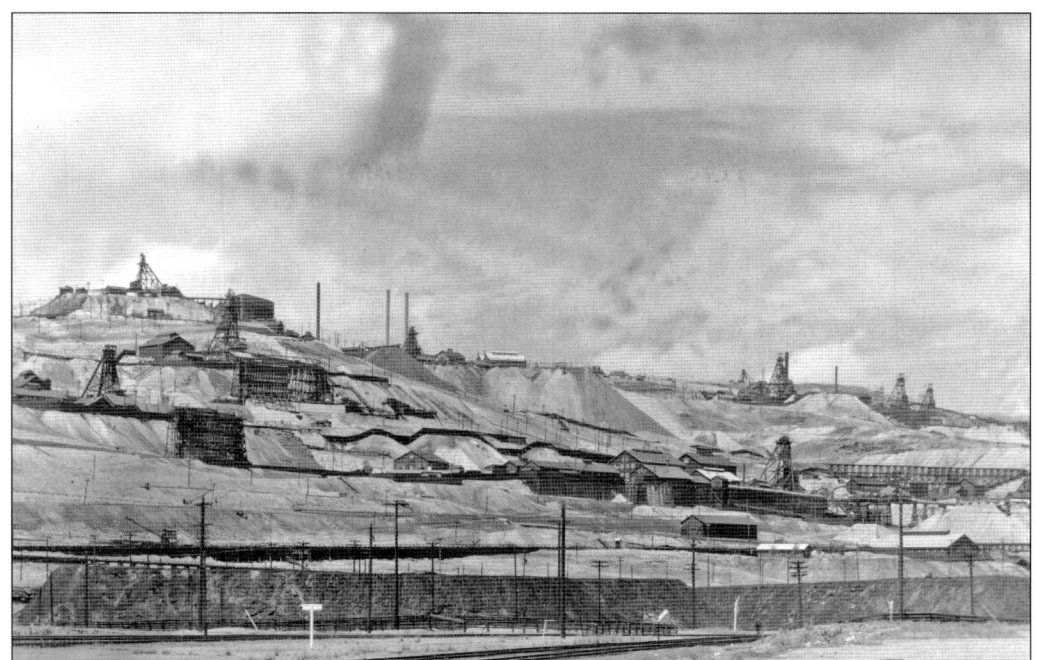

Butte's copper fueled the Age of Electricity. As early as 1882, the large patchwork of Butte mines was generating 10 percent of America's total copper output. Thanks to the establishment of Marcus Daly's world-class smelting facilities in Anaconda, The ACM accounted for 41 percent of the nation's total copper output in 1885. The company continued to grow over the next 40 years. By the early 1920s, the ACM began to broaden its markets and acquisitions: brass and aluminum plants; wire and cable companies; timberlands; and other copper, silver, and uranium mining properties in the United States, Mexico, and Chile. The ACM was the sixth-largest corporation in the United States in the 1930s.

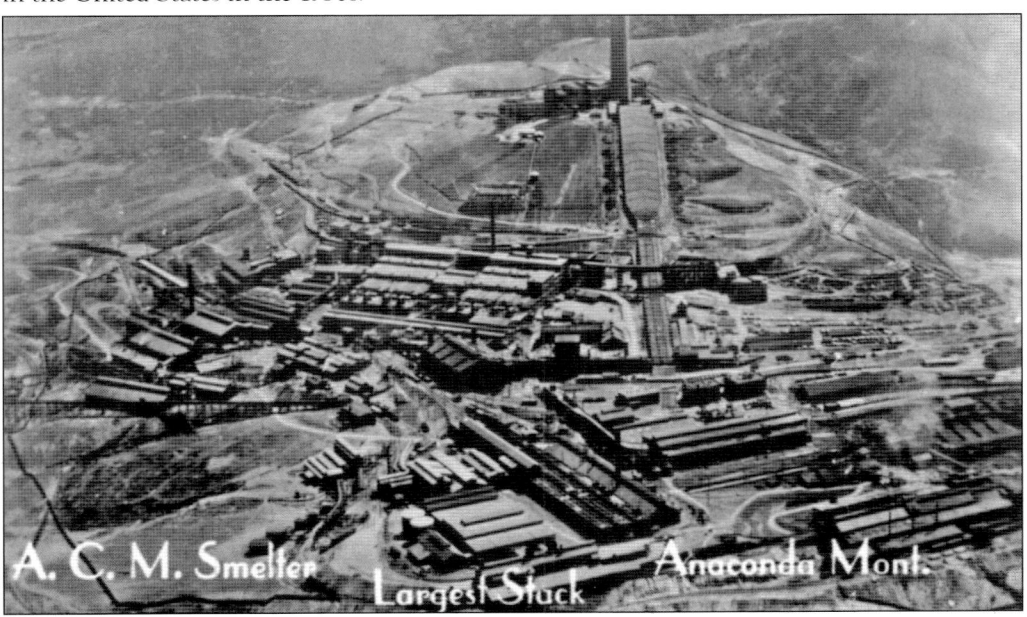

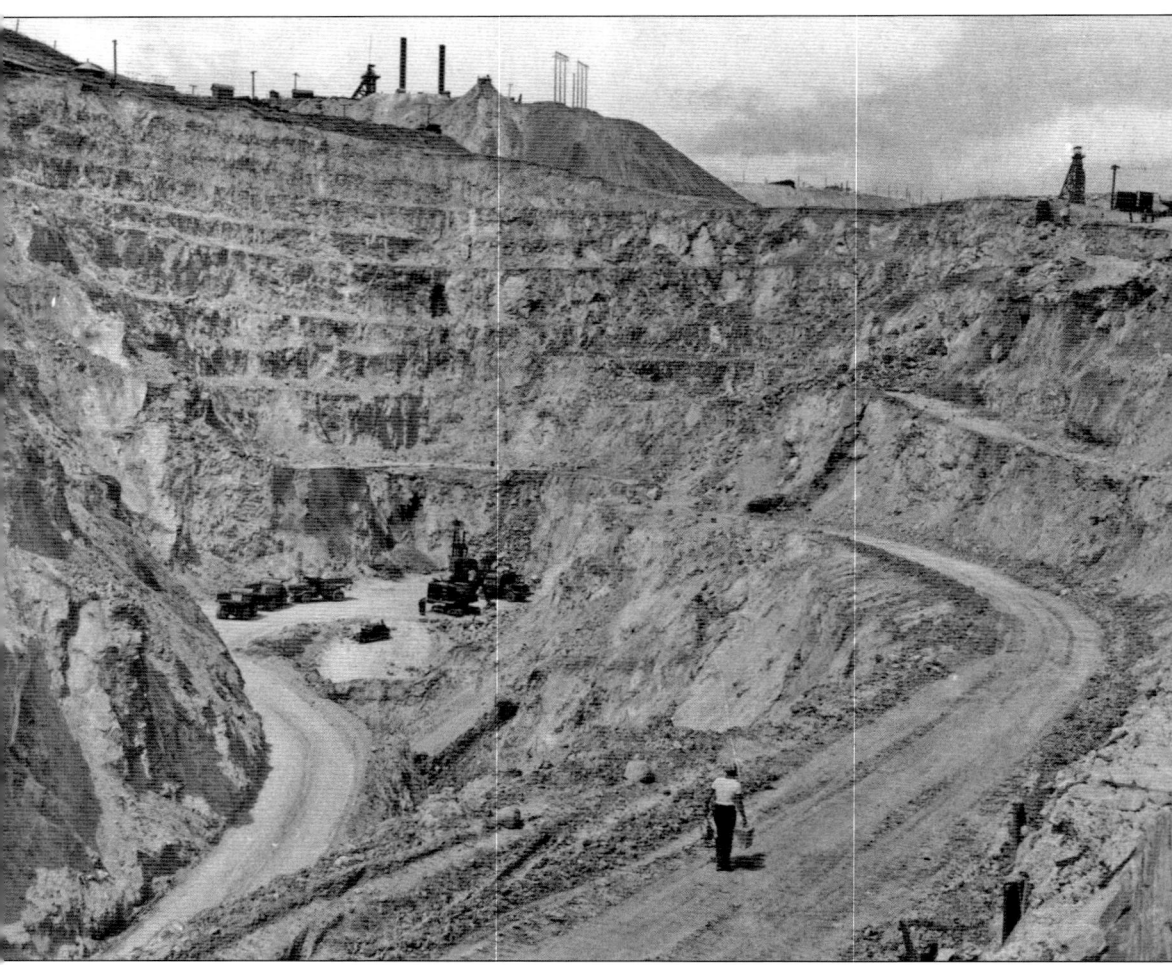

The famed Butte Hill displays some of the district's most productive mines. The Hill provided much-needed strategic metal for two world wars and copper to light the county. A mile high and a mile deep, the Hill met its match when technology could not reach any greater depths. Ore bodies below this mark are still untapped. The ACM agreed to open a pit mine on the Hill in the 1950s after other methods of large-scale underground mining failed to meet production figures. The Berkeley Pit would consume three strong ethnic neighborhoods, eliminate the work of underground miners, and leave an environmental legacy to be dealt with by future generations.

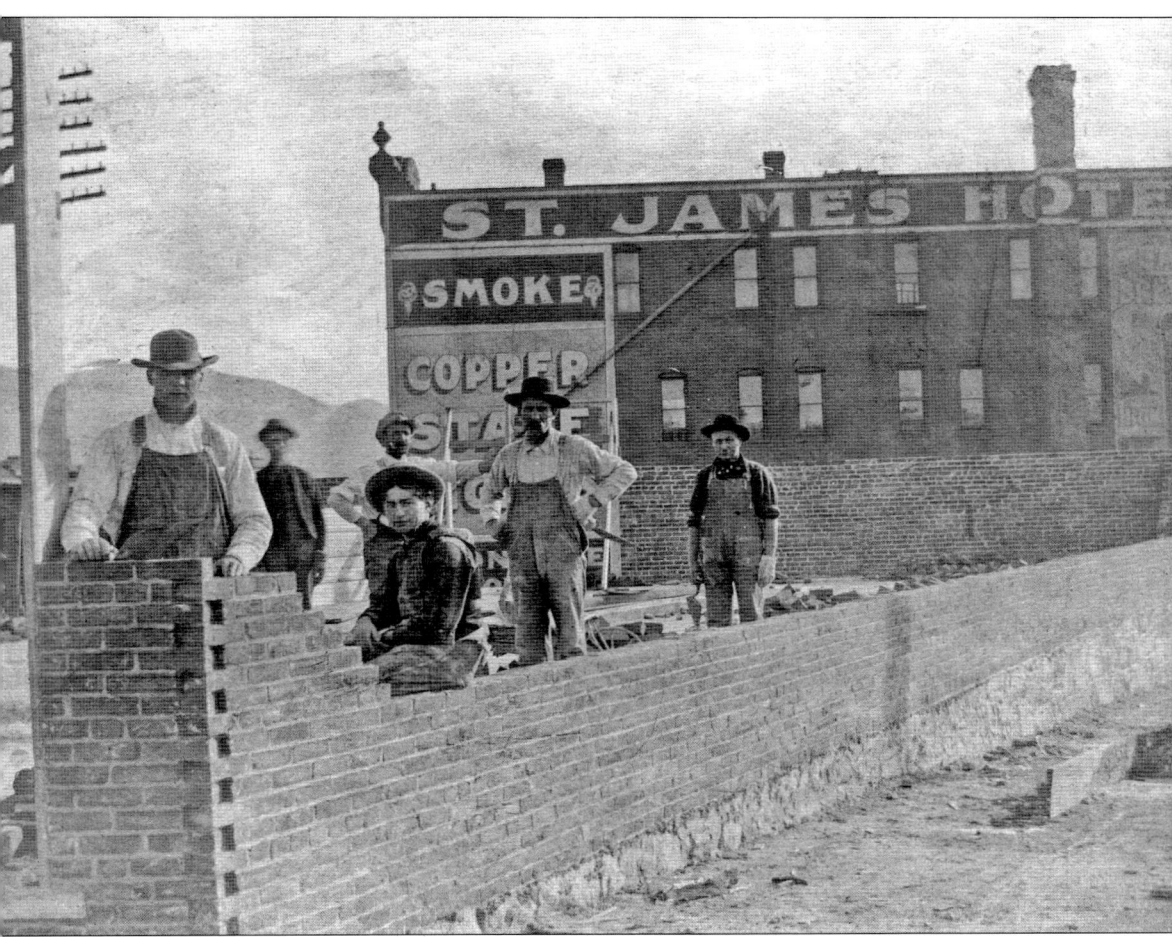

Work underground fed work on the surface. The need for workers to mine the ore created a need for housing, groceries, medical care, and other goods and services. Bricklayers, carpenters, ironworkers, bridge builders, pipe fitters, plumbers, machinists, blacksmiths, bankers, financiers, real estate developers, butchers, bakers, and druggists were just a few of the occupations necessary to build the city and to house and feed the mine workers and owners. This photograph shows bricklayers constructing a two-story building on Utah Street. The building would become the Ryan Food and Produce Company. This neighborhood was known as the warehouse district, and all goods and services were delivered to warehouses via rail and moved uptown by teamsters using horse-drawn wagons before 1915 and trucks thereafter.

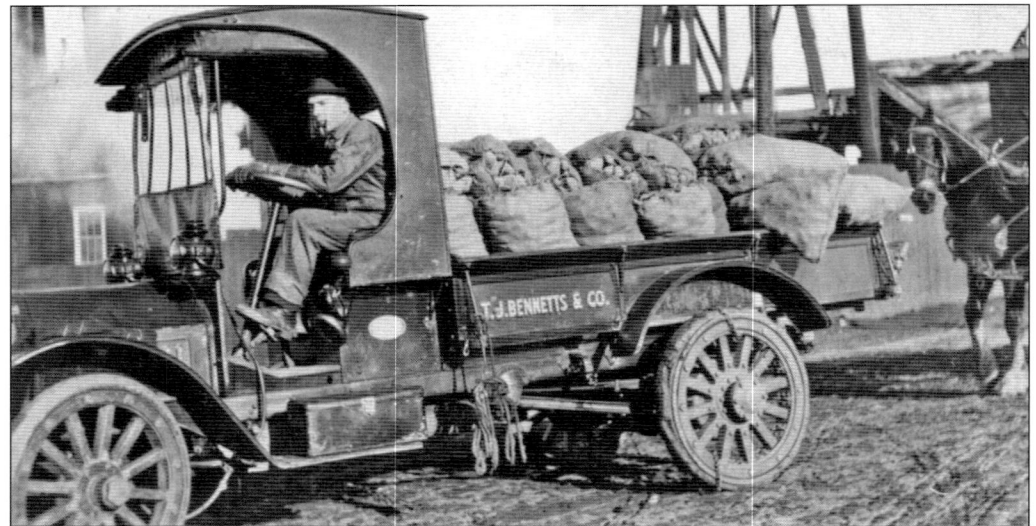

Neighborhood grocers, mercantiles, hardware stores, and coal suppliers were part of the surface activity, providing much-needed sustenance for miners, their families, and the industry itself. Miners lived right in the midst of the industrial hubbub where they worked, sharing real estate with industrial buildings. T. J. Bennett's was a Cornish grocery store that occupied the storefront of a two-story building with the Sons of St. George on the corner of Center and Main Streets, and Crescent Creamery supplied milk and dairy products throughout the city.

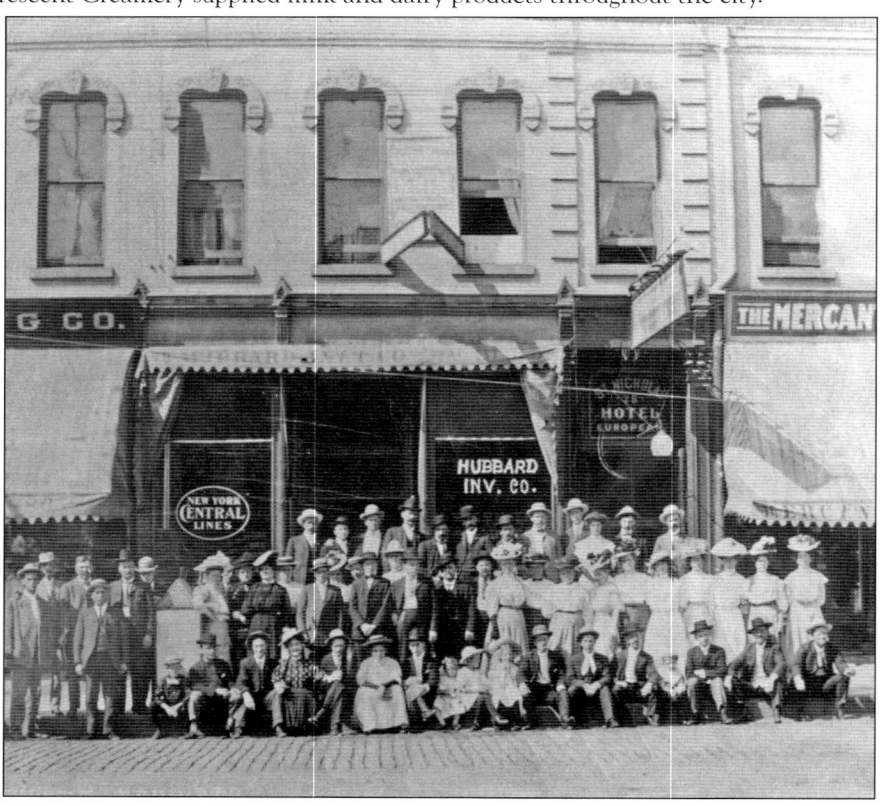

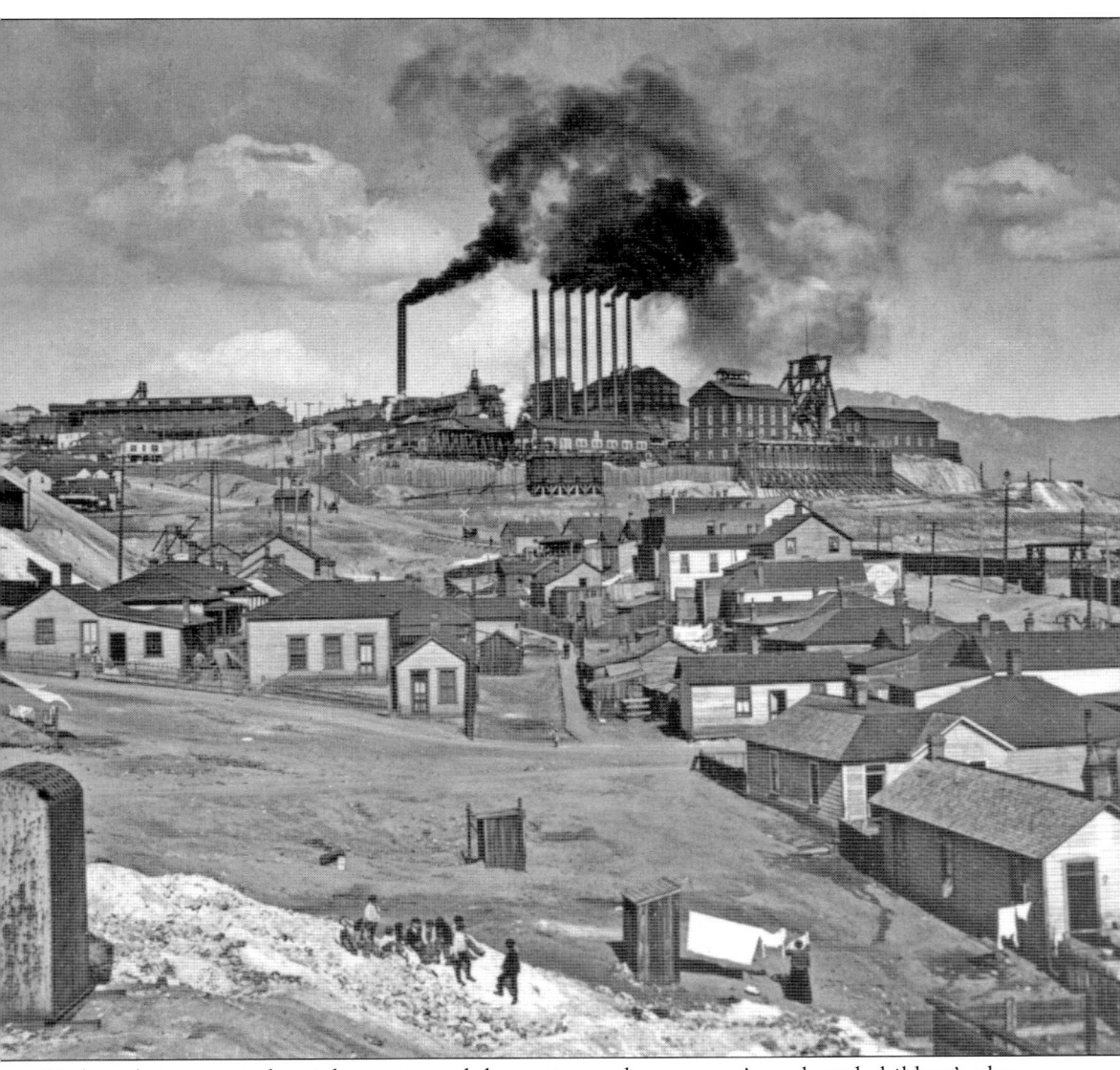

With such intense industrial activity and dramatic weather, women's work and children's play were indeed challenging. They were constantly assaulted by the sights, sounds, and smells of the industry around them. Women washed clothes on Mondays and defrosted and dusted them of soot on Tuesdays. Children played in the course slag, the sandy residue from which metals have been removed by a smelter. (Courtesy of the Montana Historical Society.)

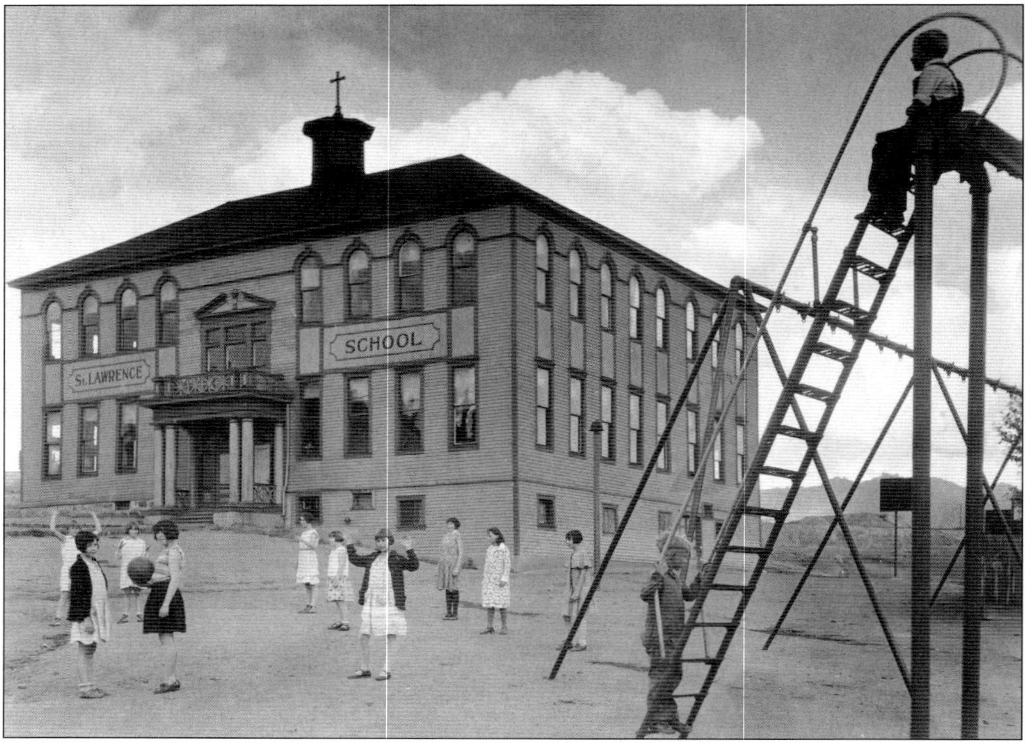

Actual playgrounds in Butte were few and far between for many years, and they certainly were not of today's variety. The hard crust of dirt under swings and teeter-totters made children all that more careful not to fall or get pushed off, although scraped knees and elbows were common occurrences. The children and young people took on the same attitude that their parents had—kids were rough and tumble. They too had to prove their worth when new to a neighborhood. They didn't dare cry when they scraped their knees and elbows on the hard ground.

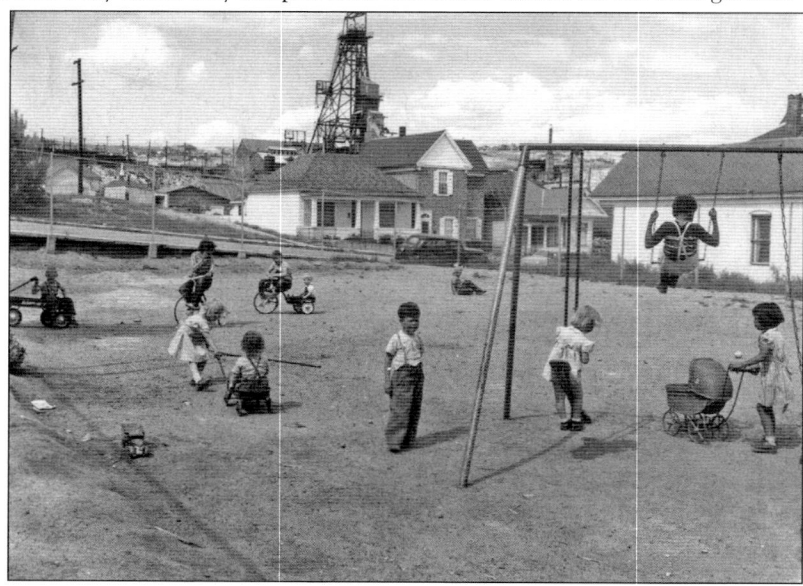

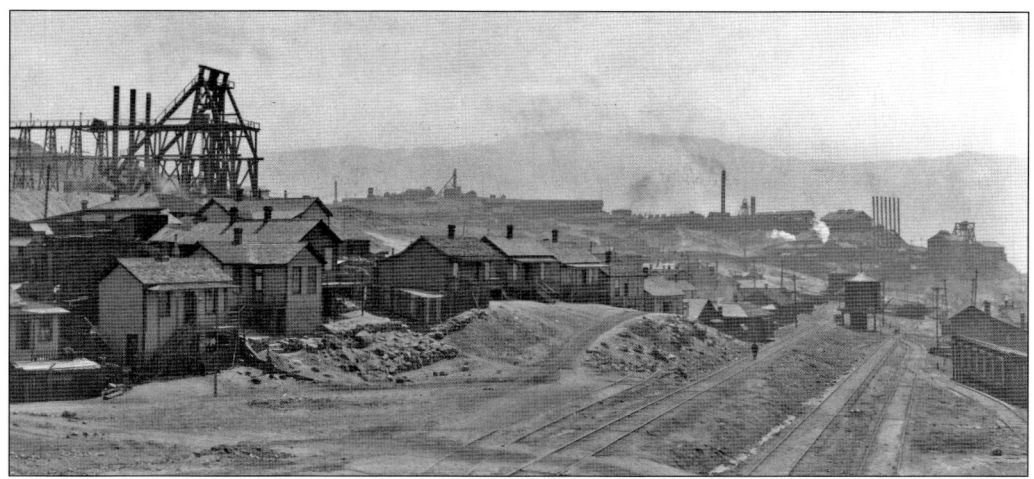

The railroad track-switching yard was right in the center of a residential area, just north of St. Mary's School. The tracks brought trains to be loaded with ore for smelting and refining. Schoolchildren would play on the cars that stood still for any length of time, walk the tracks awaiting the thunder of a coming train, and play "chicken" as the conductors would pull the whistle and yell for them to get out of the way. (Courtesy of the Montana Historical Society, photograph by John L. Maloney.)

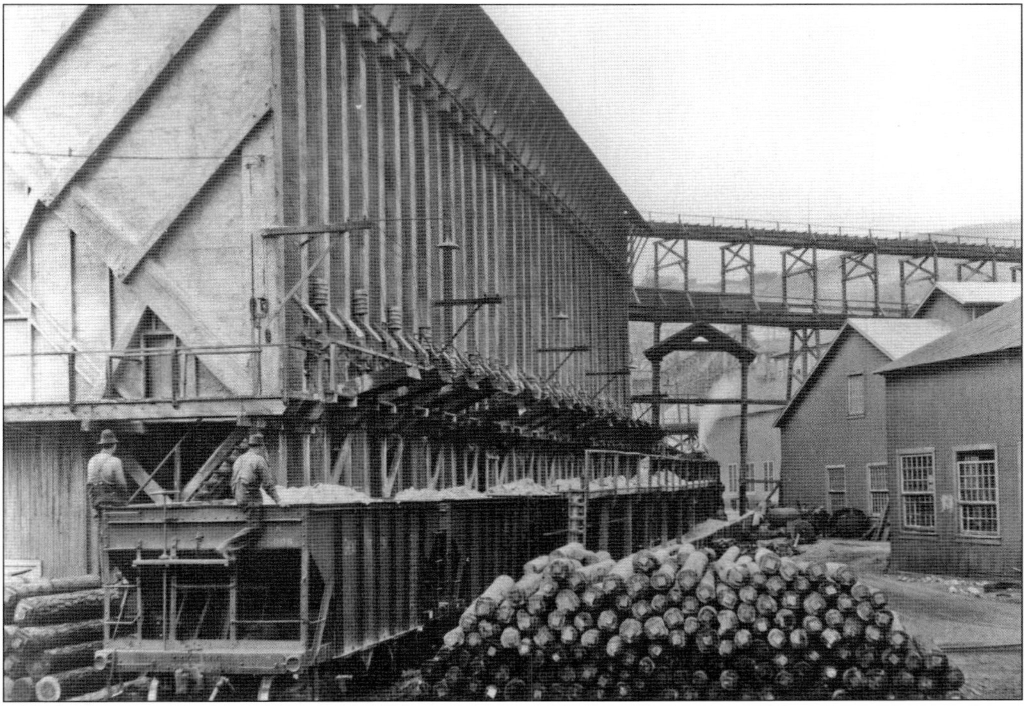

People became acclimated to the peculiar sounds of the cages being lowered and raised by the huge hoists, by the sounds of the bells and whistles that signaled shift ends and warned of descending cages, and the sound of the ore being dumped from the chutes into the railroad cars for transport to smelters. People reminisce that when the sounds stopped, they feared for the lives of the miners. There would be a huge, simultaneous sigh of relief when the noise resumed.

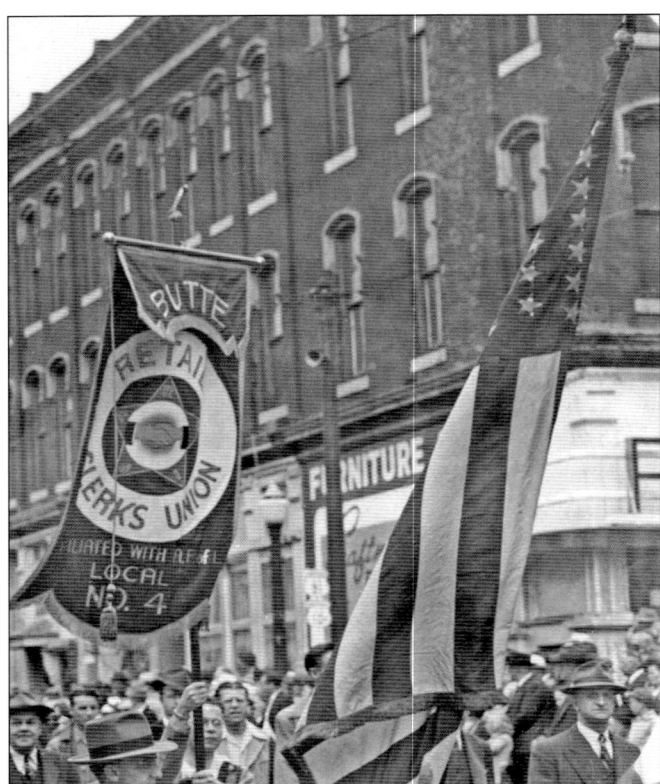

Butte was strenuous in protecting the rights of workers. Butte workers organized early in the mining camp's history, with the first labor strike occurring in 1878. The workers organized all crafts and trades in the city of Butte, and they founded the Butte Miners' Union No. 1, the mighty Western Federation of Miners, and the Knights of Labor. They also contributed to the creation of the American Labor Union, the Western Labor Union, and the Industrial Workers of the World.

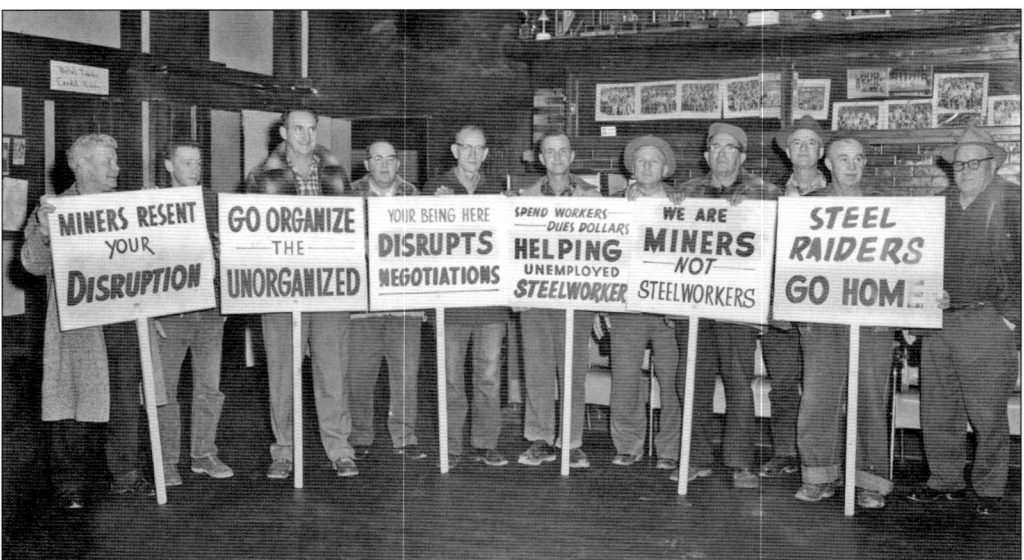

The workingmen and women of Butte all understood the strength of standing together. In Butte, every occupation was unionized into a bargaining unit. In the early 1900s, the City Directory lists over 50 unions representing most occupations. There are many firsts in Butte when it comes to labor, and the fact that they organized early gave them great influence with the ACM. The ACM may have been strong and influential, but the work force strived to be equally strong.

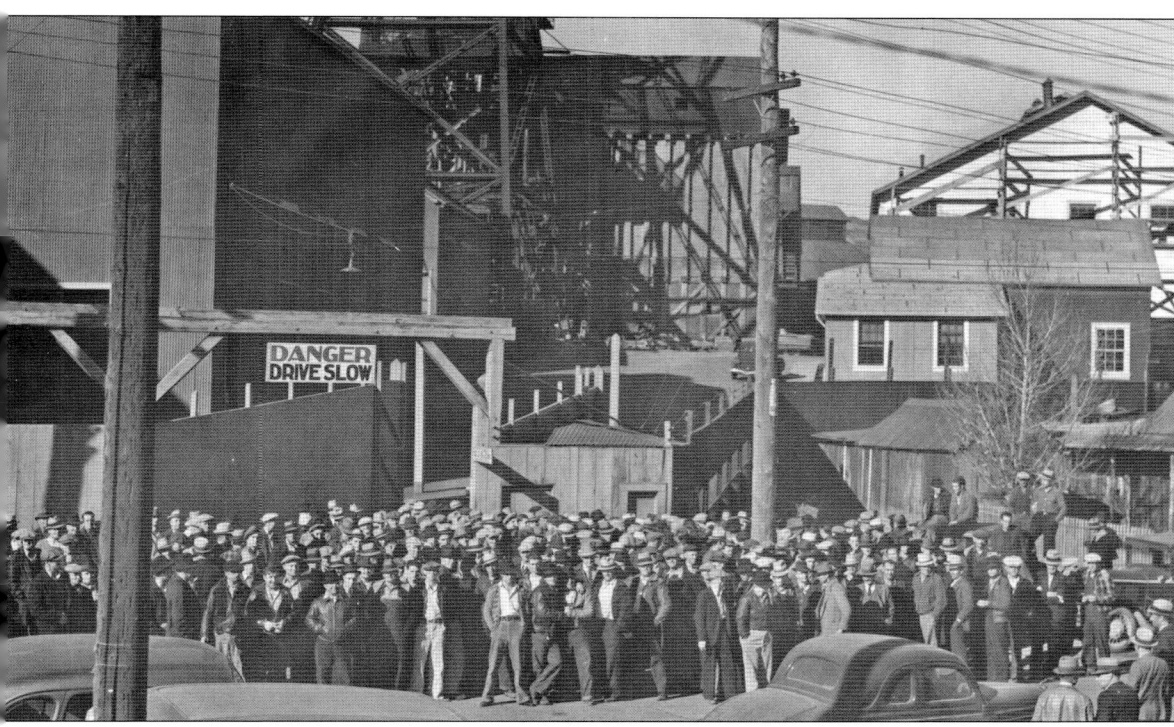

Labor strikes were a common occurrence in Butte at the start of the 20th century. Called "the Gibraltar of Unicnism," Butte saw more than its share of strikes as miners sought to improve working conditions and increase wages. Unions saved the lives of workers who would otherwise have been lost as employers put production well ahead of safety concerns. In 1934, one of the most significant strikes in the nation's history took place. The strike lasted for four months, and the ACM hired armed guards to keep strikers from mine entrances. Strikes could become ugly, as men who wanted only to provide for their families had to pit themselves against their employer in order to ensure that they received fair pay and worked in safe conditions.

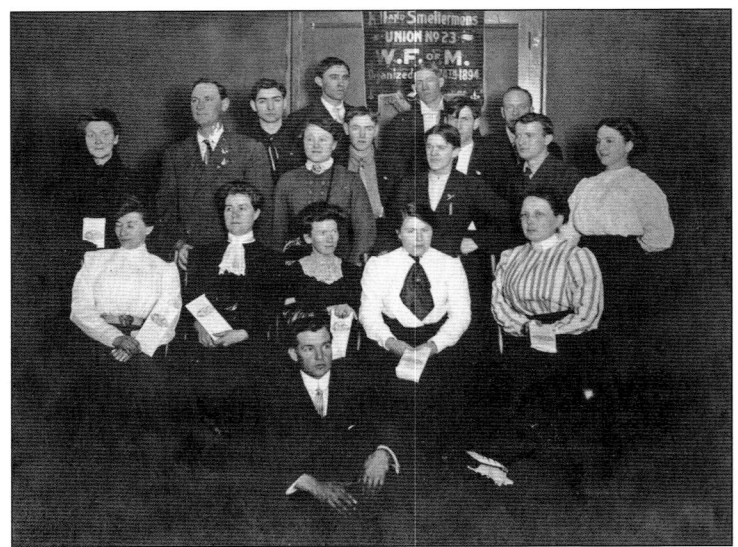

The role of women was paramount to the success of the mining industry. Were it not for the women who cared for the miners, making their homes, preparing their meals, and building a solid base for a community to grow upon, the camp would have failed. But women also worked outside of the home. The Women's Protective Union (WPU) was organized in 1890 under the powerful Western Federation of Miners.

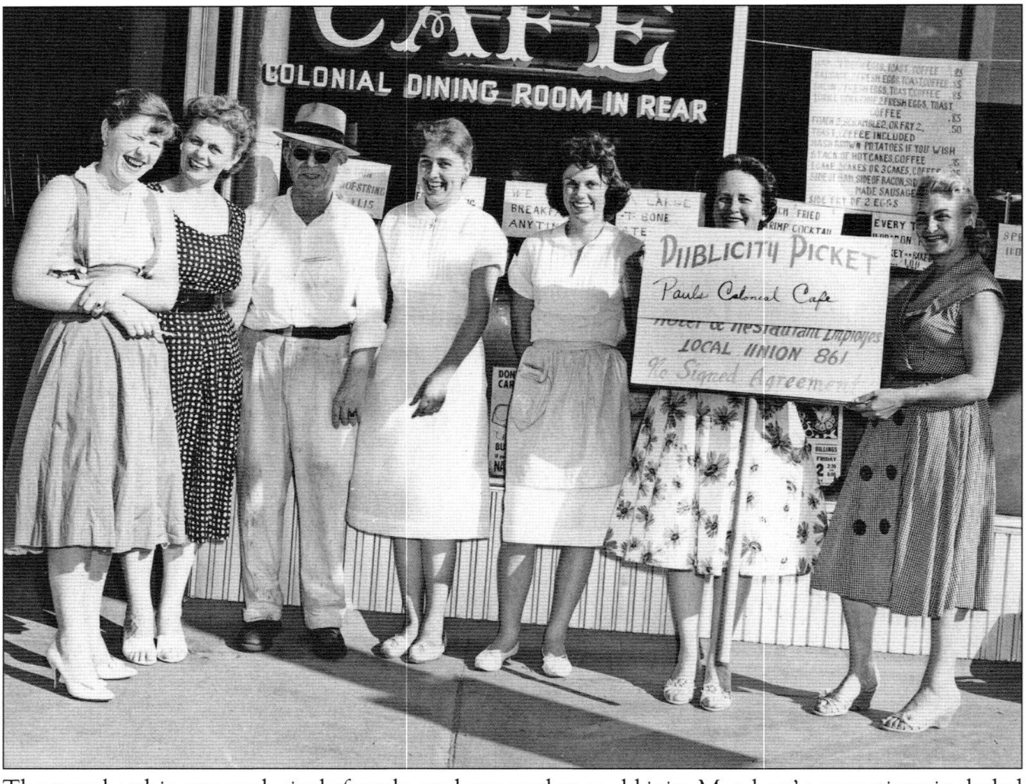

The membership was exclusively female, and any worker could join. Members' occupations included restaurant workers, boardinghouse operators, bucket girls, maids, tamale makers, nursemaids, vaudeville performers, theater usherettes, midwives, milliners, and fortune-tellers. The WPU was a very powerful organization, and in 1903, it led the nation to a 10-hour workday and increased wages in 1920. In Butte, wages for women averaged $17 to $18 per week, while the national average was $12 per week.

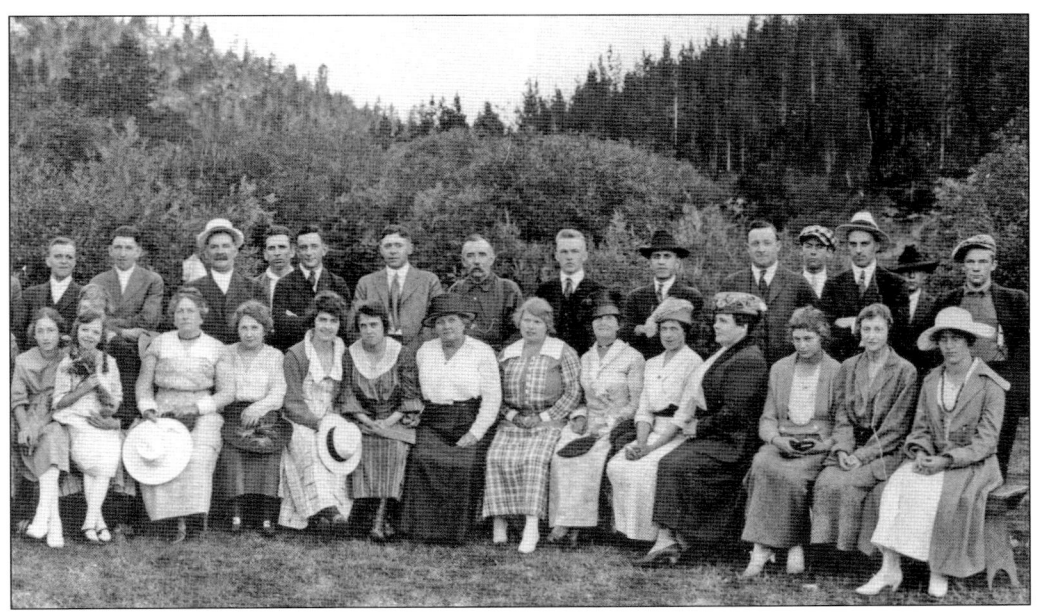

The women of Butte often were a force in the political arena as well, sponsoring candidates and rallying around issues that were important to them, such as education, health and welfare, and wages. This photograph shows employees of the county during a summer picnic in 1919. By that time, women were welcomed into the government and business worlds. The image below shows only a portion of the staff of Symon's Department Store, a majority of whom were women. (Above, courtesy of the Tracy Thornton collection.)

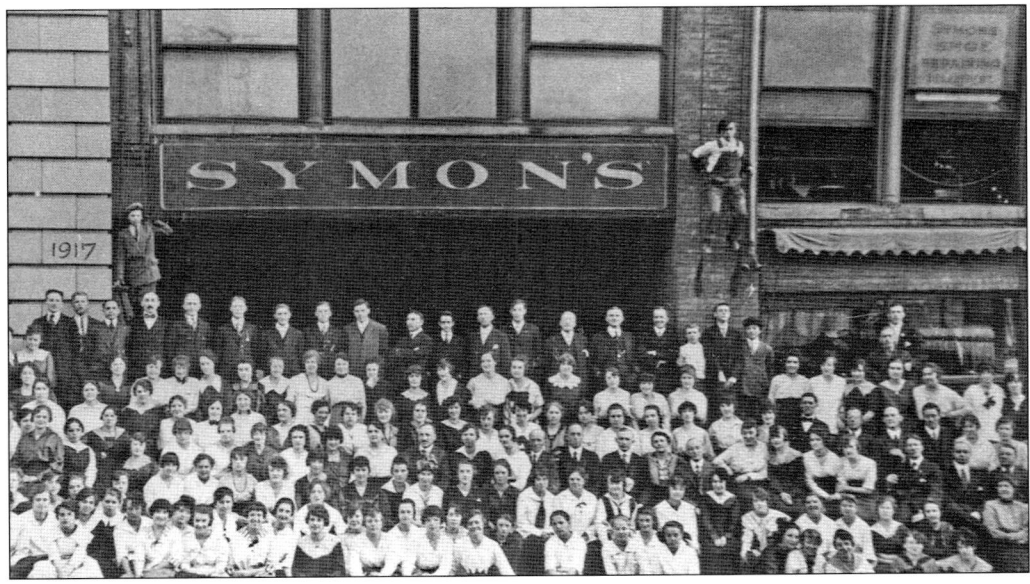

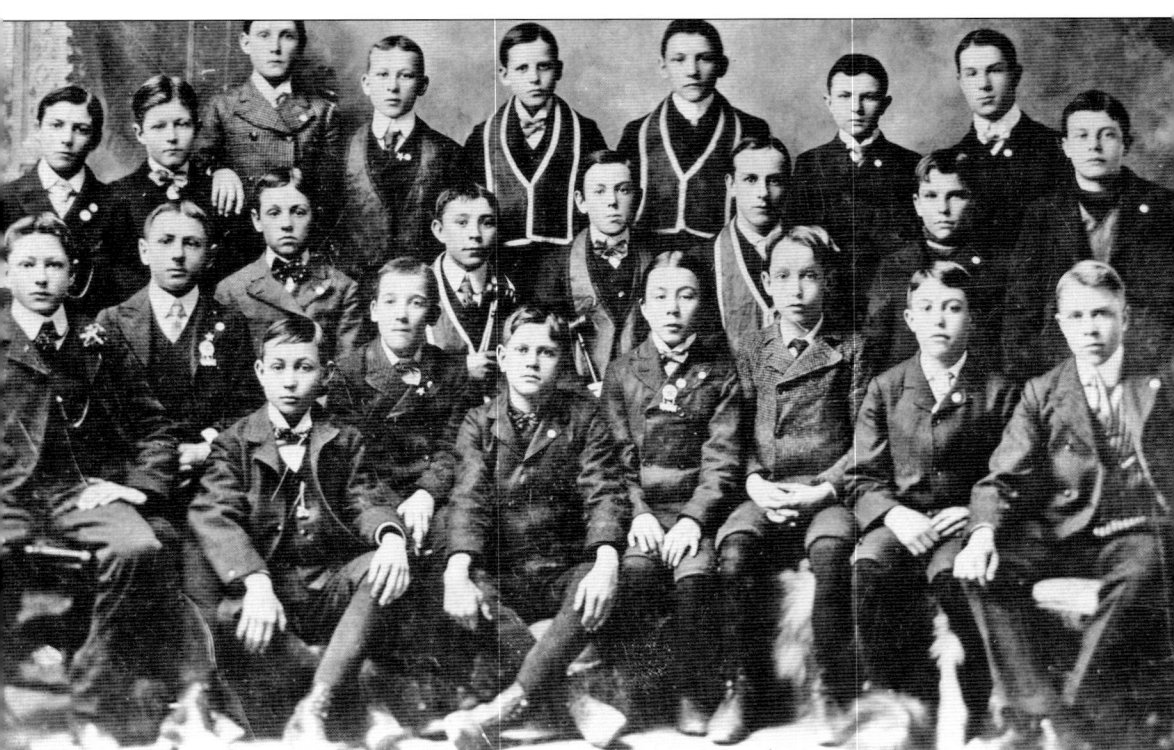

Children found their niches in the working world as well, and working as a newsboy, although not an easy duty, was a common endeavor. The newsboys were organized in Butte as early as 1900. Rather than enlisting a business agent, they had a mother who ensured they received correct payment and were not unfairly treated. A newsboys' income made a big difference in many households. With two major newspapers published in Butte, one in the morning and one in the evening, there were plenty of opportunities for hardworking young lads. (Courtesy of the William Tretheway collection.)

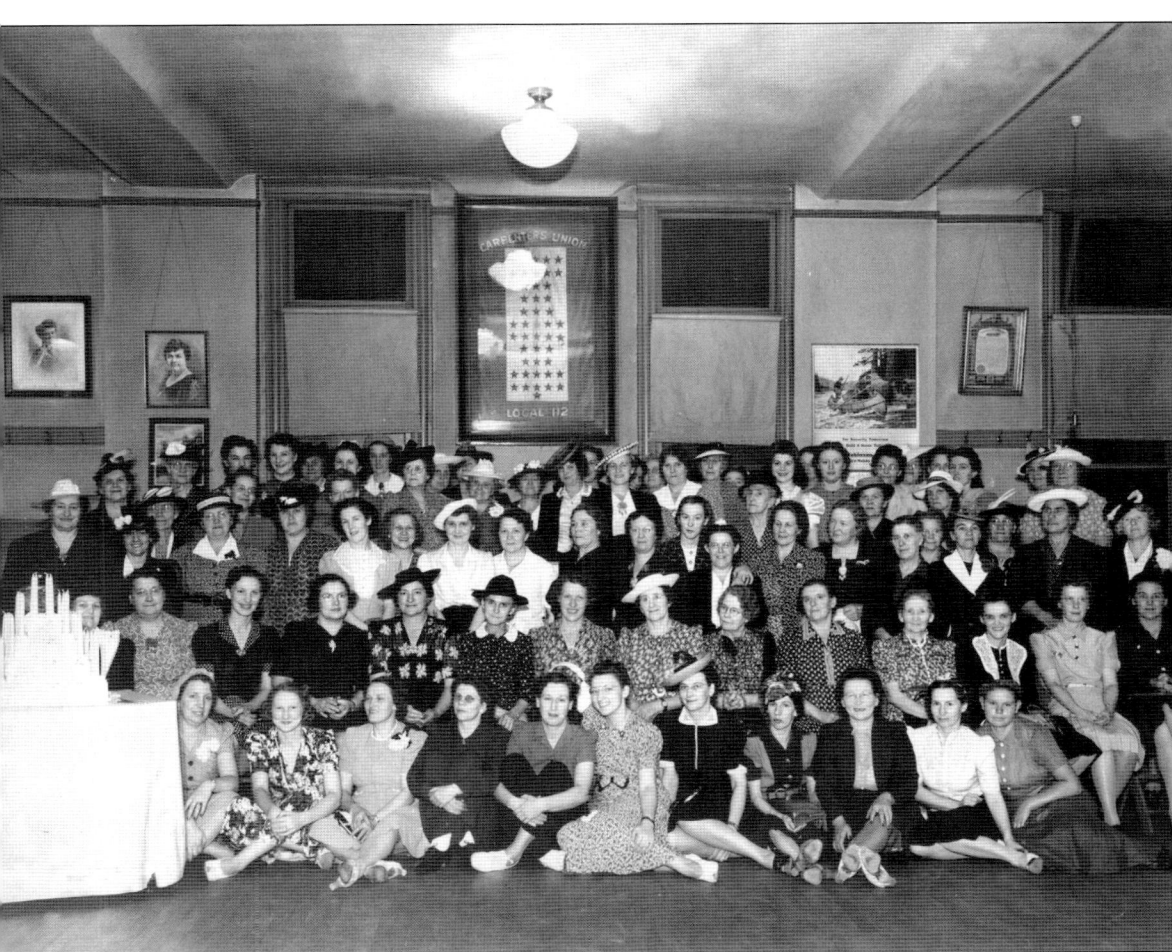

The Butte labor unions all have low numbers: Teamsters' Union Local No. 2, Butte Miners' Union Local No. 1, and Laundry Workers' Local No. 4. The low numbers are enviable because they immediately speak to the fact that many unions were established in Butte very early in labor's volatile history. Keeping those numbers becomes impossible as time marches on and work changes. The Butte Carpenters' Union Hall (shown here with members of the Women's Protective Union), the International Brotherhood of Electrical Workers building, and the Butte Teamsters' Union Hall are all still used today to hold union meetings, demonstrating Butte's continuing commitment to labor.

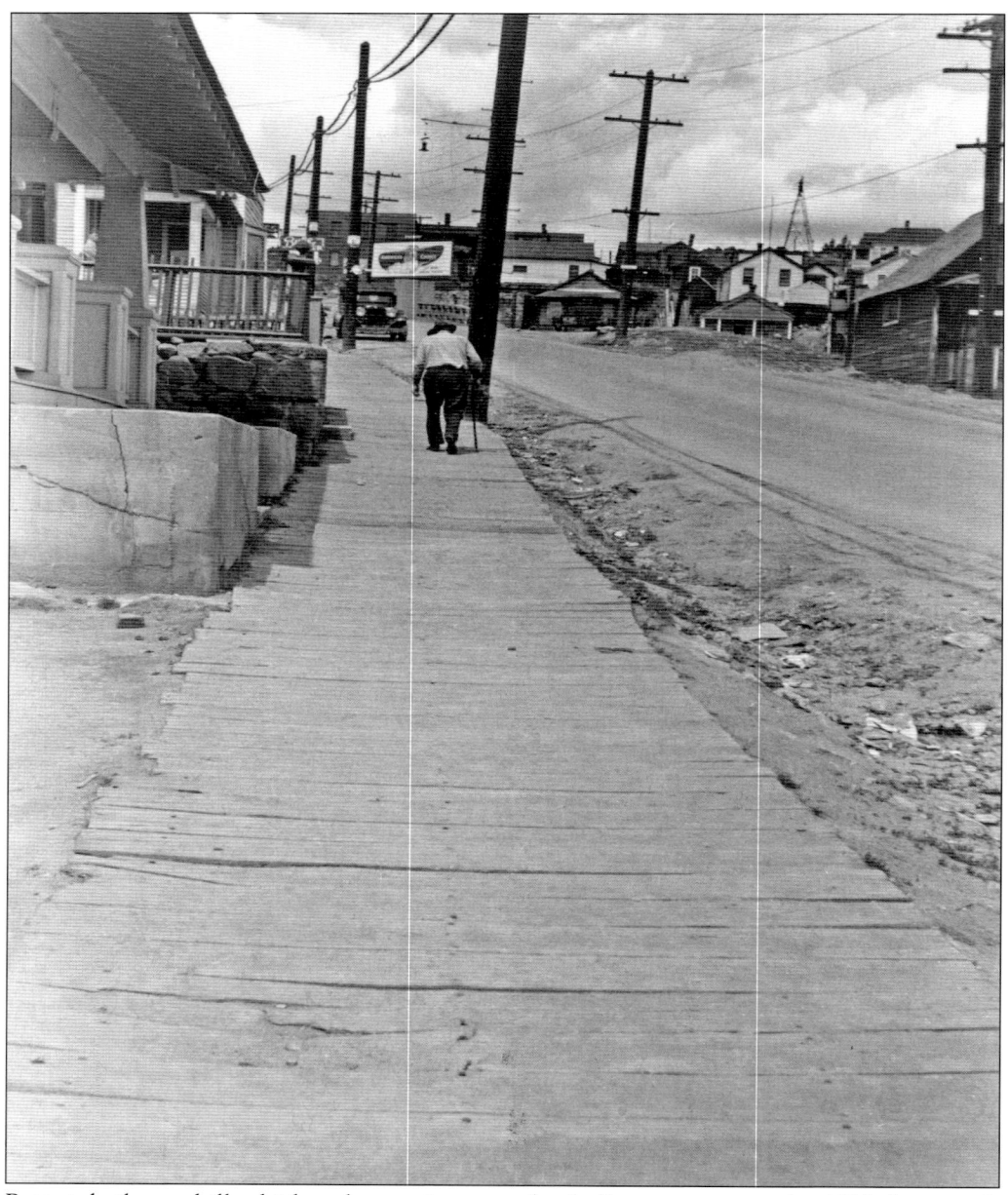

Butte is built on a hill, which makes getting around a challenge, as seen in this 1939 photograph by Arthur Rothstein of a man walking up Main Street. The elevation of this section of Main Street rises at least 280 feet every half mile, making the climb strenuous. The photograph is part of a series taken during the Works Project Administration days. (Courtesy of the Library of Congress.)

Three
BUTTE THE UNIQUE

> *In telling of the peculiarities of Butte there are a thousand and one idiosyncrasies, apropos of nothing in particular, which indicate no especial condition of affairs except that Butte is distinctive, that Butte is unique . . . Butte does not handle municipal affairs on old school political lines; it casts aside the farce of a democracy or republicanism; it elects men to office not political puppets. Like a man of independent thought, it follows a course, which gives greatest good to the greatest number.*
>
> —Thomas F. Rooney, *Butte Evening News*

In Montana, Butte has always been unique because it has little of the "Western" flavor that permeates other communities in the state. Surrounding Butte are rural towns, forest and agricultural land, cowboys, and cattle. Thirty miles down the highway, cattle ranchers kick up dust on their horses and the wheat crop waves in the starlit night. In Butte, rarely is there a cowboy other than the drugstore variety, and neon signs illuminate the night in the city center. It may be small, but it is as urban as any city in the country. From the shoe-shine boy on the streets to the president of large companies, each person had a place in Butte, and Butte had a place for them. Many people considered it to be a classless society. Rich mingled with poor, white-collar worker blended with laborer in the same organization, and the mayor's wife enjoyed the same sorority as the steel worker's wife. It meant little that one had steak and one had Cornish pasties. In a community like Butte, where the tide of economics could shift without warning, people had to stick together. Regardless of its external idiosyncrasies, Butte was a stalwart community that claimed its place among the larger, more urbane communities in the country. Butte the Unique learned, and quickly, how to mold its fortunes out of what it had and how to take solid rock and turn it into a marketable commodity.

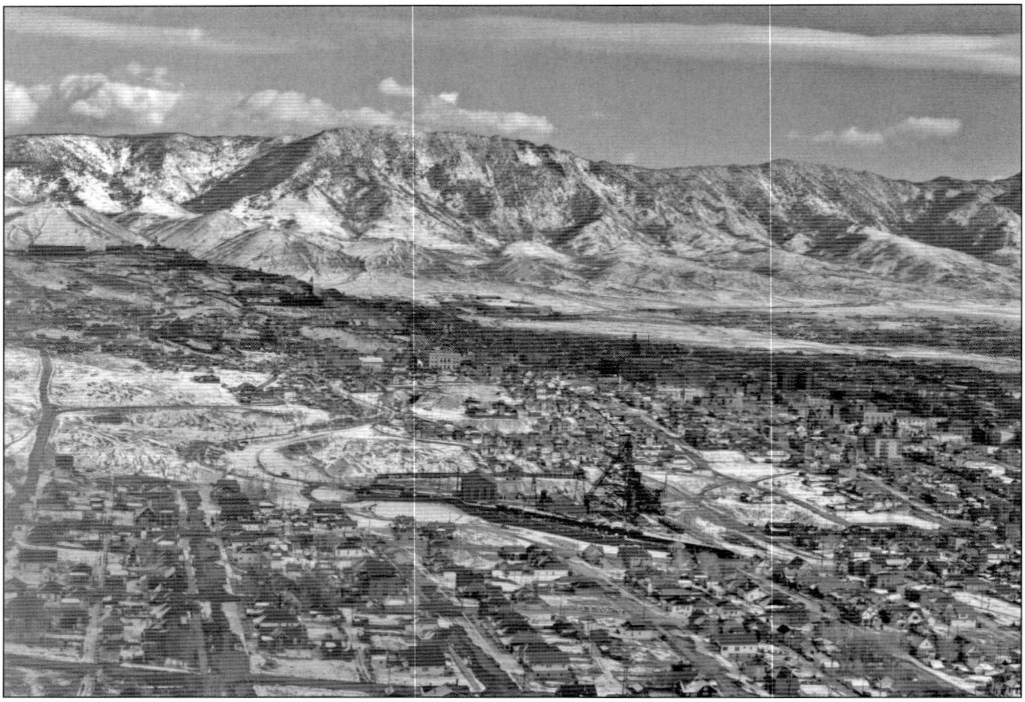

Surrounded by the Continental Divide, Butte is dotted with magnificent buildings, industrial remnants, and miners' cottages—making the built environment one of a kind. The fact that Butte survived the mining camp phenomena is unique to mining towns throughout the world. Butte had a run of 50 years as the nation's greatest copper-producing center, and it still is producing a good share of the world's copper supply. In addition, Butte residents were, and still are, fiercely loyal to their community. Often dubbed "Butte, America," the city has an attitude that is nourished by the steadfast, unfaltering confidence of its people. (Above, courtesy of the Montana Historical Society.)

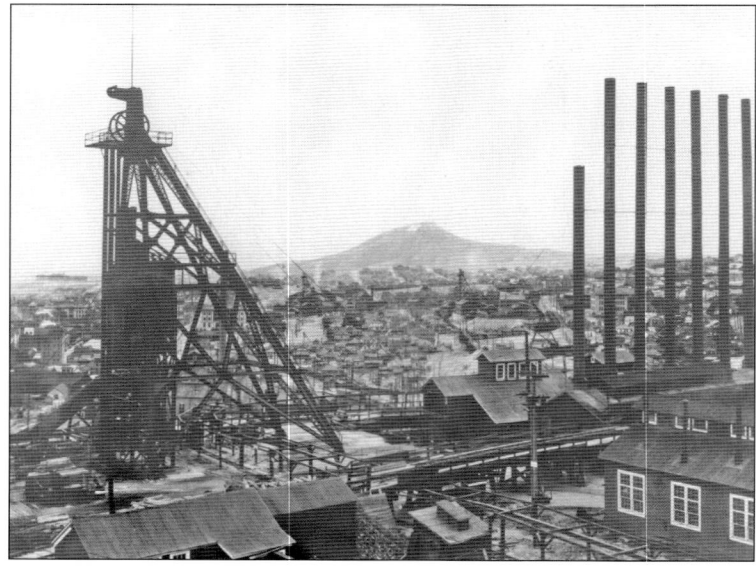

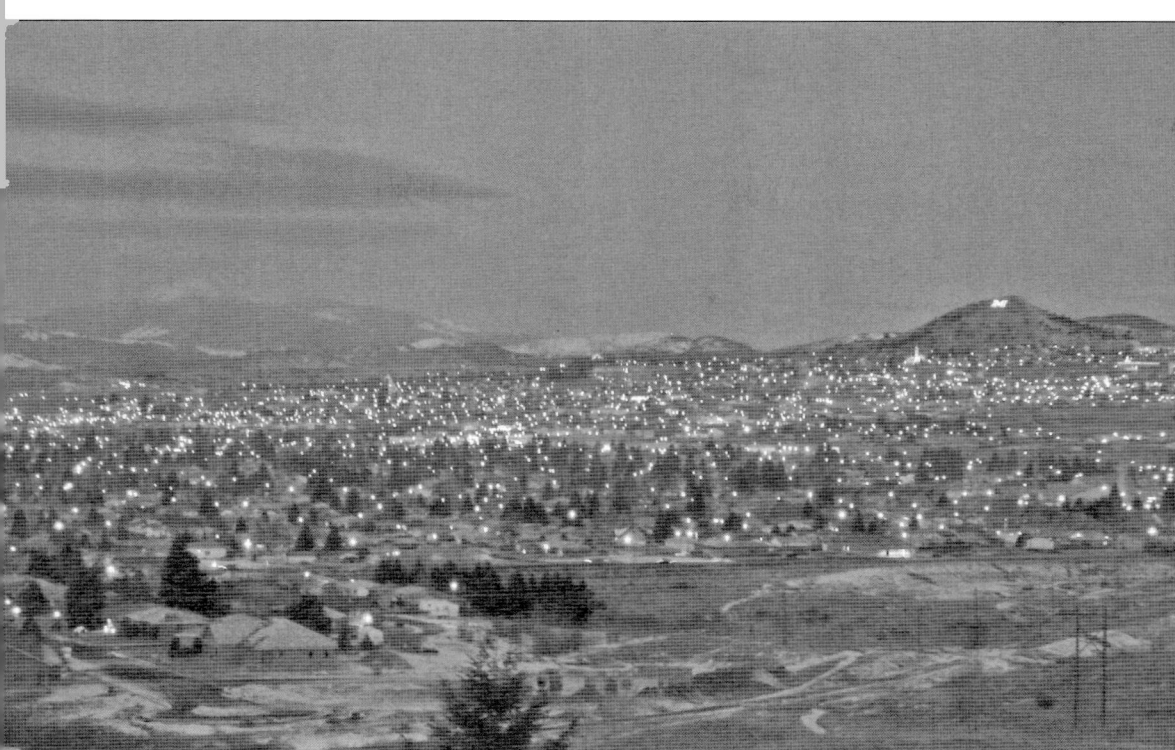

Butte has been called unpredictable. As described in the Writers' Program of the WPA in 1941, the city was "virtuous yet wanton, vindictive and forgiving, hard headed or charitable, kind, cruel, religious, agnostic, sordid, exalted, gay and tragic." Butte is viewed as a diamond in the sky at night and by some as the "perch of the devil" by day. There is no end to the adjectives that can be attributed to Butte, some fitting, some not so. Few would have called Butte an attractive town, especially when the smoke from the smelters decimated everything green in the early 1900s. Yet the city sparkles like a cluster of diamonds at night, and everyone in Butte knows that it isn't what is on the outside but rather what is in the hearts and minds of its people that keep Butte alive. (Courtesy of Rose Sladek.)

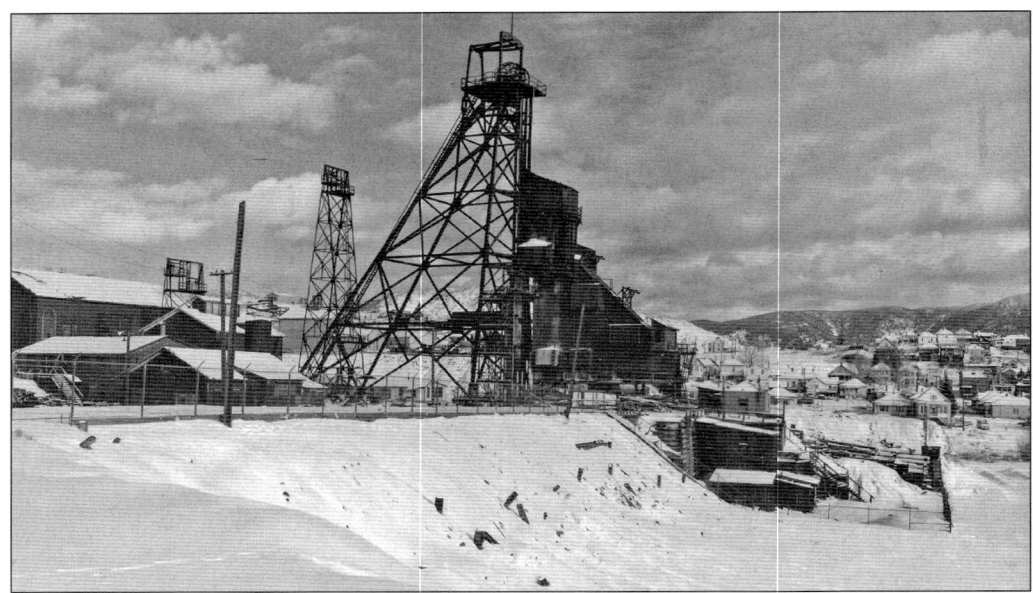

Butte has a dramatic and unique landscape. Rugged in its own right, the landscape is home to towering headframes that reach majestically toward the sky, unequivocally identifying it as having been a major industrial power. The statuesque headframes add a degree of sophistication to the landscape and tell a story wherein words are unnecessary.

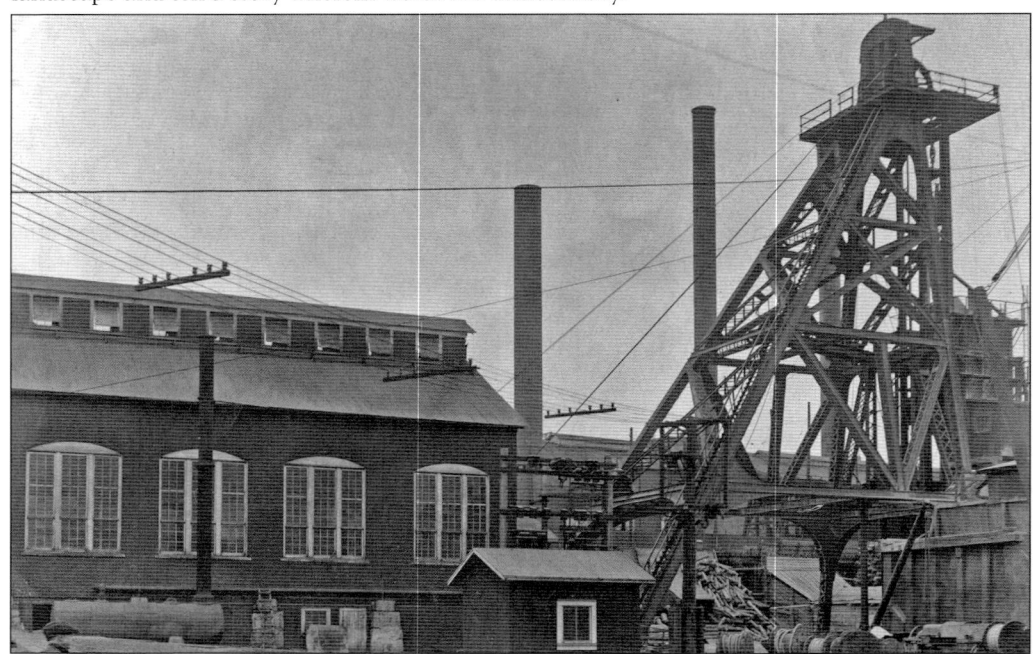

The first steel headframe to appear in Butte was the 100-foot structure erected at the Diamond Mine in 1898 at a cost of $8,940. That same year, steel headframes were erected at the Original and Steward Mines. In both cases, the steel structure was erected over the wooden headframe, which continued to operate until the new structure was complete. By the start of the 20th century, the four-part steel headframe was a familiar sight on the Butte Hill.

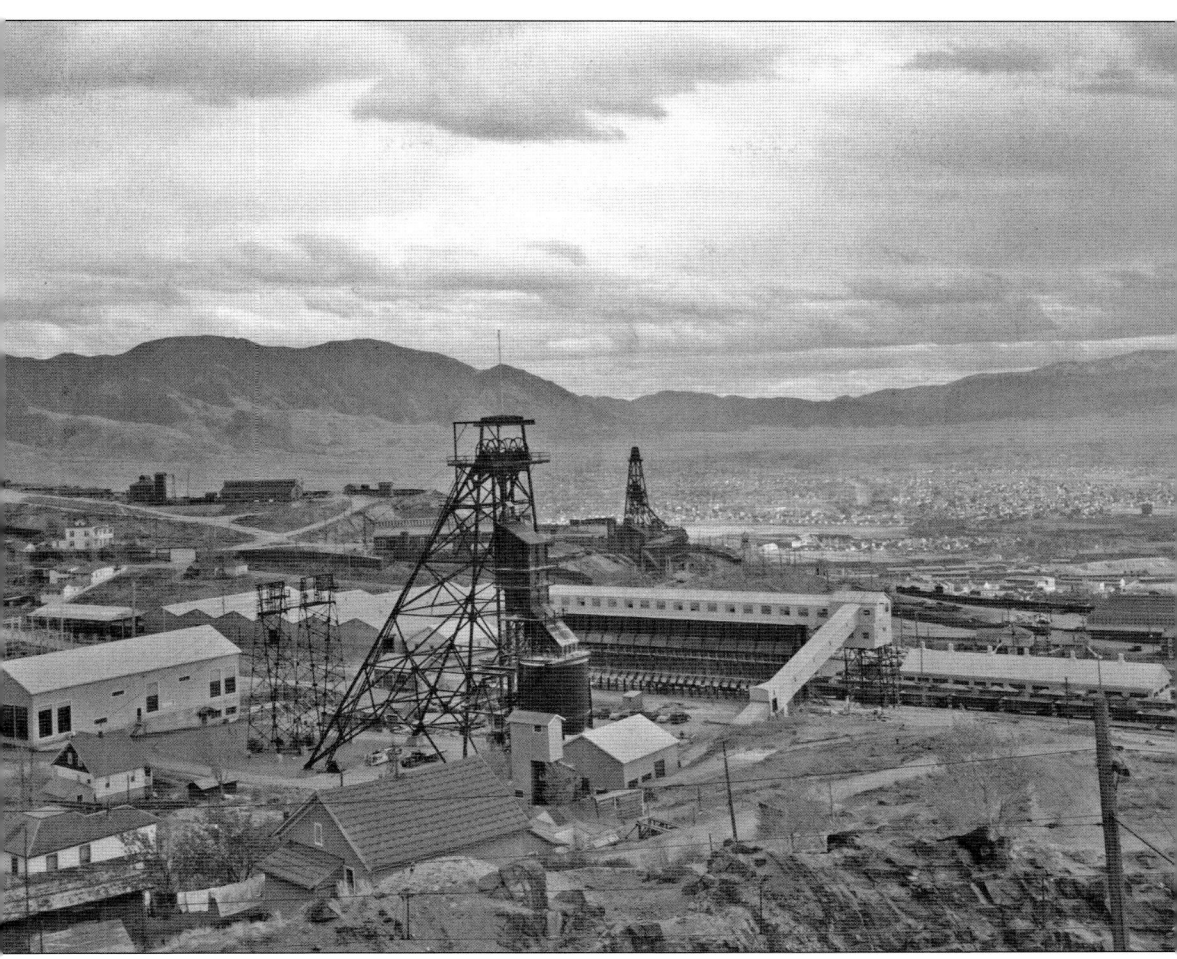

Butte's landscape was dramatically shaped by the copper industry. In addition to the headframes, hoist houses and smokestacks covered large areas of the Butte Hill, immediately impressing the visitor with the enormity and sophistication of the industry. "A very striking feature of the camp is the works and houses of the great Anaconda group of mines," remarked Prof. Arthur Lakes in 1900. He continued, "It consists of lofty plant houses and numerous groups of exceedingly tall black chimneys. Seven in a row of these belong to the Never Sweat Mine alone." The Kelley Mine, shown here, illustrates a 1947 evolution in underground mining using block caving to offset the cost of extracting ore of continually diminishing grade and to increase profit. Many of the structures that made up the Kelley Mine, including the headframe, warehouse, and office, still exist.

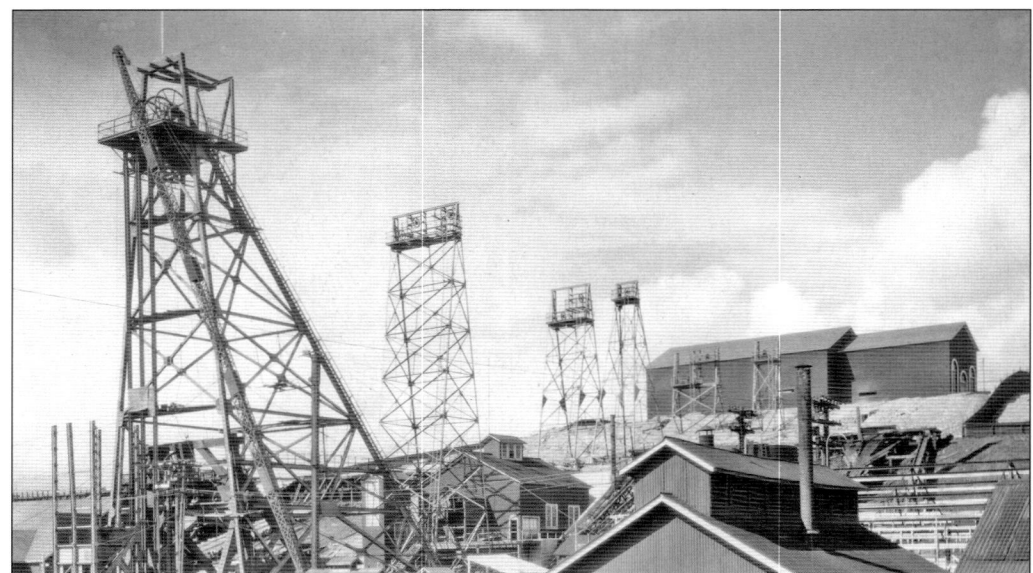

The various sizes and shapes of the buildings on the Hill reflected their different functions and the complexity of the mining process. In 1900, all of the machinery necessary to transform the copper sulfide into metal to be used for electric wire could be seen working in Butte. The various compartments contained everything necessary for production. There were timbering and carpentry shops, ironwork stations, planing rooms, blacksmith shops, machine shops, and large warehouses. The entire mining process could be viewed through the operation of the mine buildings: the hoist house (equipped with a four-cylinder steam engine), ore bins, machine shop, change house, blacksmith shop, ice house (to supply miners with cold water), framing shop, pump house, rope house (for repairing steel hoisting cable), and assay office.

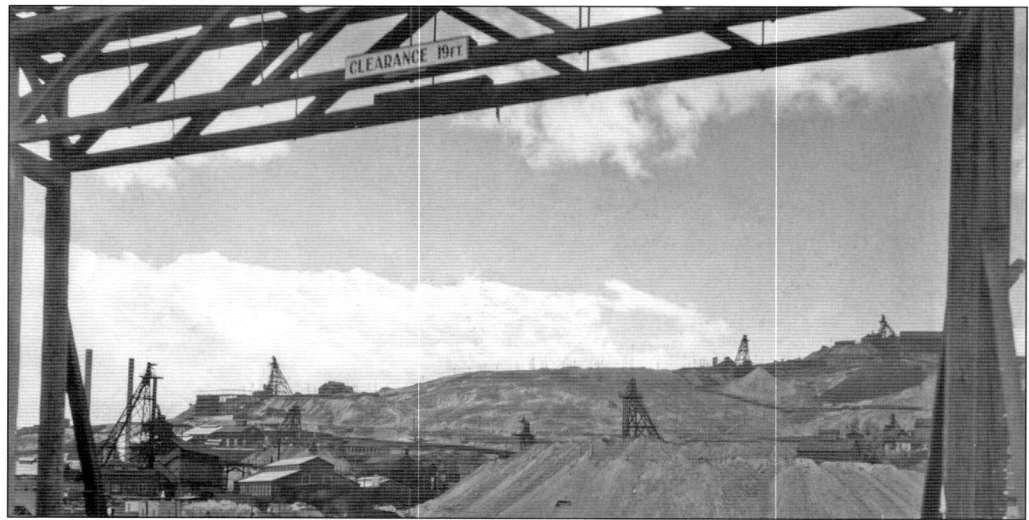

Remaining on the Butte Hill are 14 headframes—2 wooden and 12 steel. They vary in size from the 70-foot Orphan Girl to the 178-foot headframe standing over the Kelley No. 1 shaft. The steel structures offered greater permanence and resistance to environmental deterioration as well as the advantage of portability. They could be disassembled and reconstructed at different mine yards and, over time, the headframes were frequently moved.

The headframes that survive are reminiscent of the more than 80 that punctuated the landscape in 1925. Now protected by a local ordinance, the headframes and their associated buildings are being preserved through grants and volunteer efforts. In the past four years, individuals, corporations, and families have sponsored the lighting of the headframes to honor their past and provide an exceptional vision dotting the landscape at night. Through the efforts of preservationists and retired mine workers, these industrial sites have seen some unique adaptive reuses.

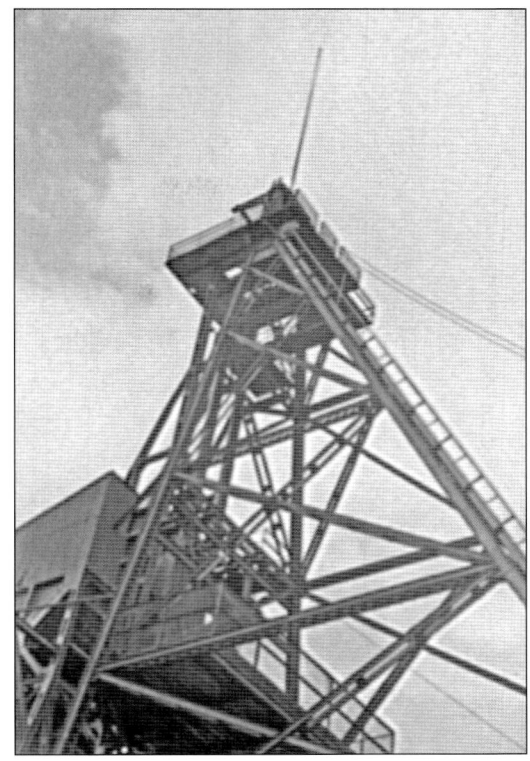

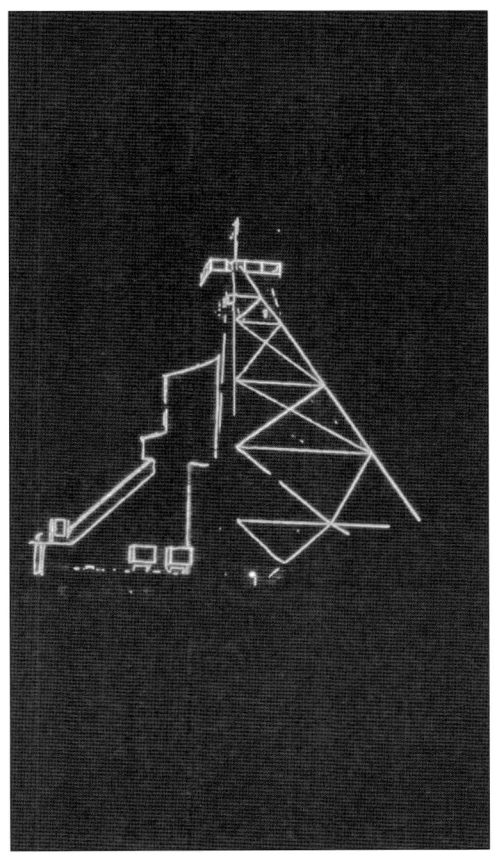

For example, the Original Mine Yard serves as an outdoor theater venue in the summer months, and the Orphan Girl Mine is the home of the World Museum of Mining. The museum offers an impressive underground experience with retired miners, rope men, and hoisting engineers sharing their work history with tourists and schoolchildren. (Archives staff photograph.)

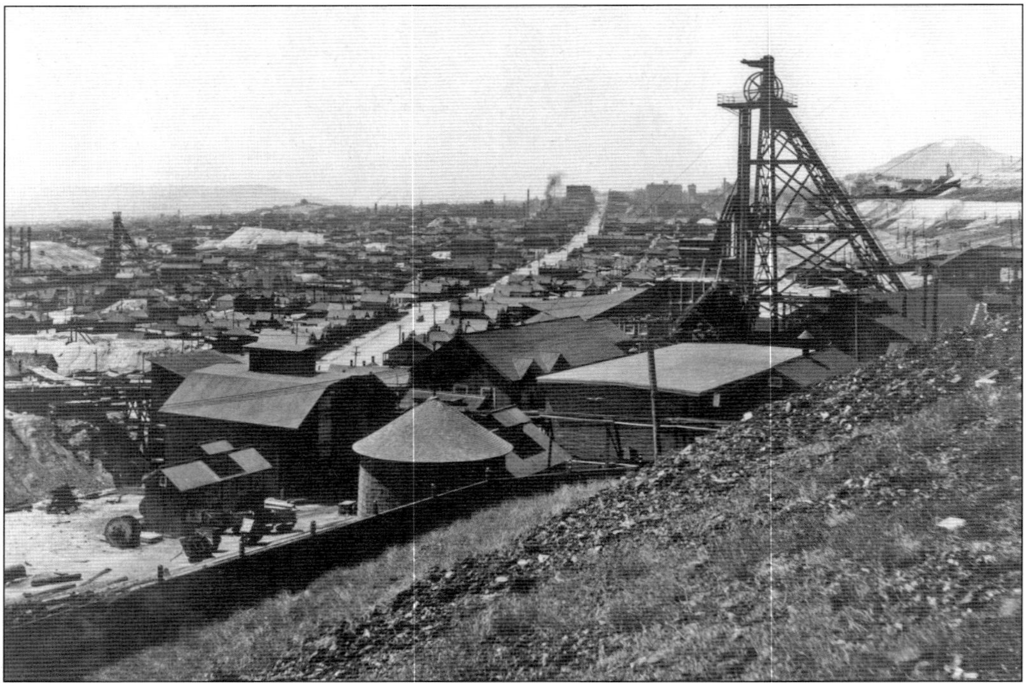

Much of Butte's vast mining landscape lies hidden from view, deep within the Richest Hill on Earth. In most western mining camps, the mine workings were some distance from the settlement area. In Butte, the ore reserves were so large that the community had to build on top of them. This mix of industrial and residential space is an attribute unique to Butte. It also accounts for the fact that beneath the surface of industrial as well as residential areas are mazes of underground tunnels that can cause subsidence at any time. Subsidence occurs when the ground sinks or settles downward into a hollow area, such as a mine shaft, a feared result being the collapse or major shifting of a home or business above the shaft.

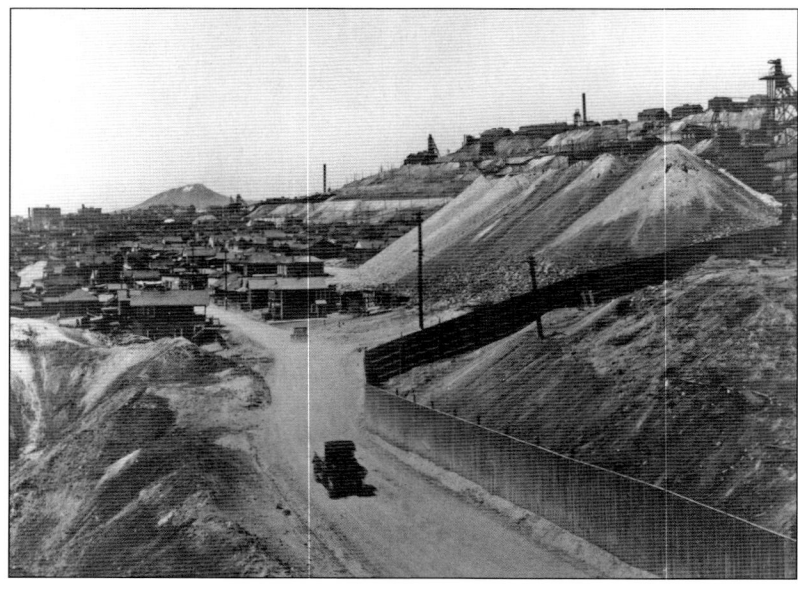

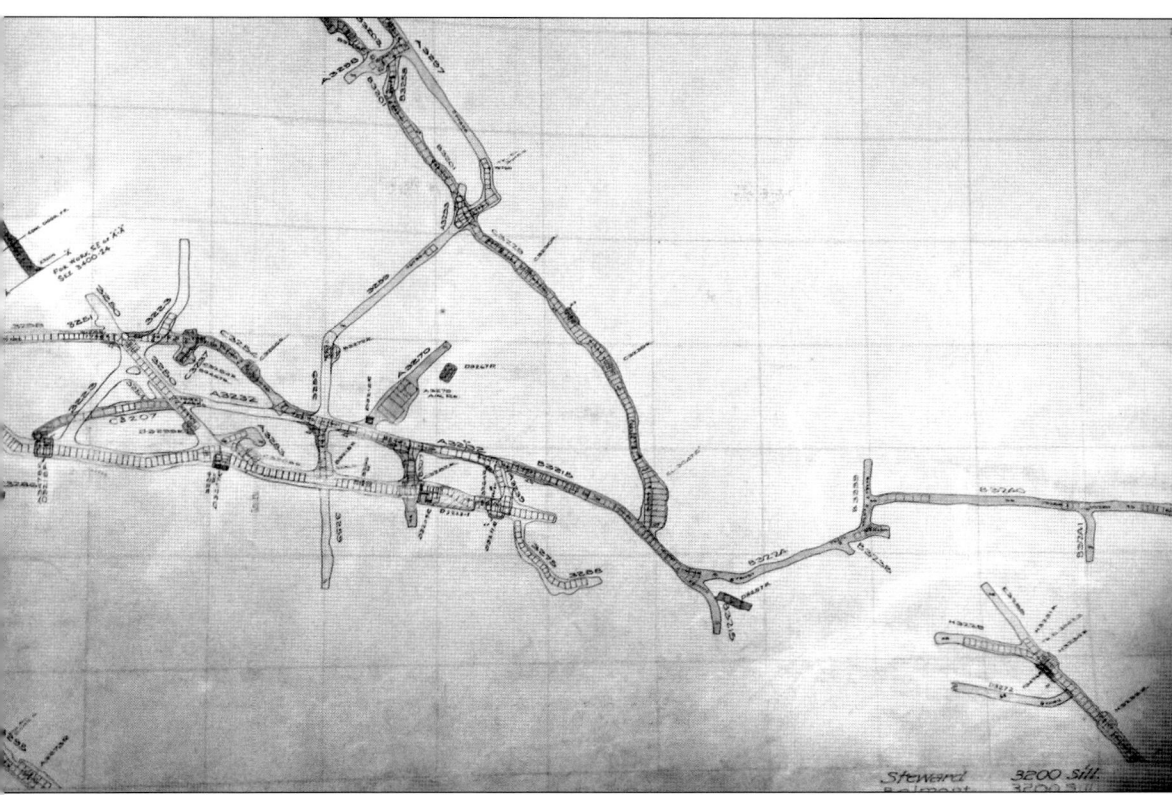

While the headframes are the most obvious sign of the city's industrial nature, they pale in comparison to the scale and magnitude of the engineering required to form the estimated 3,000 miles of tunnels and shafts that underlie the town. Depicted here is a hand-drawn map showing the web of tunnels below a portion of the city. These hand-drawn, color-coded maps were created by geologists for the ACM, which at one time employed over 50 geologists to chart its massive underground workings.

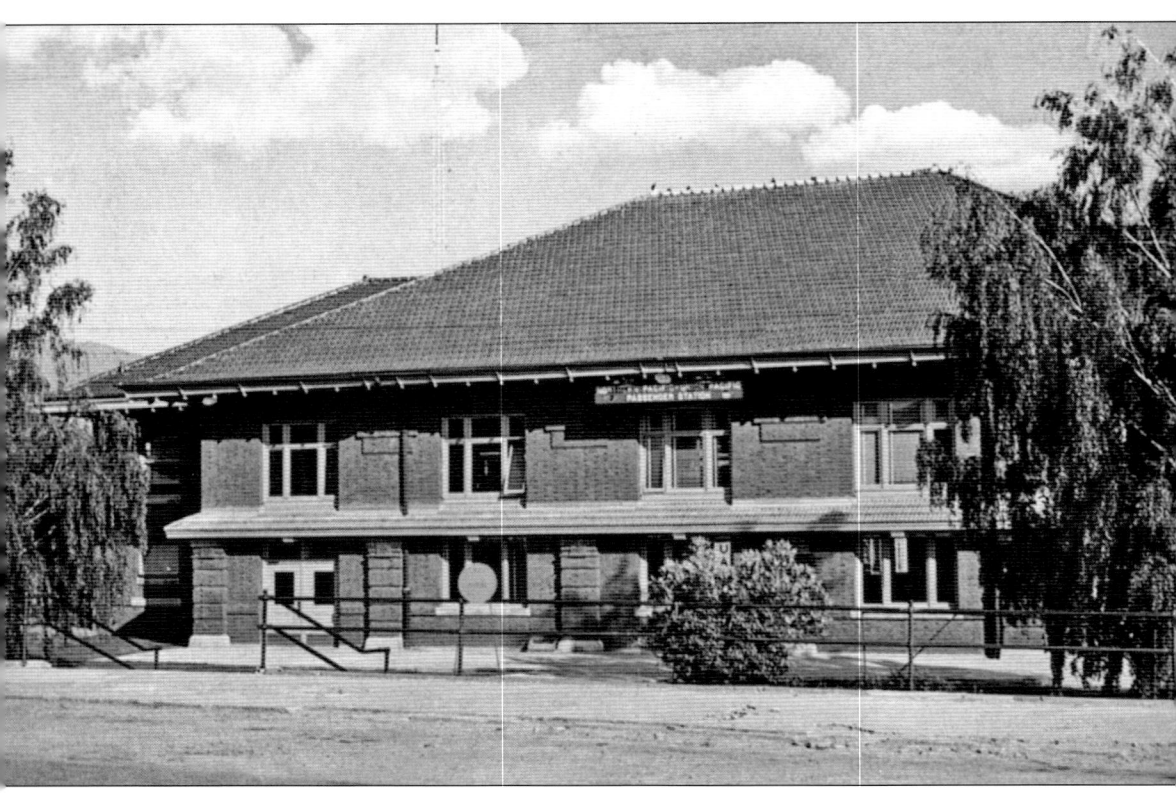

Butte's full-scale industrialization crystallized in December 1881 when the Utah and Northern Railway connected it with the rest of the industrializing United States. Rail transportation made the mines viable and brought needed technology, capital, and labor into the city. In 1883, the Northern Pacific arrived, and the following year, the railroad constructed a narrow-gauge line between Butte and the newly formed town of Anaconda. By the mid-1880s, Butte was one of the busiest cities in the West. And at that time, developments at the Anaconda Mine were about to elevate Butte to the ranks of America's foremost mining center.

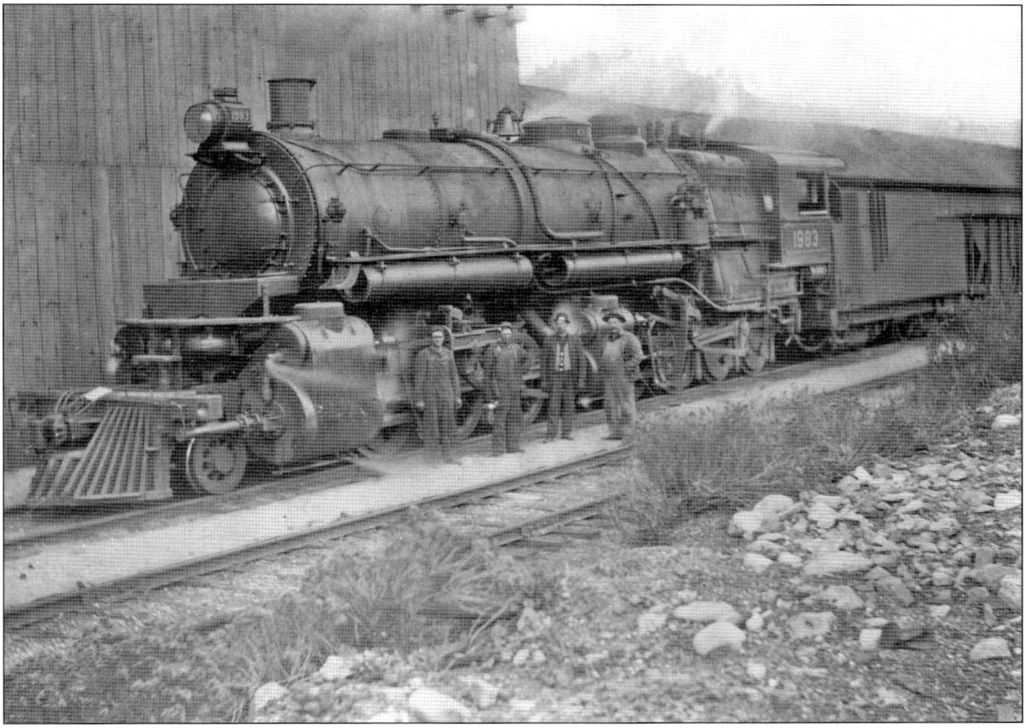

Butte grew rapidly from 1880 to 1910, and that growth can be directly linked to the arrival of the railroad. The presence of five major railroads bringing travelers, news, and goods into the city was also unique. From the 1880s to the 1960s, Butte was served by the Union Pacific, the Northern Pacific, the Milwaukee, the Great Northern, and the BA&P Railways. The railroads were not only responsible for bringing fast and efficient service to the mining industry but also the corporate structure that controlled transportation.

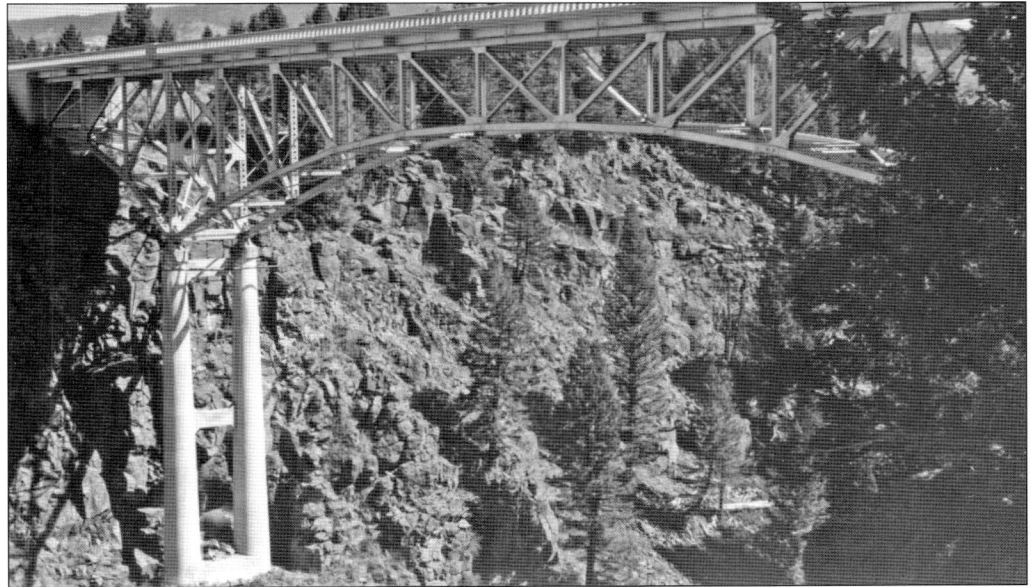

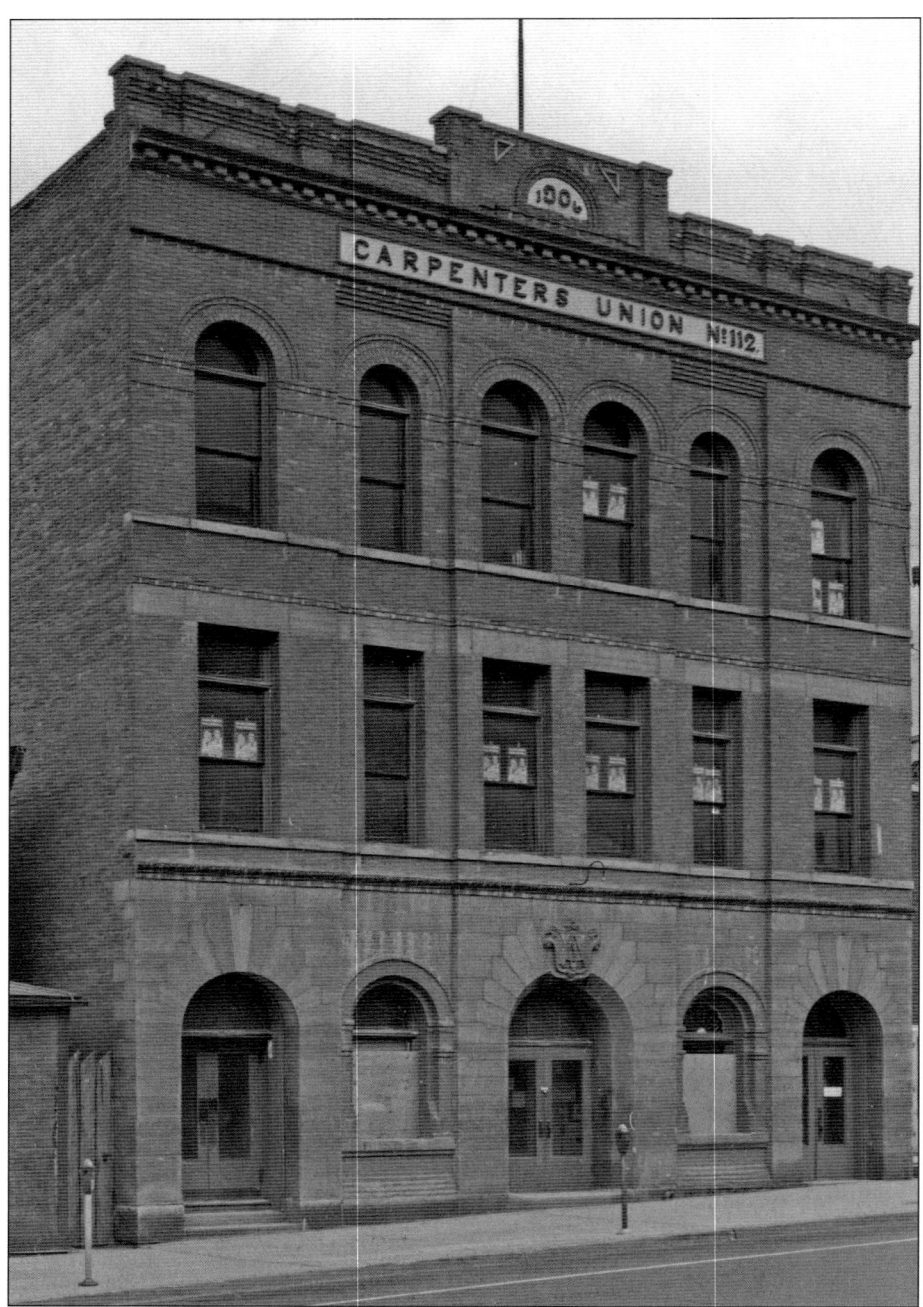

The Butte area is a unique and outstanding element of America's built environment critical to understanding and appreciating the nation's extractive mining and labor history. Closely affiliated during the late 19th and early 20th century with the rapid industrialization of the United States and labor's collective response to this process, the area possesses exceptional value in illustrating the dramatic changes that resulted from America's emergence as the world's leading industrial nation. This is a photograph of the Carpenter's Union Hall that is still functional today as union headquarters.

The meteoric rise of Butte to the pinnacle of world copper production was inherently linked to the advent of the Age of Electricity and the corresponding industrial revolution. By providing vast reserves of red metal just when it was needed most, Butte helped transform the United States into a modern economic superpower.

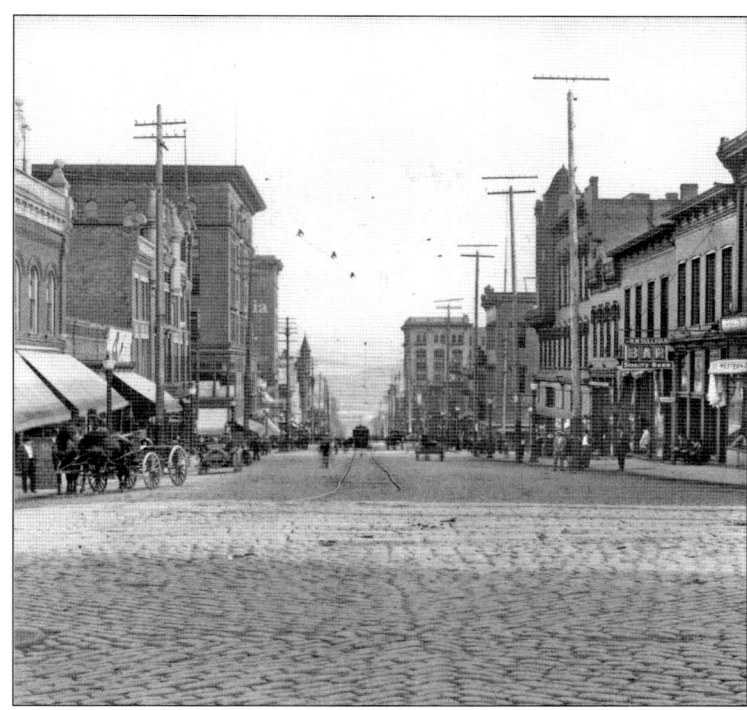

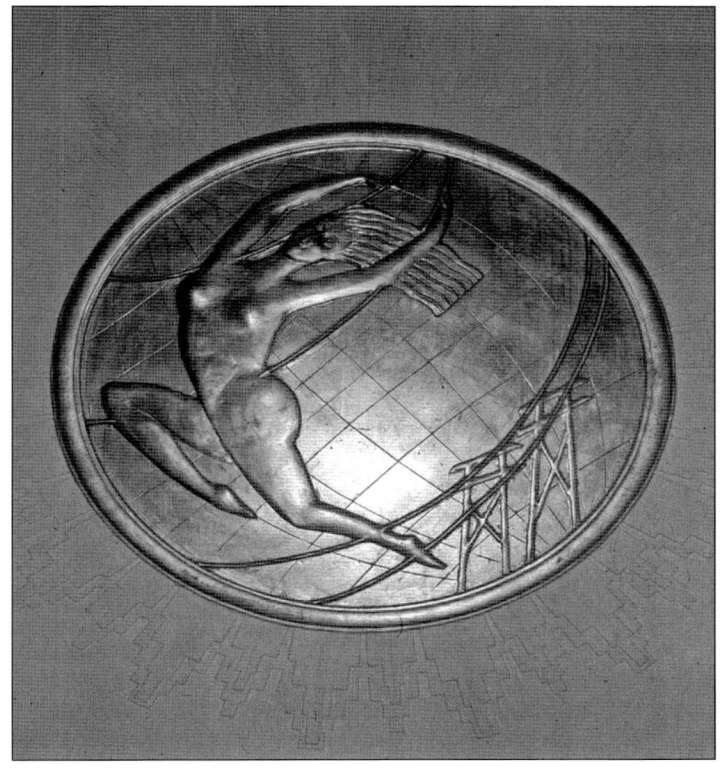

In 1912, a Butte company, the Montana Power Company, consolidated all power generation and distribution in the state of Montana. The Montana Power Company provided power to Montanans for the next 80 years, when it would begin to sell off its generation and distribution assets to various interests—a controversial and interesting story yet to be told. The image on the medallion shown here is that of Electra, the Greek goddess of electricity.

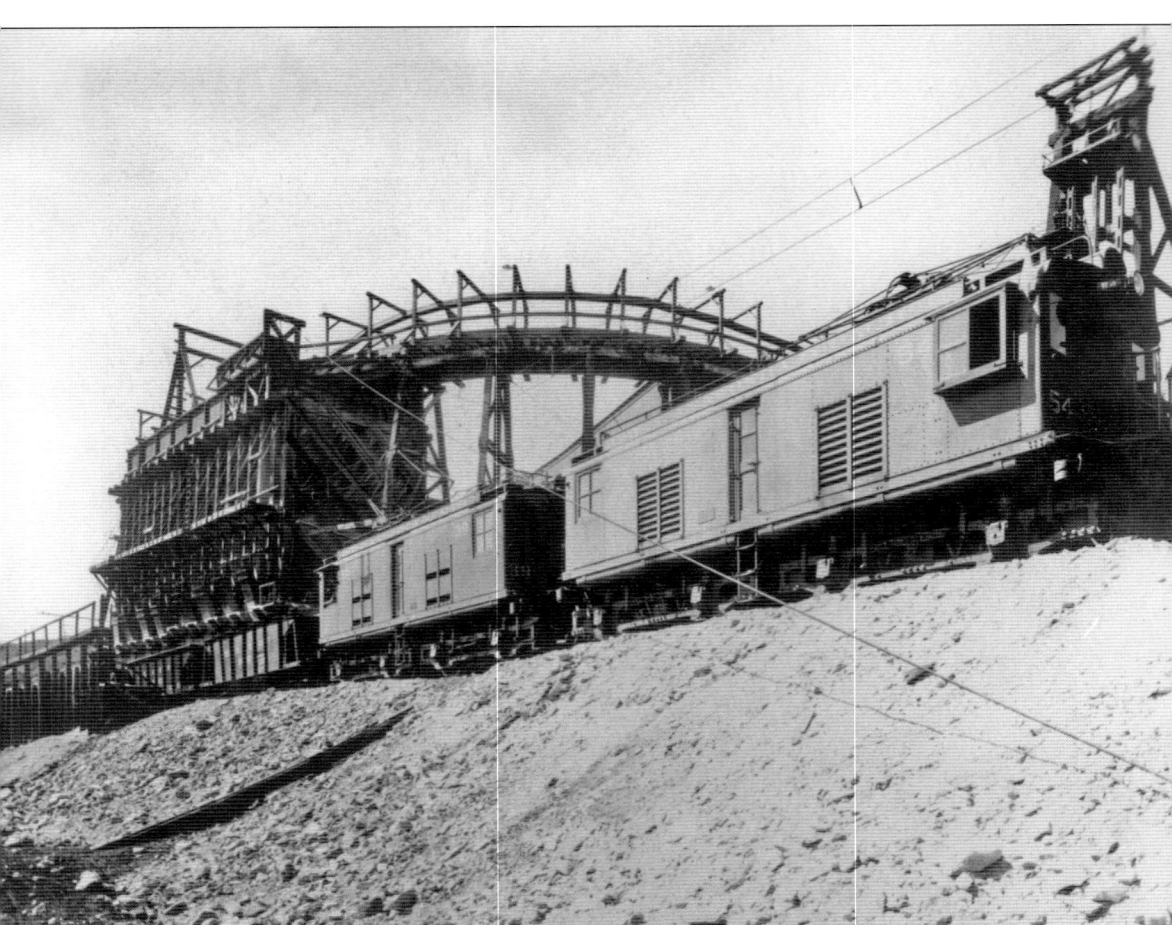

Butte is the story of electricity. At the same time Edison was playing with electric transmission, the mining men in Montana were unveiling large reserves of electrolytic copper in Butte. These two discoveries catapulted Butte into position as a major player in the copper mining game and changed how the nation would work and play for the next two centuries. Butte utilized this technology to its greatest potential. Electric engines were unable to effectively pull the railcars up the grade of the Butte Hill though, so General Electric was asked to provide a solution, which was a small booster engine to assist in those heavy hauls up the Hill. The rail men affectionately called the engine "the cow" and the booster "the calf." Electrification was abandoned in 1967 as it became cheaper to operate diesel-electric locomotives.

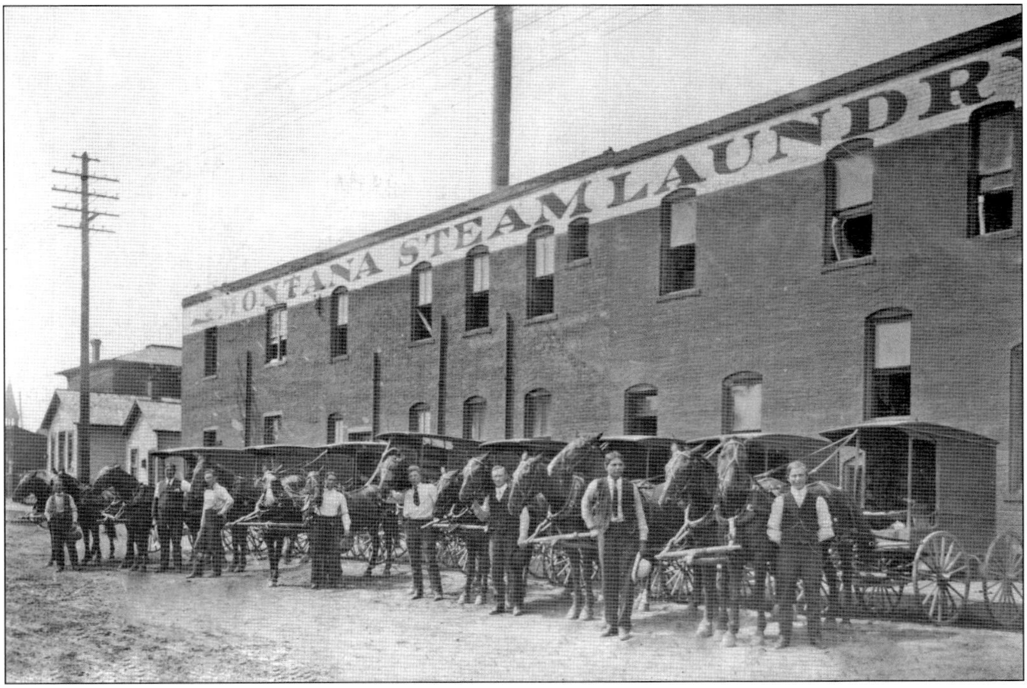

Unlike many other mining communities, Butte was not a company town. Businesses were as independent as the union members who worked the Hill were. In other places, miners ended up owing more to the company store than they earned. That was not the case in Butte. Although the ACM, when consolidated in 1910, had every tool, machine, method, and procedure in place necessary to extract and process the ores being mined, it did not own the businesses that supported it and its workers. Butte people were uniquely independent in that regard.

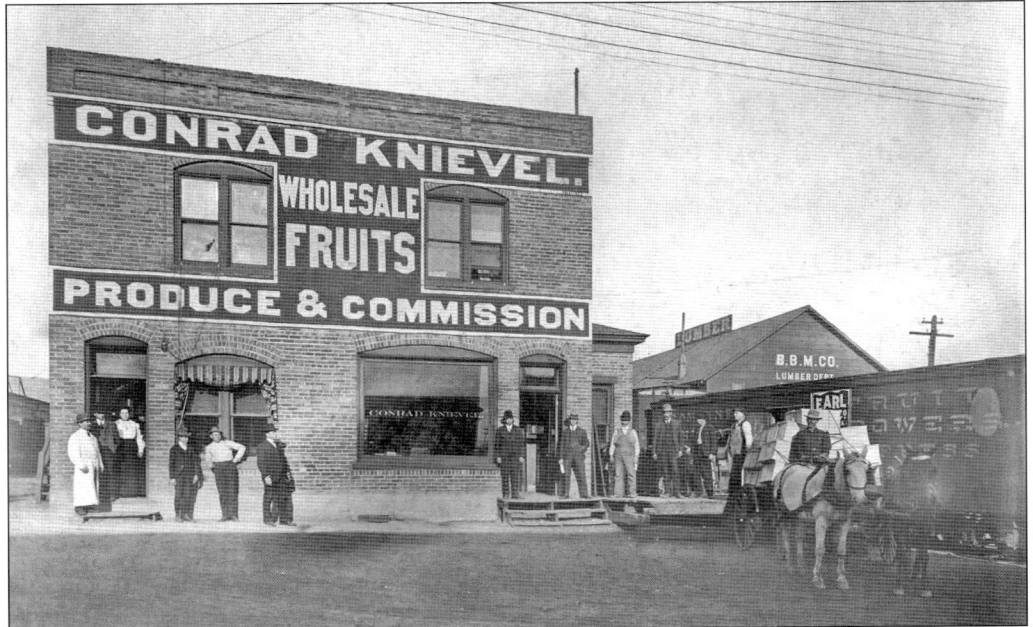

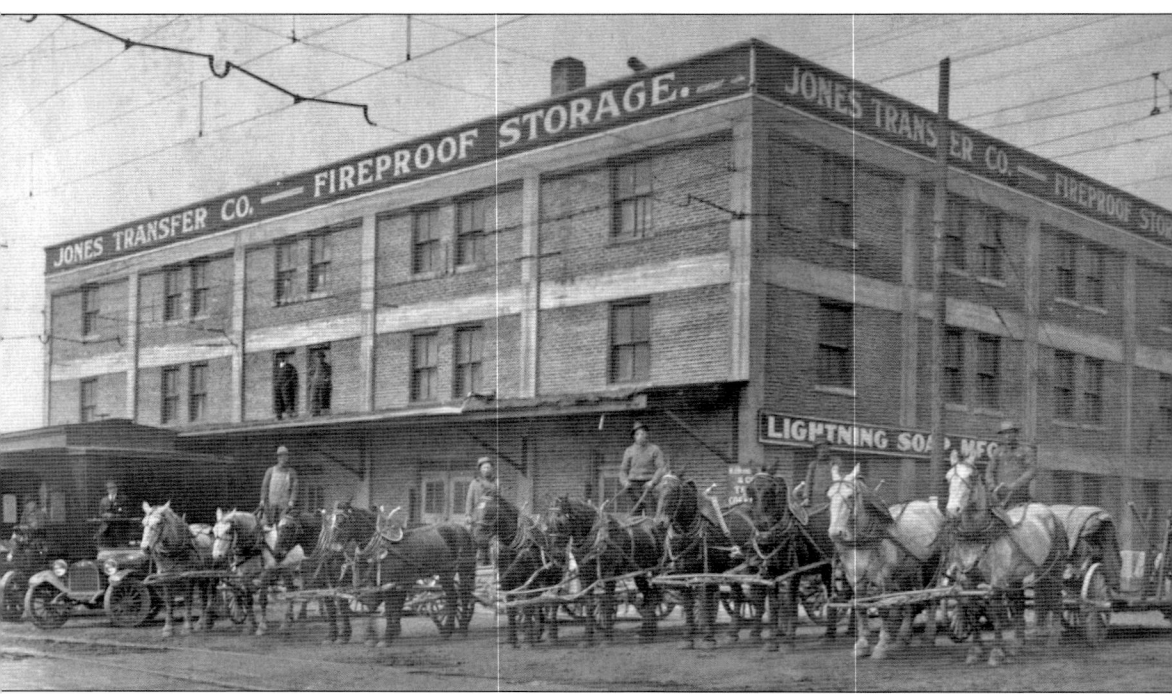

Butte as a rail center encouraged the growth of a distinct warehouse district. This area was an impressive wholesale distribution center. Warehouses were built out of brick and steel and served as ironworks; coke and coal storage; meat, poultry, and dairy processing; as well as for the distribution of lumber, building supplies, bricks, and other goods. The warehouse district remains intact and still functions as a distribution center in Butte, now served more by truck than rail.

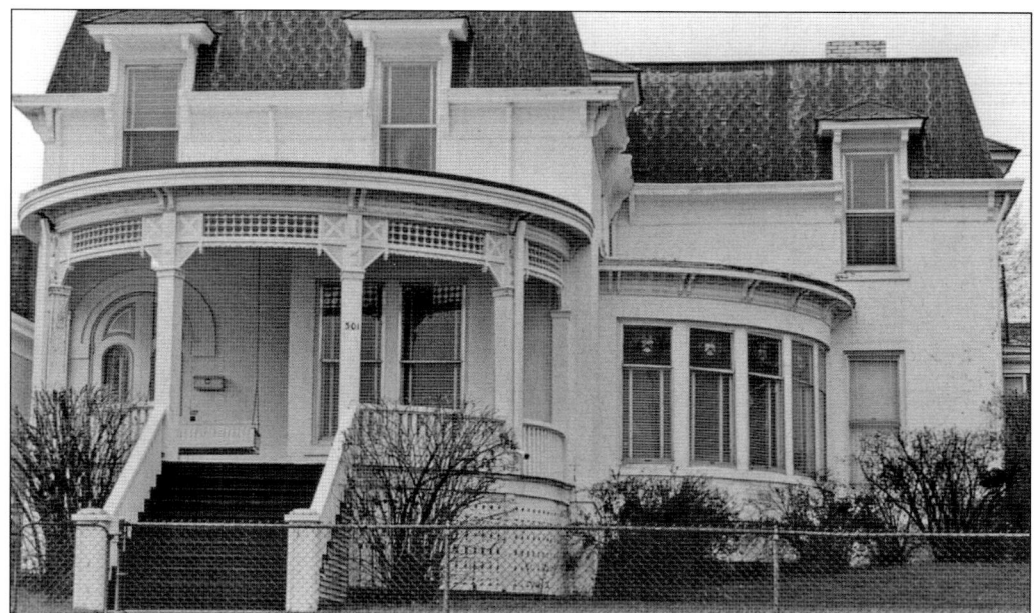

In other communities, class was distinctive, an influence that created divisiveness and disjointedness. In Butte, class meant little. As long as a man worked hard for his pay and was straight up in his dealings with people, he was accepted. Beautiful mansions are interspersed with cottages and bungalows. The mine superintendent lived in a house surrounded by workers' cottages. The owner of a bank lived across the street from a railroad employee.

In *The Battle for Butte*, Michael Malone observed, "Millionaires, bums, working stiffs, well-groomed ladies, and whores all bumped elbows on common terms, and Butte seldom bothered to make any pretenses."

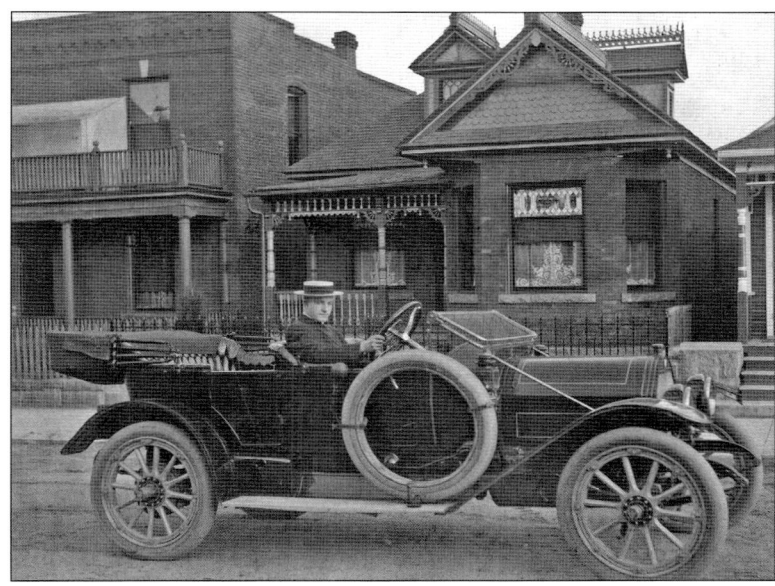

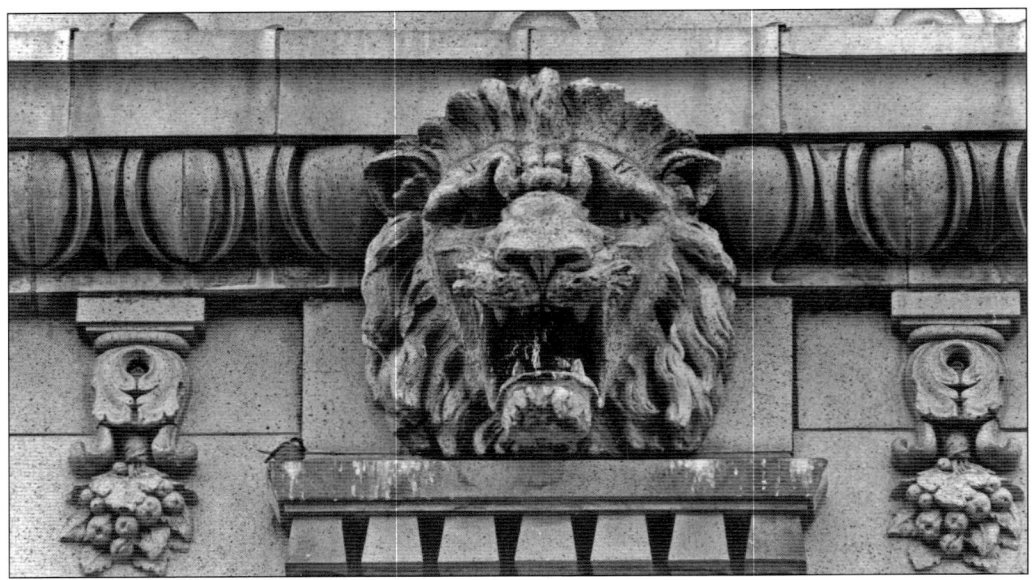

Butte's central business district has the feel of a large city with architecturally masterful buildings, watchful gargoyles perched atop multistory buildings, and the impression that one is immersed in another distinctly historic period of time. Although there is the occasional new building or modern renovation of an historic building, Uptown Butte looks remarkably like it did at the dawn of the 20th century sans the cobblestone streets and trolley cars.

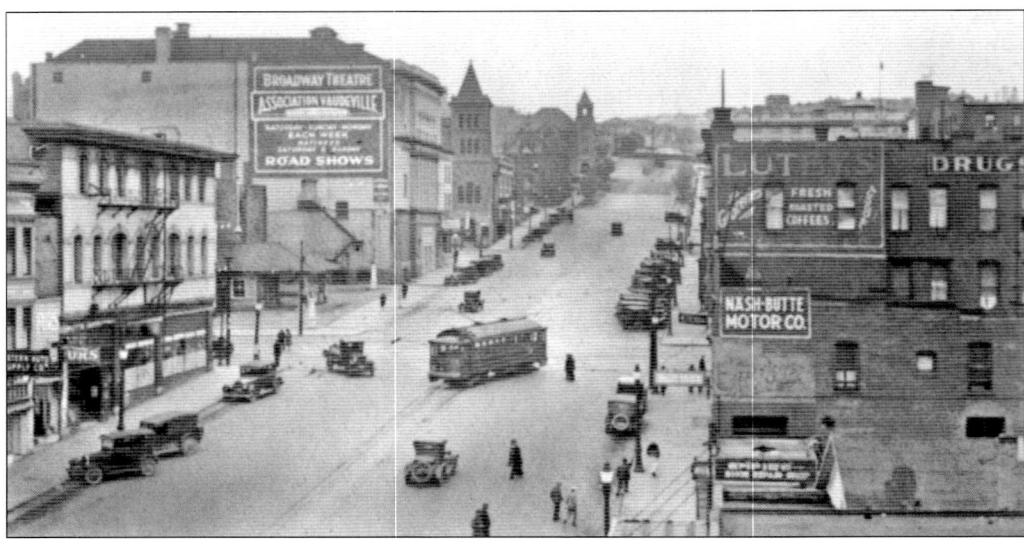

Butte was home to religions of all types. In 1910, Butte boasted 41 churches, 7 of which were Catholic with a membership of over 20,000 people: St. Patrick's, St. Mary's, Immaculate Conception, St. Joseph's, Sacred Heart, Holy Savior, and St. Lawrence. Church life extended beyond Sunday services with much of the congregations' social and civic lives tied to church activities. Young girls joined sodalities and sang in the choir, boys became altar boys, women congregated to create community feasts for the holidays, men joined organizations that encouraged humanitarian activities, and families enjoyed bingo night. (Courtesy of St. Patrick's Parish.)

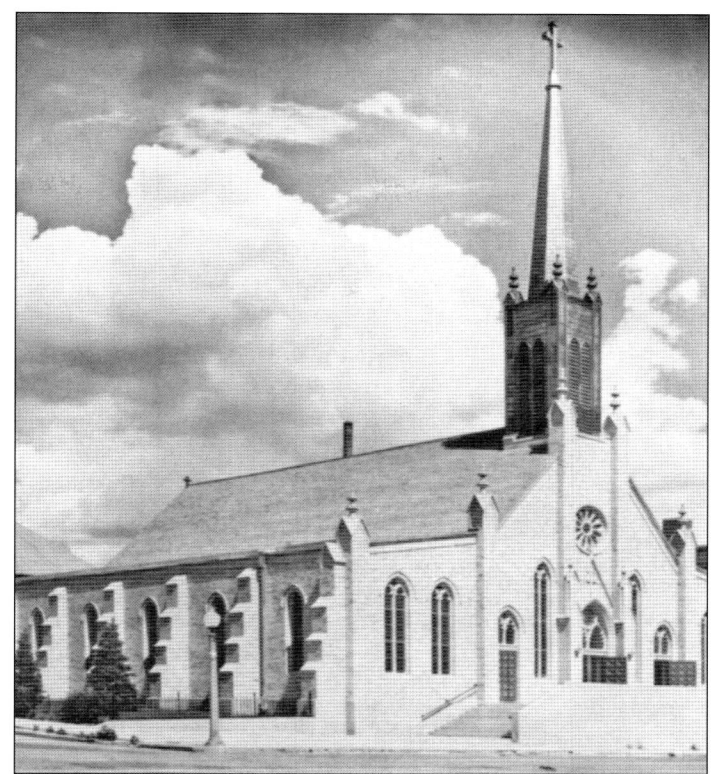

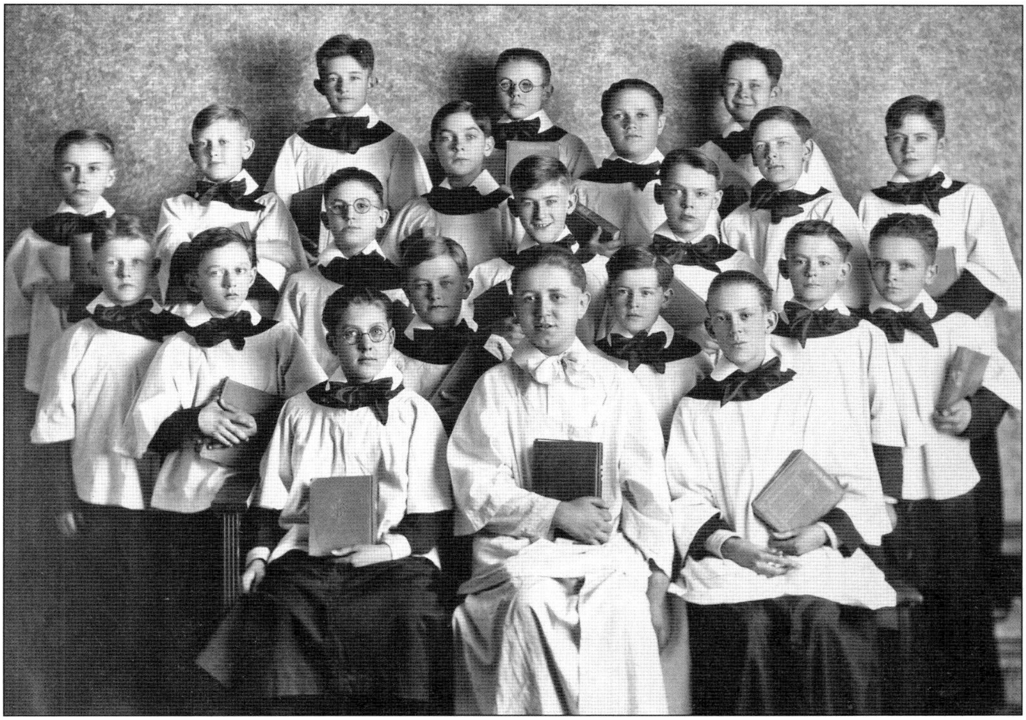

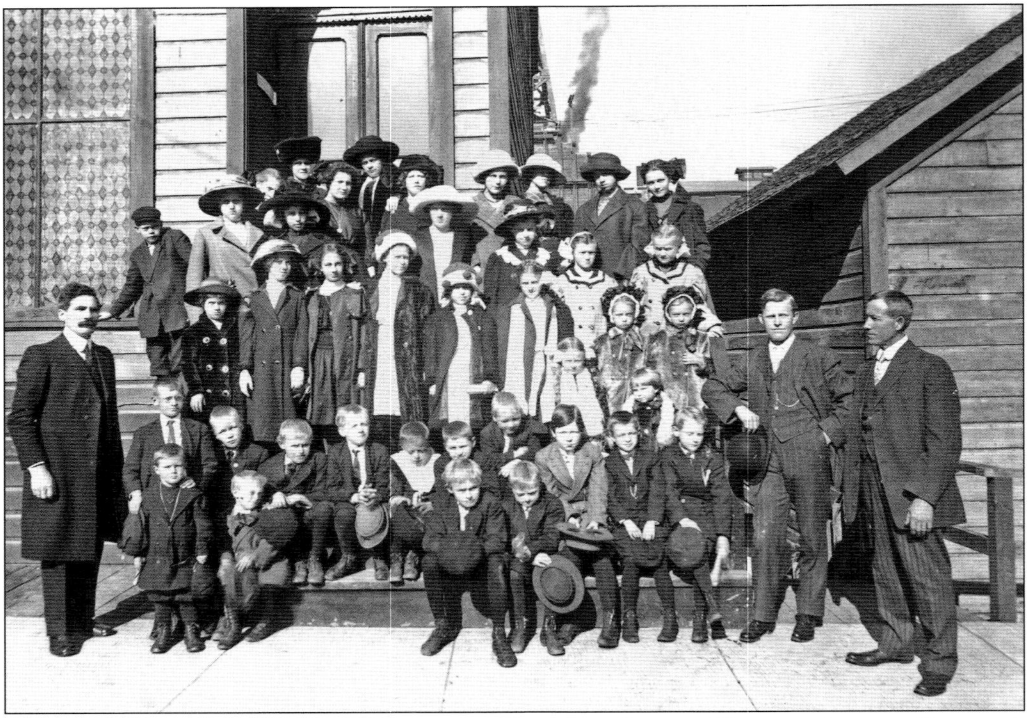

Numerous other religions were also represented, such as Baptist, Christian Science, Episcopal, Methodist, Lutheran, Presbyterian, Jewish, Eastern Orthodox, Unitarian, several other Christian sects, and Mormon. There were a number of Lutheran churches, including the Norwegian Lutheran Church, the German Evangelical Lutheran Church, and the Swedish Evangelical Lutheran Church. There was even a Buddhist Temple that existed for over 60 years. These churches embodied not only the religious mores of their congregations but their social and civic lives as well. The Trinity Methodist Church on North Main Street is shown below.

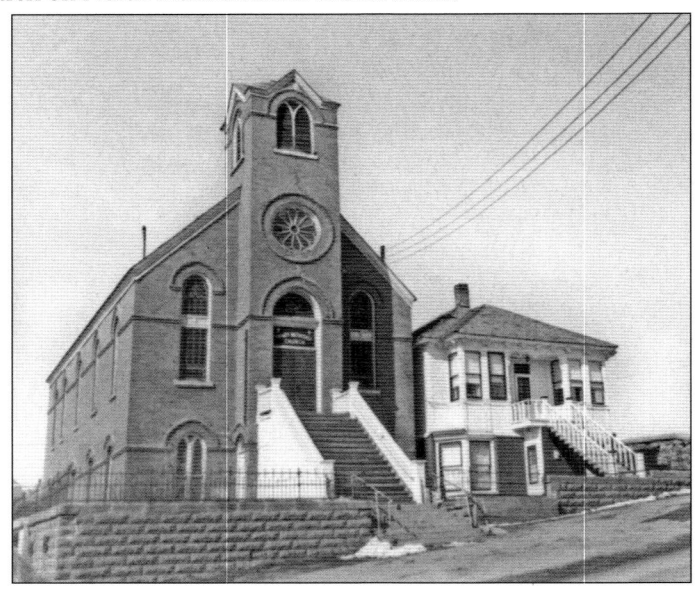

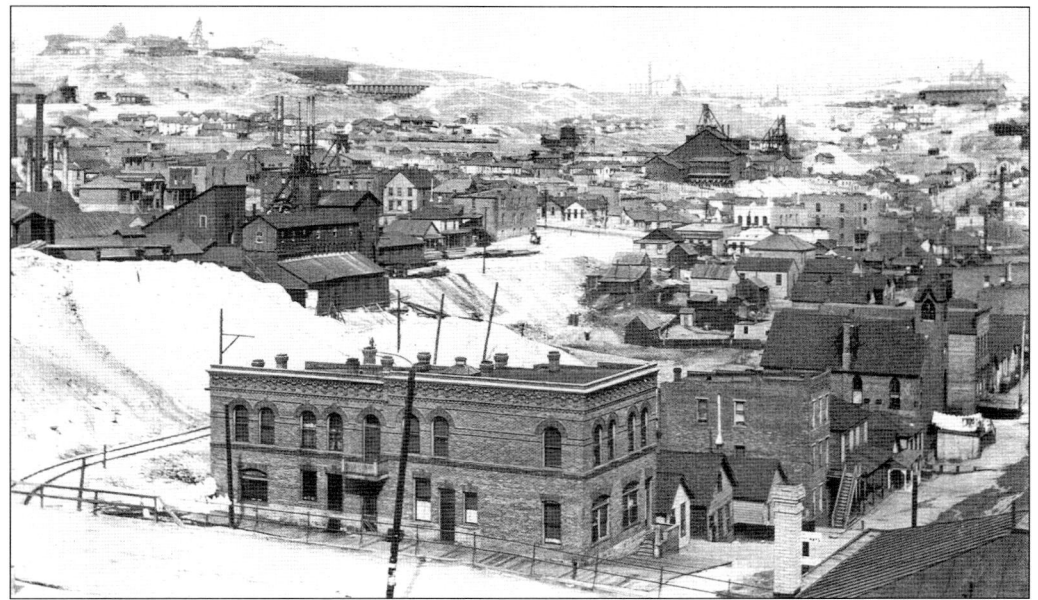

Butte no doubt seemed a chaotic, unbalanced place to newcomers. And in many ways, it was. As Thomas F. Rooney described it, "Butte is like a fast-growing child. Its clothes become too small for its body before there is time to make new ones." It lacked predictable development that could be found in more mature towns and the niceties of picturesque East Coast towns. Even many of its streets seemed disjointed and unplanned, and much of Butte was not laid out in a systematic or regular pattern. Neighborhoods cropped up around the ore bodies and the mine entrances out of convenience, not logic.

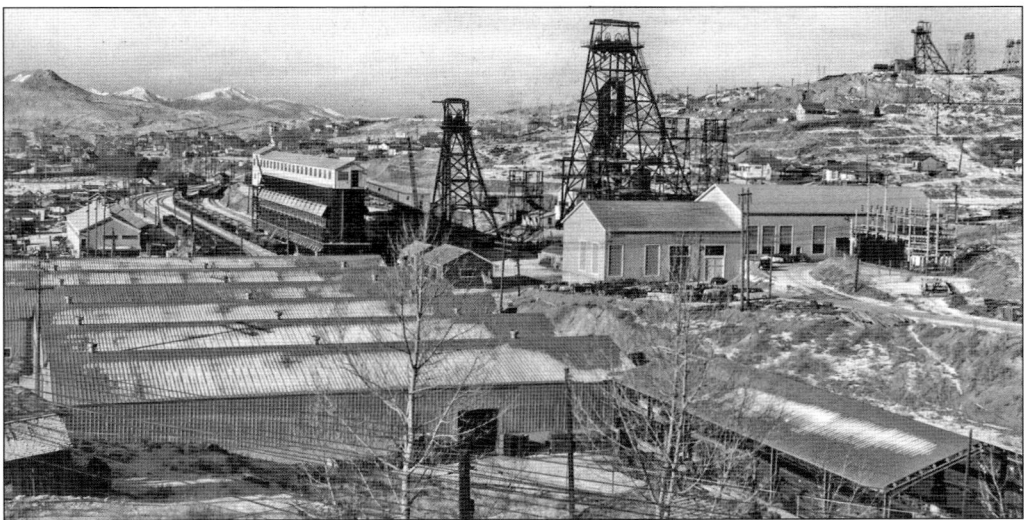

Because most people in the late 1800s and early 1900s traveled by foot, neighborhoods developed around the mines where people worked. Dirt streets followed hill and gulley, curving this way and that, with houses on either side. Houses were built on flat ground regardless of traffic flow or how difficult it might be to find them. As time passed and many of the wooden structures succumbed to fire, it was common to see a single house at the top of a hill. What appeared to be a loner's wish for privacy had actually been the only one of several wooden houses that survived.

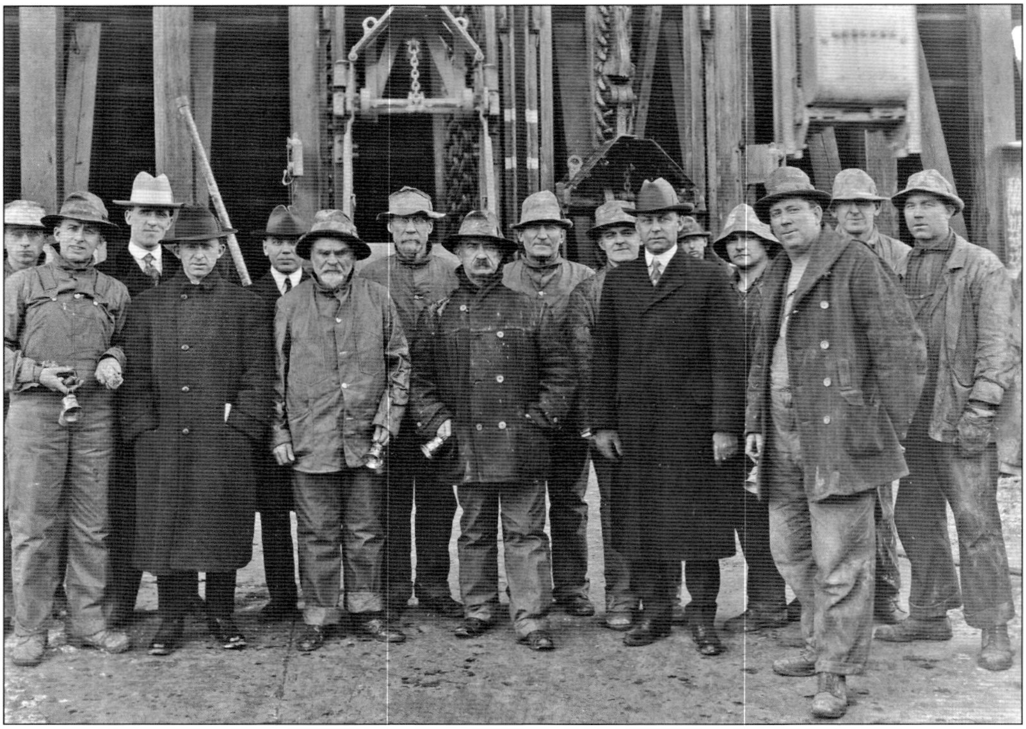

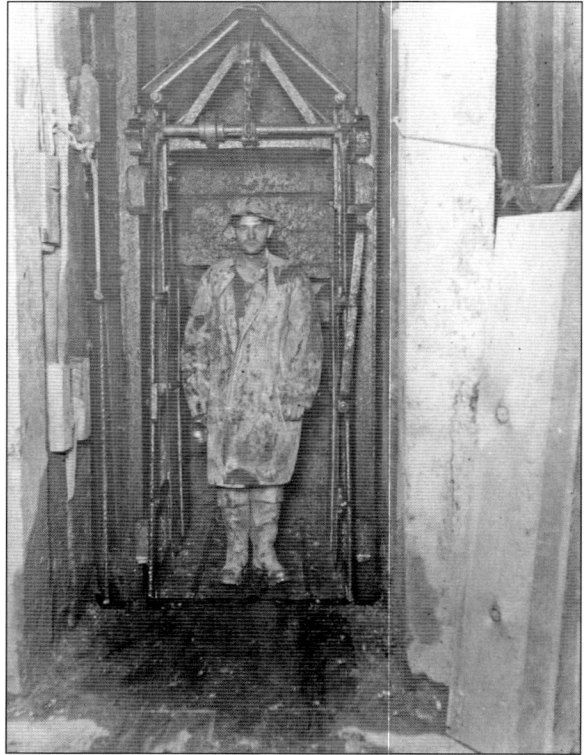

Butte was not a place for the docile soul. People had to be tough to weather the work, the terrain, and the weather. Although a welcoming place in many ways, Butte had the reputation as a tough town where newcomers had to prove their mettle. The rugged miners and sophisticated investors did not take kindly to strangers who came to town to make an easy buck. People worked hard, played hard, but most of all, they were honest—there was no in-between.

Butte profoundly affected the nation's labor movement. It embodied the strengths (and periodic weaknesses) of the industrial working class, spread the gospel of unionism, and spearheaded the formation of the Western Federation of Miners (WFM) and Industrial Workers of the World (IWW). This photograph shows a miner about to be lowered in a cage to underground workings.

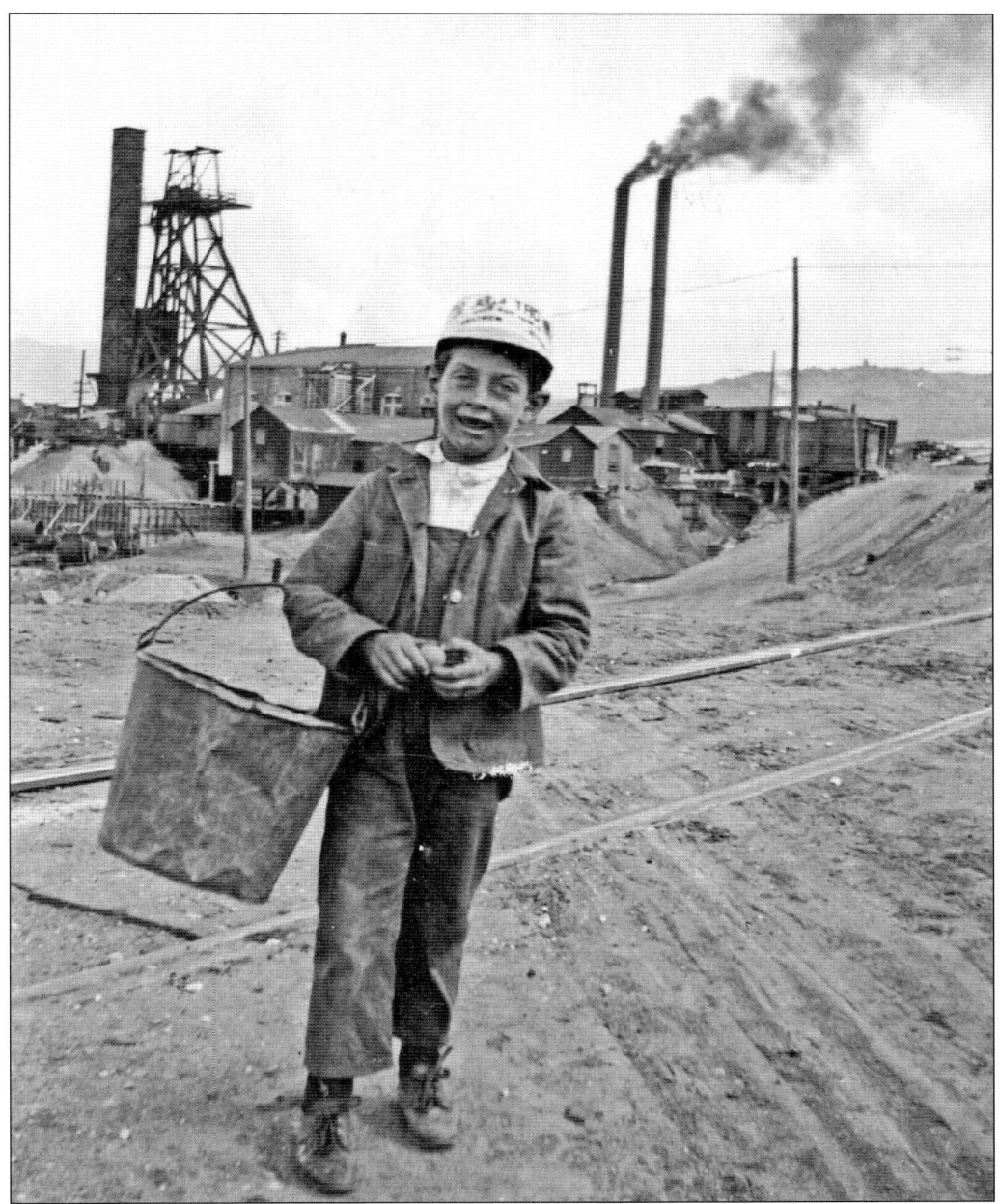

Equalitarianism was the norm in Butte, a true democracy in which social parity and respect for the individual within the community was as important as the community as a whole. Michael Malone in *The Battle for Butte*, observed, "Mining-camp democracy meant, in other words, social commonality, wide-open tolerance of drinking, whoring, and gaming, and a peculiarly unrestrained kind of individualism." Regardless of size, intellect, or wealth, people in Butte mattered. To this day, a man who has been a shoe-shine boy for 53 of his 60 years is still taken care of by the people of Butte. He may be different, he may be slow, but when he scurries down the street at his fast pace, people wave, offer him rides, and protect him. He is accepted, and he will always have a sense of place and dignity. He is a Butte boy after all. (Courtesy of Chris Fisk.)

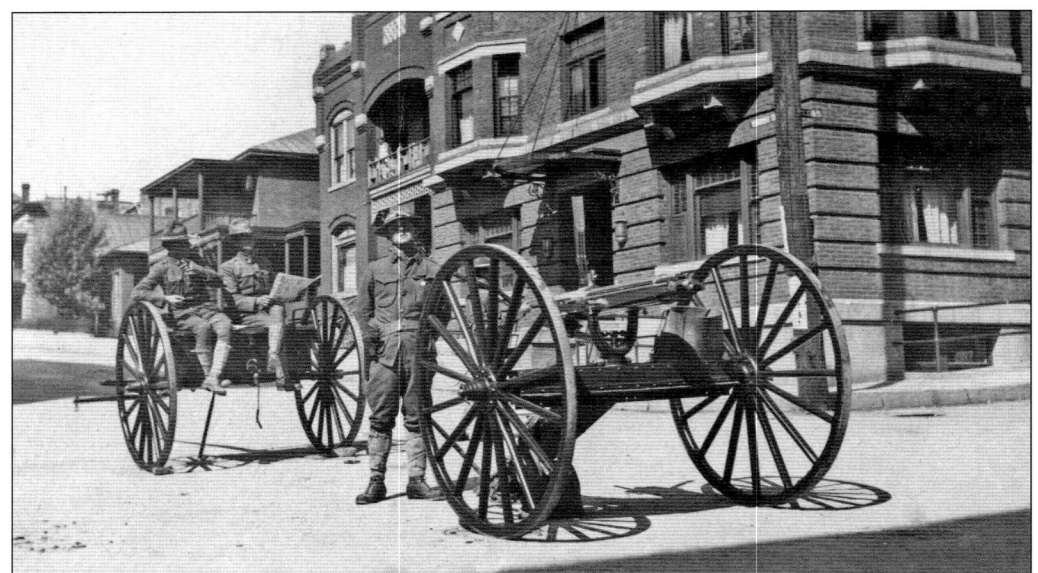

The Butte Miners' Union had been affiliated with the Western Federation of Miners, and the rank and file of the Butte Miners' Union was leaning toward the philosophy of the Industrial Workers of the World. In 1914, when union officials supported the ACM's rustling card system, irate miners protested by blowing up the union hall on June 13, Miners' Union Day. The government called for help, and martial law was imposed on Butte.

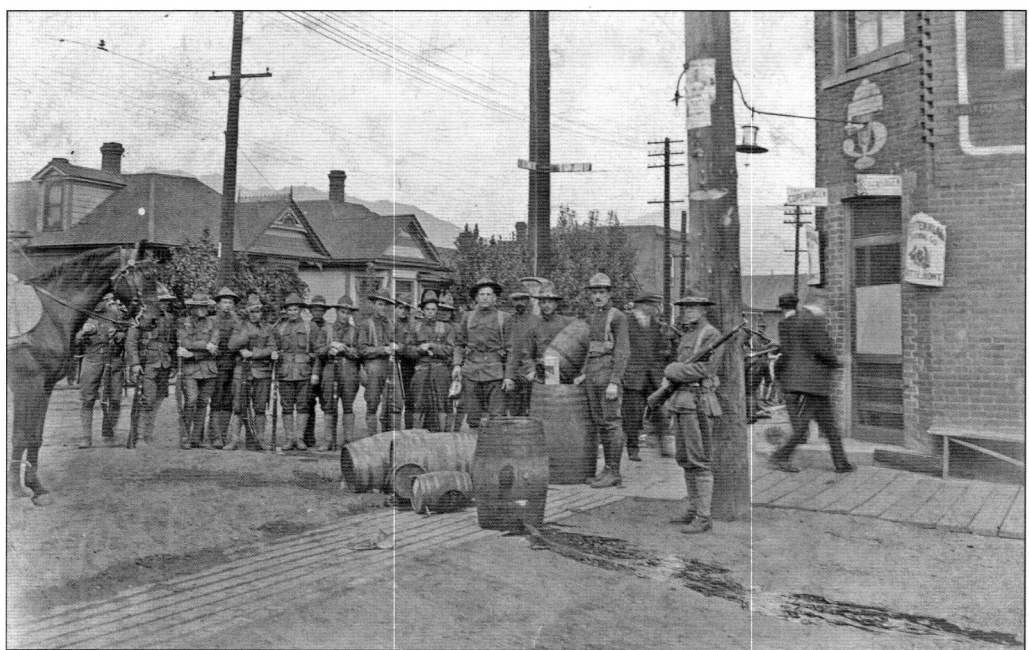

Between 1914 and 1920, National Guardsmen and federal troops occupied Butte six different times to quell domestic disturbances. National Guardsmen not only maintained order on the streets, they also enforced laws prohibiting the sale of alcohol and imposed a curfew of 9:00 p.m. to keep the streets quiet and safe.

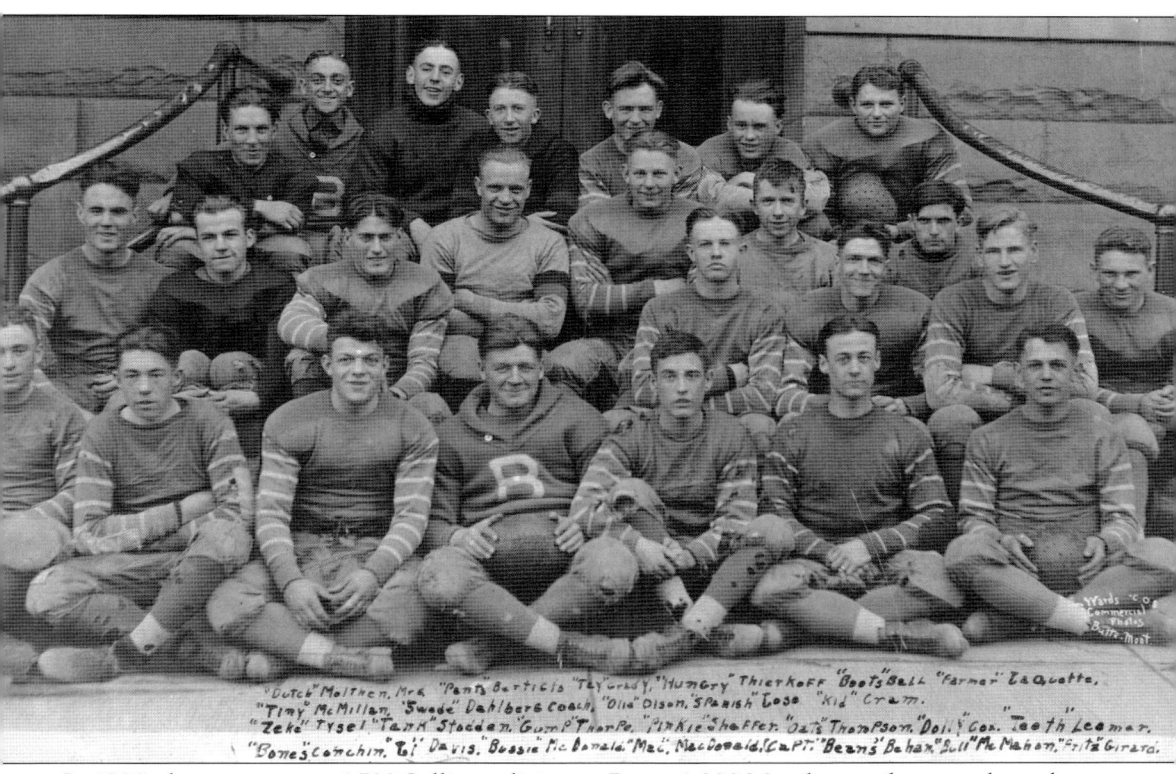

In 1900, there were some 1,700 Sullivans living in Butte, 1,000 Murphys, and an equal number of Sheas and Harringtons. With this number of identical surnames, some related to each other and some not, keeping them all straight required creative naming. Nicknames became the norm. The Sheas could be identified as "Jazz," "Tubba," "Finny," "Mooch," "Monk," "Calla," "Weenie," "Raggs," "Gub," and "Smart Alec." Some of the Harringtons were named by their occupation, "the Butcher" Harringtons, or by their clothing style, the "Fur Bearing" Harringtons. Nicknames could be earned or given based on looks, occupation, residence, nationality, or athletic prowess. Many a Butte lad wore his nickname proudly and replaced his given name with it: "Harp" Cote, "Red Neck" Kelly, and "Dublin Dan" McCarthy. The caption handwritten on this image is a perfect example; each one of these players had a nickname.

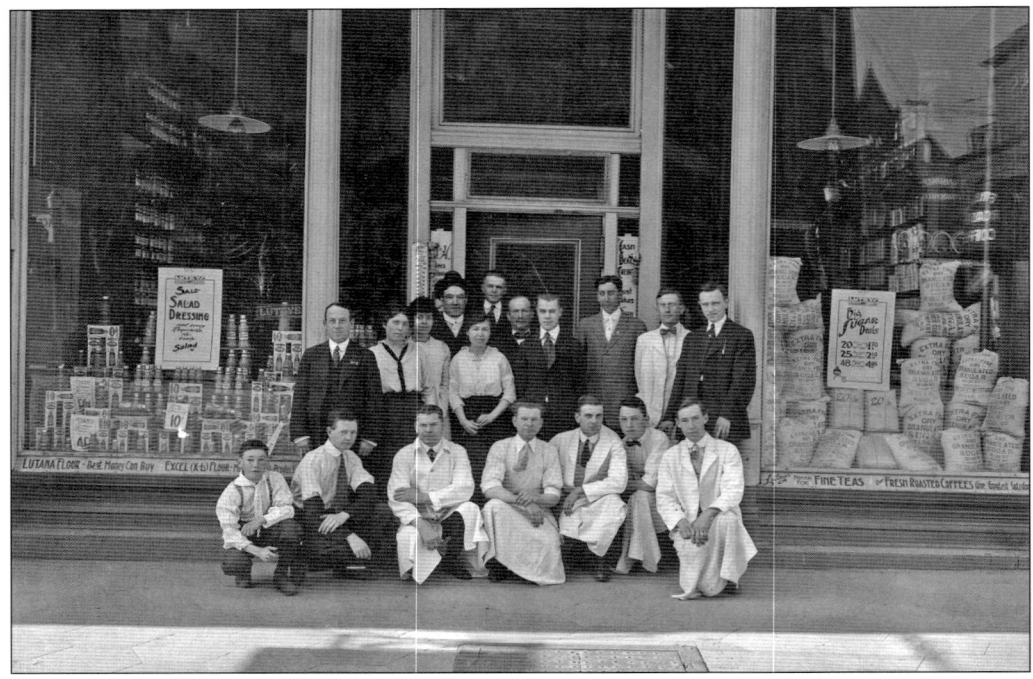

In his *Butte Evening News* article, Rooney stated, "The Butte laborer—the man who works on the streets with a pick and shovel—earns more than the ordinary follower of the 'elegant pursuits' in the East. The messenger boy here earns more money than the clerk who has worked for years behind the counter in New York, Chicago, or Boston. The girl who works in a Butte store earns more than does the New England streetcar conductor."

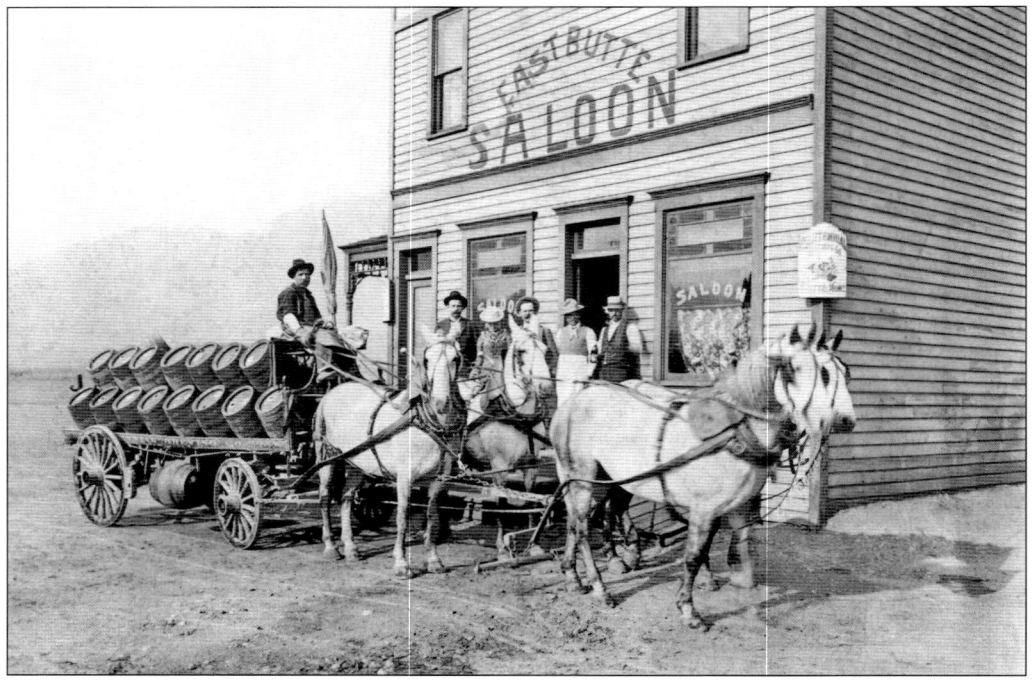

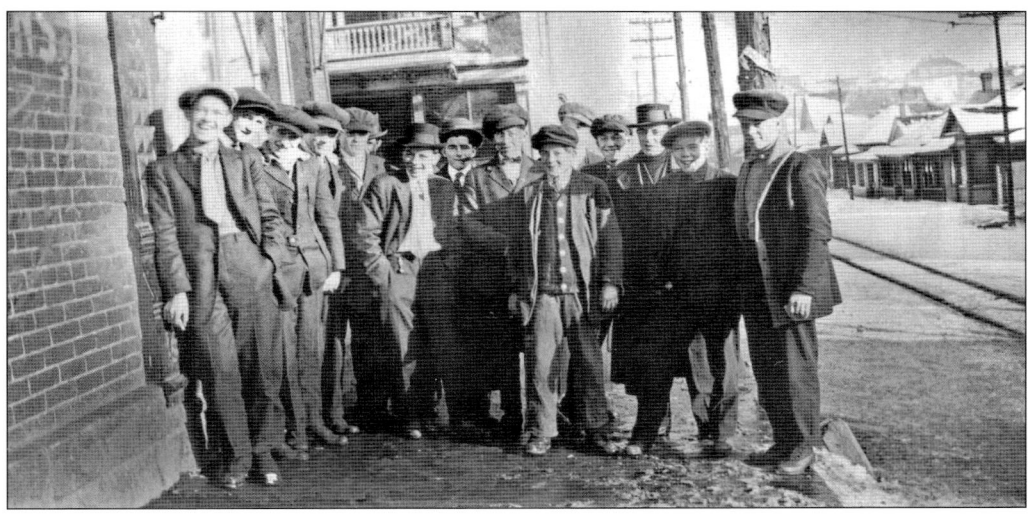

Old movies that depicted the Wild West as cowboy country did not know Butte. There were horses, of course, for that was the common mode of transportation, but the pioneering families who lived in the country and wore cowboy hats and spurs were not part of Butte's culture. Working boots, known as loggers, and fedoras or newsboy caps (Gatsby's) were items of male clothing most common on the streets of Butte. (Above, courtesy of Chris Fisk.)

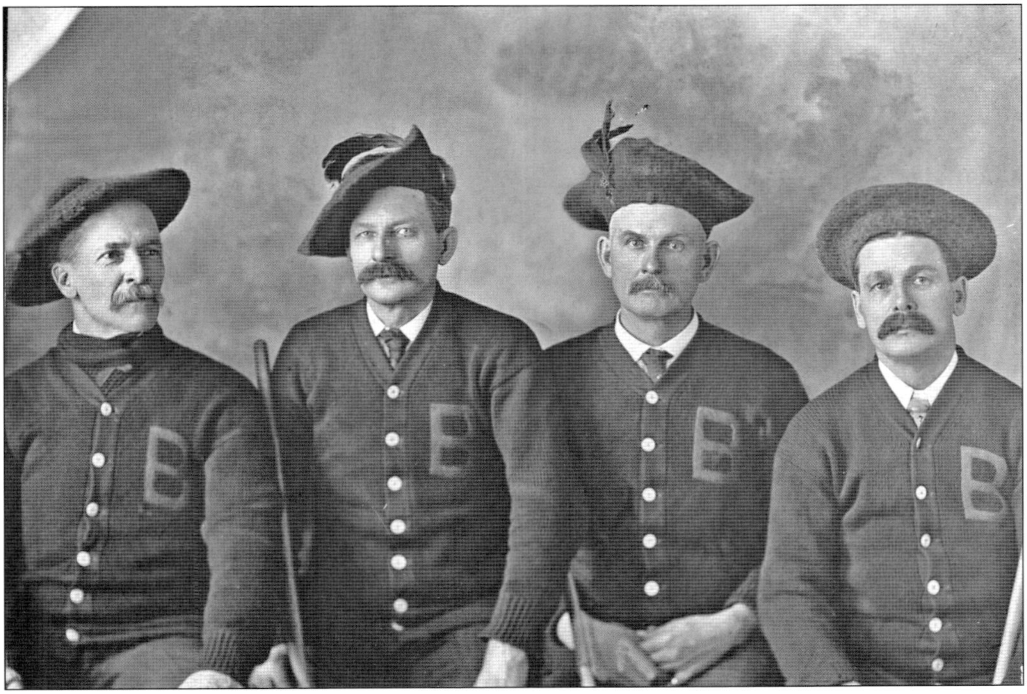

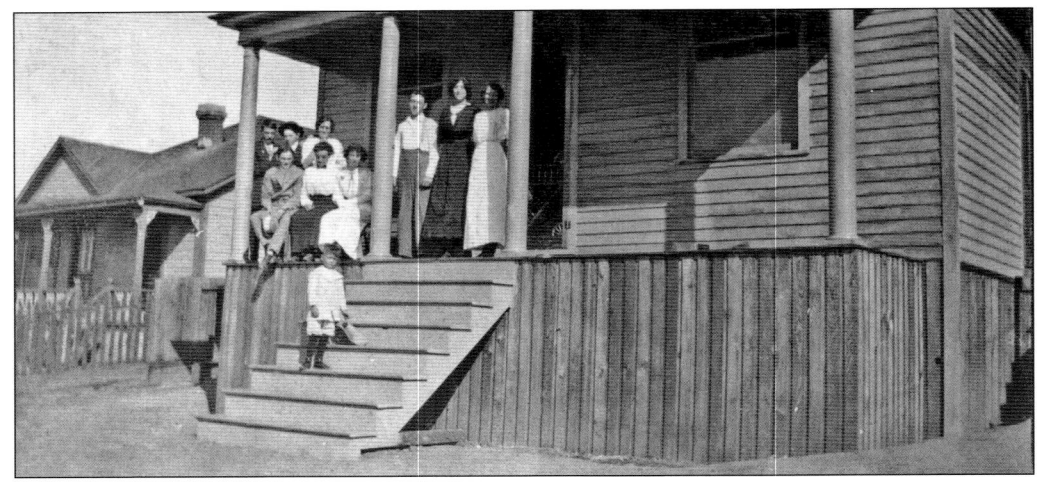

The makeup of Butte's families was often at odds with conventional structure. Many women became widows at very early ages. Life in the mines took its toll, and many men succumbed to accidents, tuberculosis (or "black lung" as it was called), and often the harsh realities of living in a town that took pride in its toughness and encouraged a fighting spirit. It was not uncommon to meet a woman with five to eight children and no visible means of support other than taking in laundry or boarders to support her family.

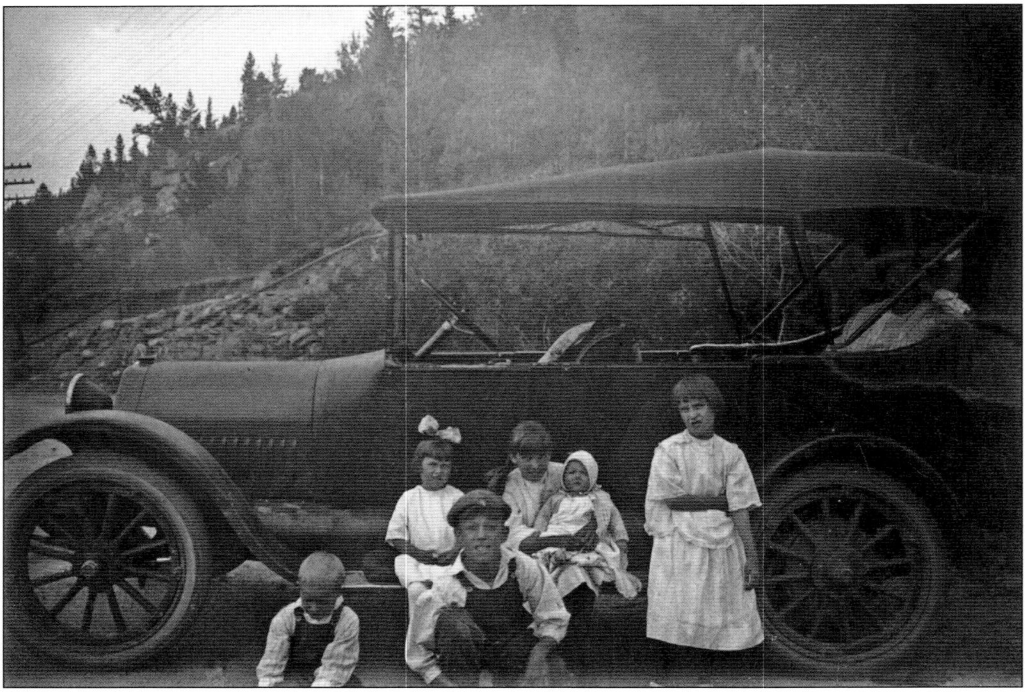

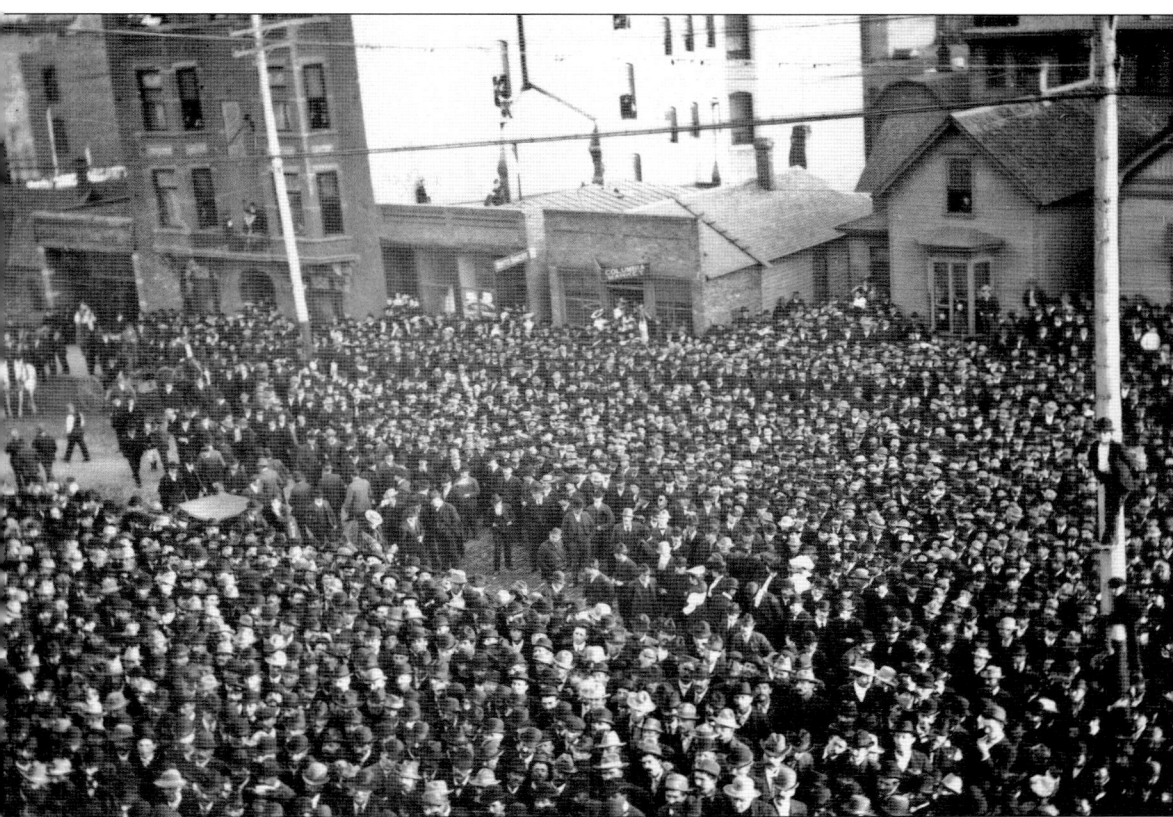

Politics is another arena in which Butte is an anomaly. Butte was a demanding and powerful force in the politics of the state and the country for decades. Its entrance into the world of politics began with the War of the Copper Kings. Marcus Daly, F. Augustus Heinze, and William A. Clark all wanted bigger and bigger pieces of the Butte Hill and its sister city of Anaconda. As the "war" grew, so did the issues that were the subject of rivalry. What began as a financial struggle turned into a full-blown battle for social and political power. This group of men was gathered in front of the courthouse to witness Pres. Theodore Roosevelt during his visit to Butte in May 1903. Roosevelt was placed in the awkward position of mediating the various factions at the banquet in his honor that evening.

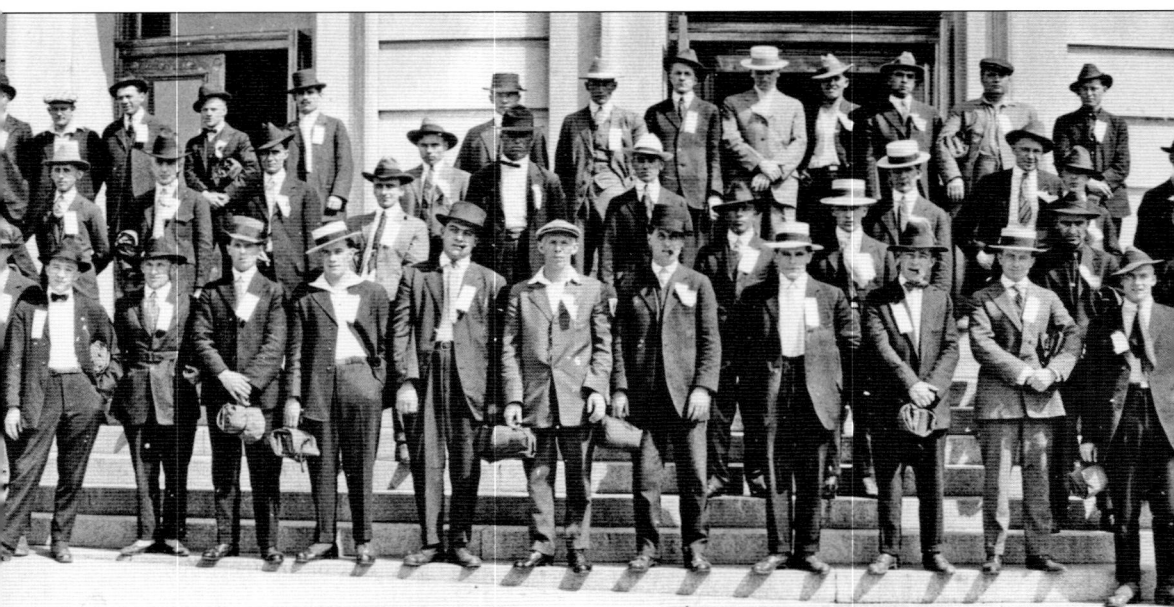

In the true meaning of the word, Butte was democratic in every way. Thomas F. Rooney described the city's level of equality when he stated in his *Butte Evening News* article, "In the East, the man can reach out and see the horizon of his possibilities. In Butte the teamster may go to the legislature." Butte was singular among the other cities of the state and region and kowtowed to no one. It not only fought but won the fiercest battles in the political playground. Might and power in its makeup begat might and power in the political arena.

Four

BUTTE THE PROSPEROUS

Every budding community in the entire country can take a lesson from Butte. . . . The spirit of molding one's fortunes out of what you have is in the breast of the Butte newsboys. True she is richly endowed by nature—but most of the nature that is worthwhile is in her sons who wrestle fortunes from what has been set before them as a task.

—Thomas F. Rooney, *Butte Evening News*

Not everyone would find the reference to Butte's newsboys complimentary, for the young men could be an unruly group. They were eager though and fought mightily for the chance to earn their keep in a hard world. Like their fathers and their mothers, the young men learned quickly to wrestle their fortune from what lay in front of them. The immense mineral wealth of the mining district accelerated the growth of Butte and its sister city Anaconda. By 1900, this mining complex made kings of many men, most notably the infamous Copper Kings: William A. Clark, Marcus Daly, and F. Augustus Heinze. Butte the Prosperous had kings and it had king makers, such as the workers who made mining such a lucrative business. These king makers were the highest paid industrial workers in the nation in 1900, earning twice the daily wage of most industrial workers in the United States. Yet Butte's prosperity is also evident in the contributions of its women and their work building churches, libraries, schools, playgrounds, and gardens. Women served the community and the family. They were the teachers and the caretakers. Women passed down the cultural heritage through food and celebration and gave their families lessons in measuring wealth in the richness of their culture, their value as workers, and their strength in family and friends. The kings would flourish for a time, but the king makers' prosperity would be more intrinsic, more valuable, and more lasting.

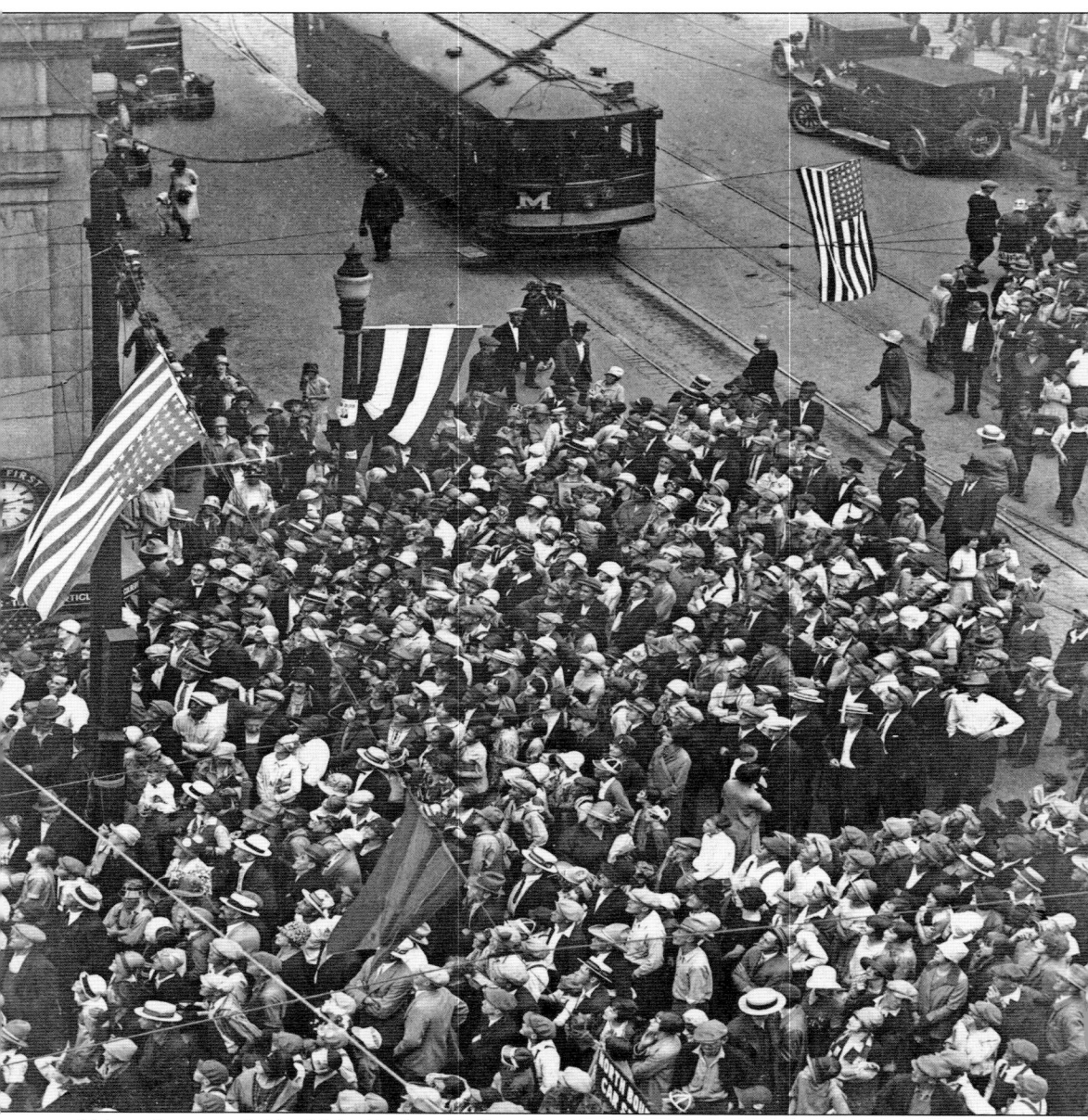

Although it was dubbed "the Richest Hill on Earth," financial prosperity in Butte has been an elusive concept for many people and the community in general. The resources of the area, although plentiful, are at times in demand while others are not—important one day, insignificant the next. Butte's true prosperity comes from its people. This group of people is standing at the corner of Park and Main Streets to listen to the news being broadcast over loudspeaker to determine how the nation's economy and politics will affect them.

Marcus Daly, one of the Copper Kings, was the founder of the Anaconda Copper Mining Company, the firm that at one time owned all of the mines on the Butte Hill. In 1900, he invested $20 million in his Anaconda Smelter to make it a showcase of smelting technology. By 1912, Butte mines were valued at $500 million and represented over 900 miles of underground workings. (Courtesy of the World Museum of Mining.)

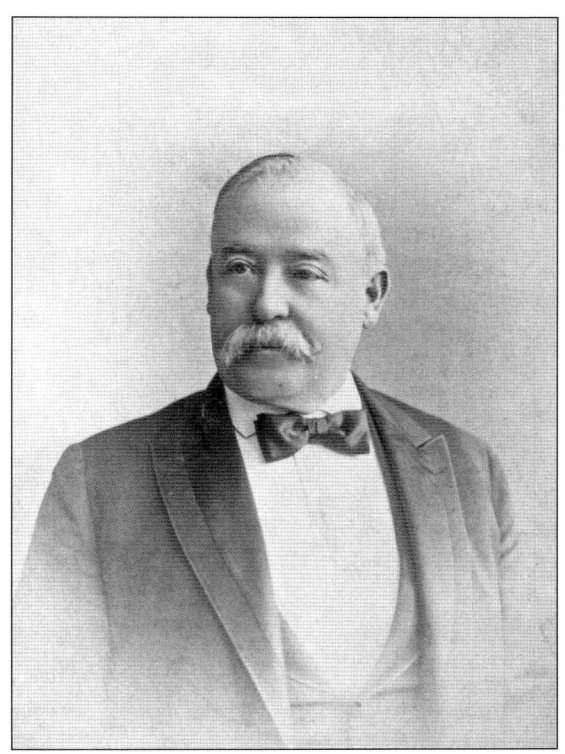

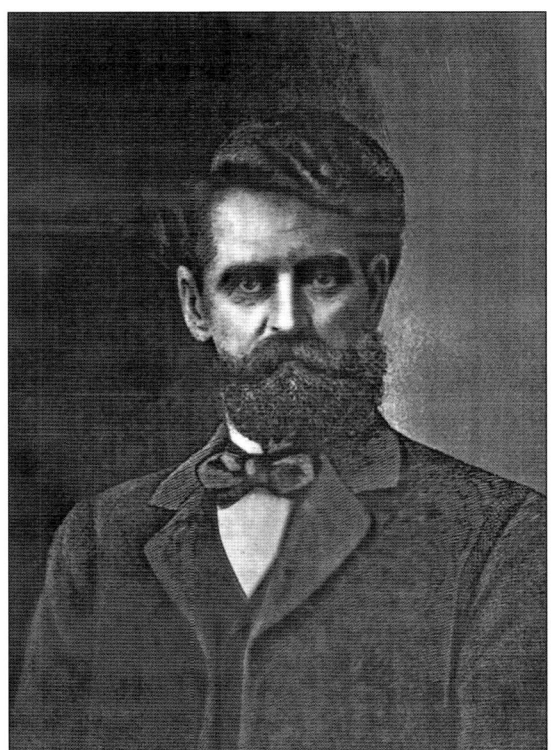

Another Copper King, William A. Clark, was reputedly worth some $50 million with a mining empire that stretched from Montana to Nevada and Arizona. Clark was notorious not only for his dominance in the mining field but also for purchasing a U.S. Senate seat. Although most of the money he made in Butte left the area, Clark was credited with erecting the Columbia Gardens and Clark Park for the children of Butte. (Courtesy of a Newspaper Reference Work, 1914.)

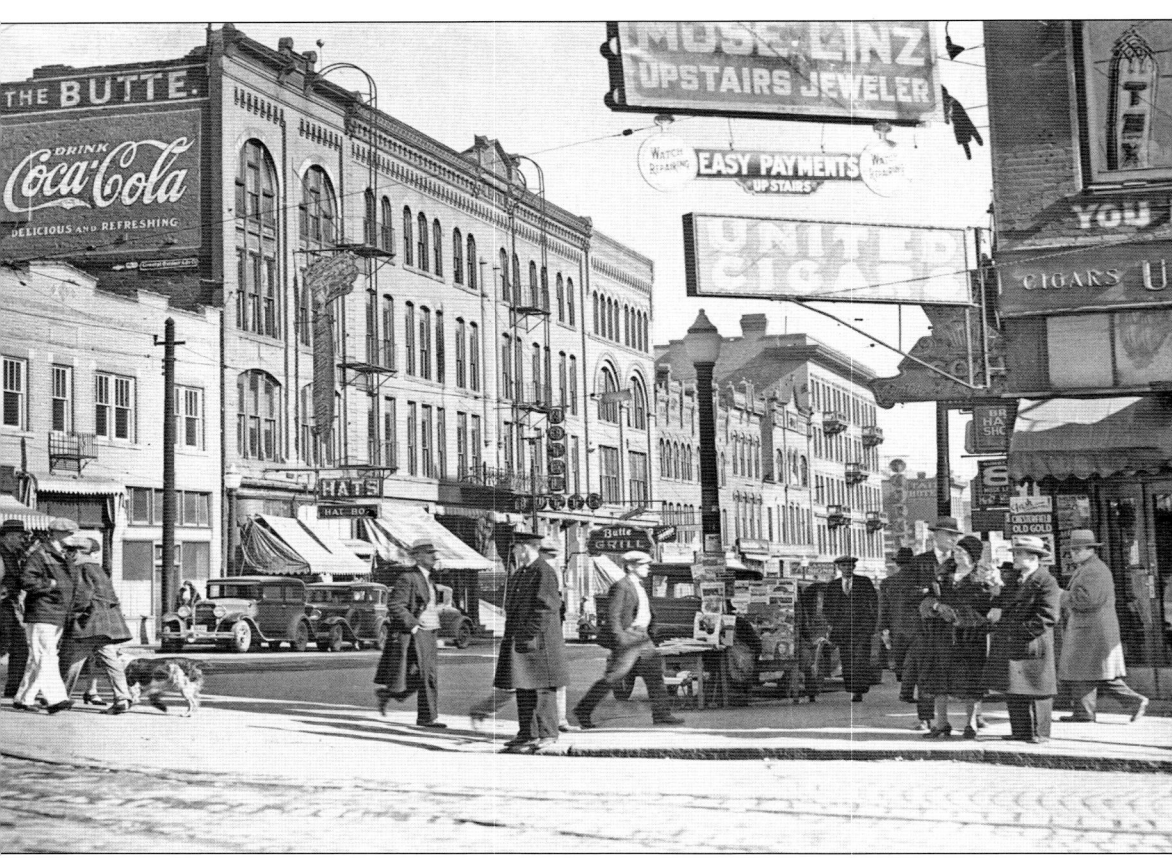

The city grew and became prosperous on silver, the metal of choice in the late 1800s. People (and the money they needed) came from the East to mine silver, and from 1864 until 1870, they reaped the riches of the silver veins. It was this silver boom that pushed William A. Clark to the top of the Hill, literally and figuratively. Clark and his bank provided the much-needed capital to develop the technology necessary to extract the precious metals and gain major control of the silver resources in the area. By 1880, the once-ramshackle mining settlement was the most prosperous city in Montana, a trend that continued well into the 1900s.

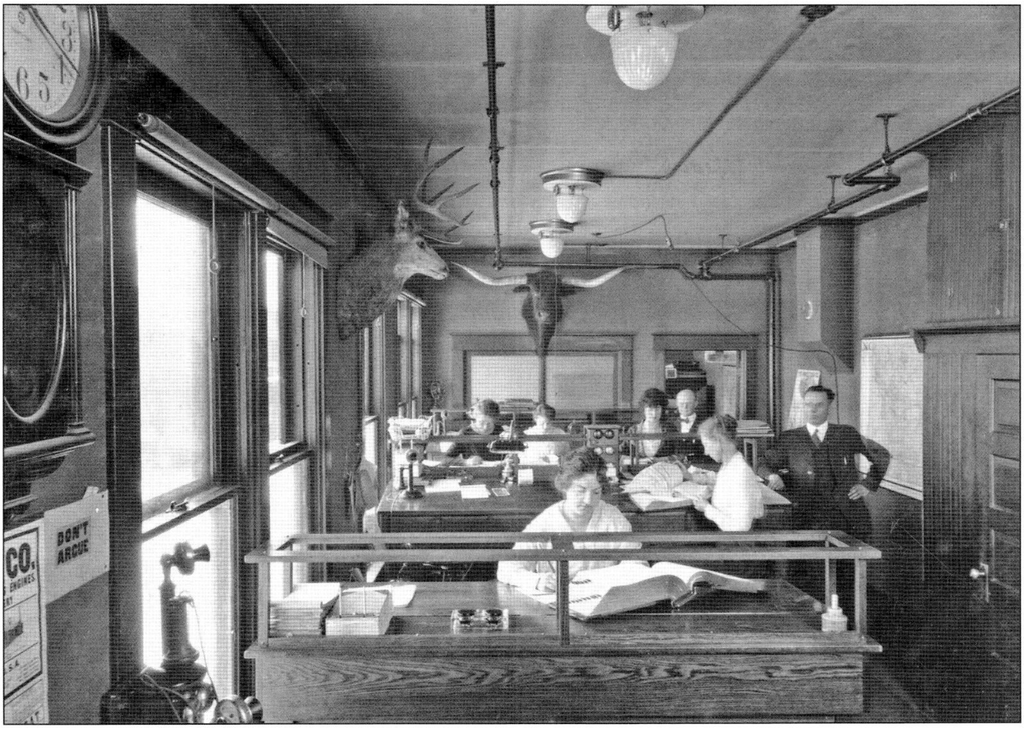

As mining prospered, so did the secondary businesses that were established to support the mines: foundries, brick factories, hardware stores, and banks. In 1905, there were seven banks, all of which were owned by millionaires. There were hydroelectric plants that provided electricity, and five major railroads came to Butte to move ore and cattle to eastern markets. Businesses such as the Peterson Sauerkraut Factory, Hansen Packing Company, Butte Carriage Works, Butte Tombstone Company, and Butte Brewery all contributed to the growing economy.

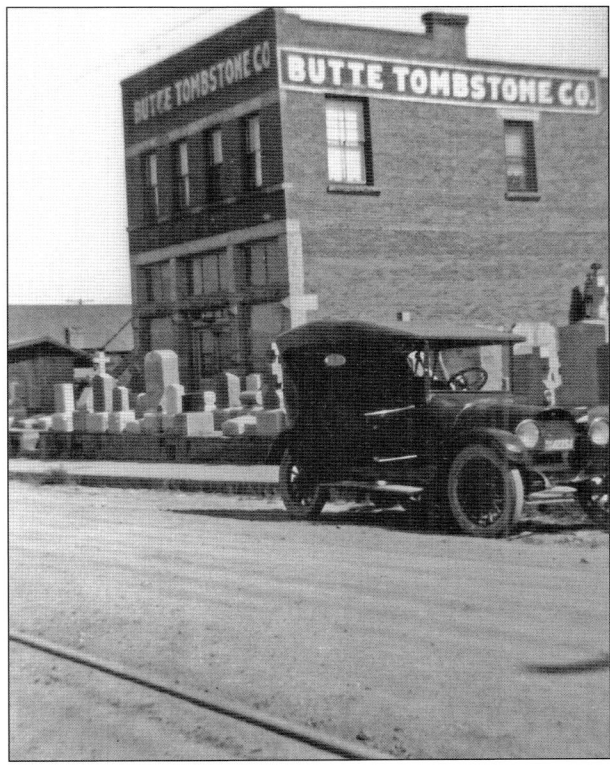

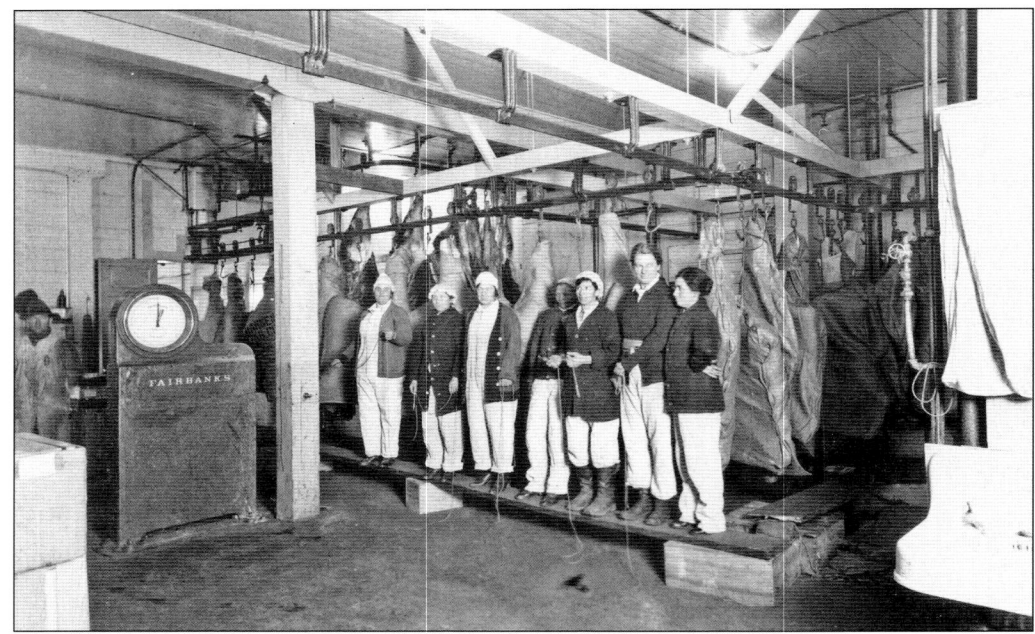

The Hansen Packing Company was first established in Butte in 1915 at Timber Butte. The company was established by Walter Hansen, who built the slaughterhouse at the junction of the Beef Trail and the rail spur of the Milwaukee Road, an ideal site for transport. In 1929, the company employed 300 men and 50 women. Payroll for the company amounted to $55,000 per month, according to the January 12, 1929, edition of the *Montana Standard*. The Hansen Packing Plant sent beef to Britain during World War II and shipped 400 to 500 railcars of beef and pork every month.

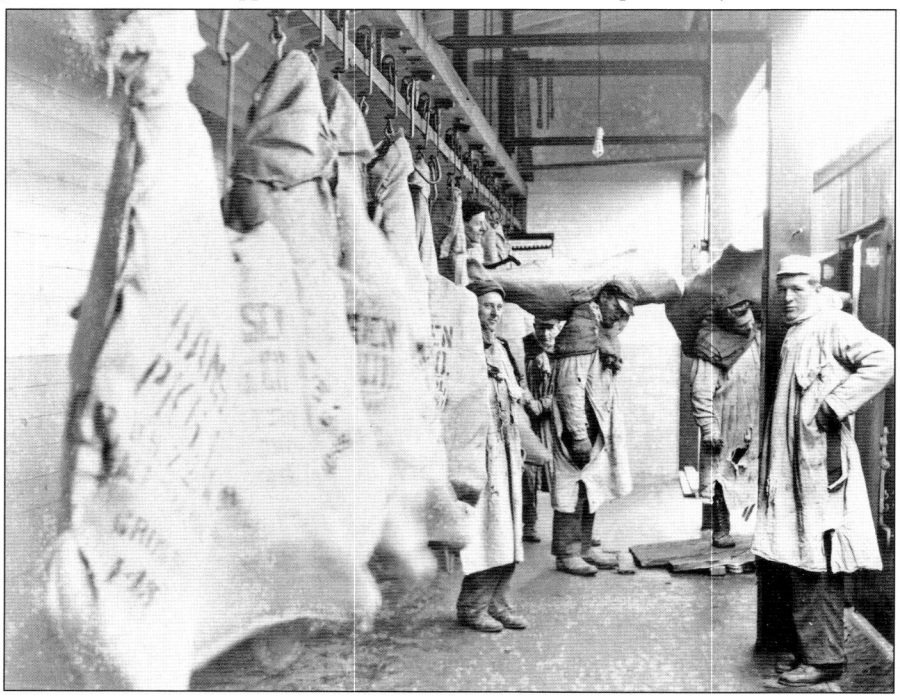

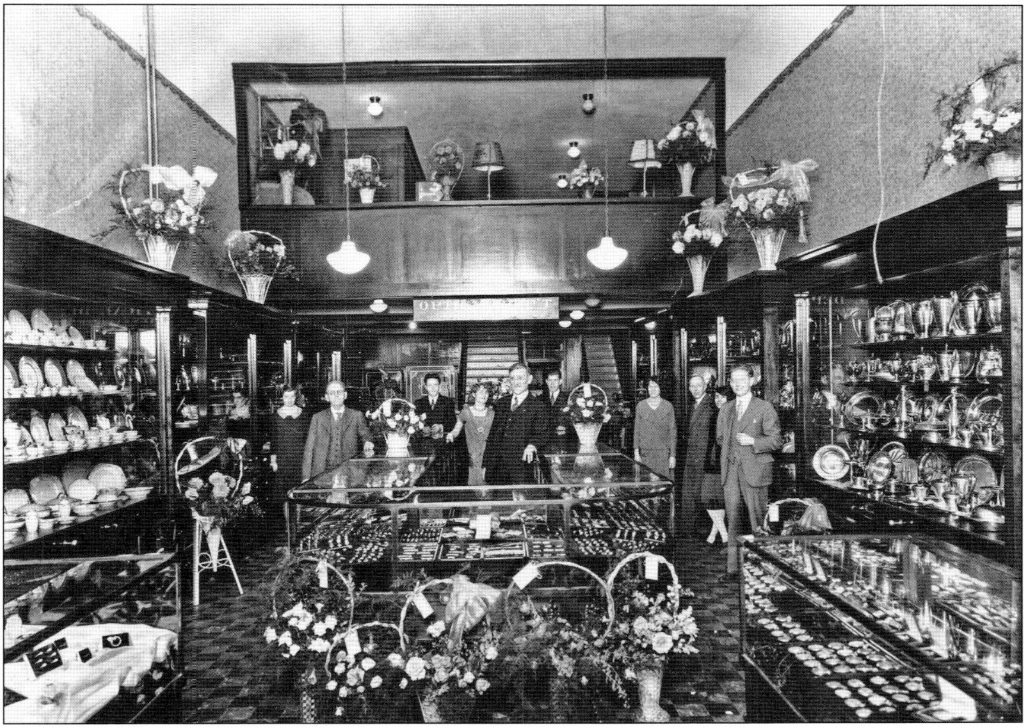

Hannifin's Jewelry Store was a well-known establishment for almost five decades. The store began as a partnership that included Dr. John Hannifin, a local optometrist. When he died in 1935, his daughter Dorothy, a practicing attorney in Butte, took over management of the struggling shop. Dorothy and her only sister, Lucille, operated the store until 1977 when they retired. In addition to being successful entrepreneurs, an unusual accomplishment for women at the time, the Hannifin sisters were involved in the community, their church, and various civic organizations.

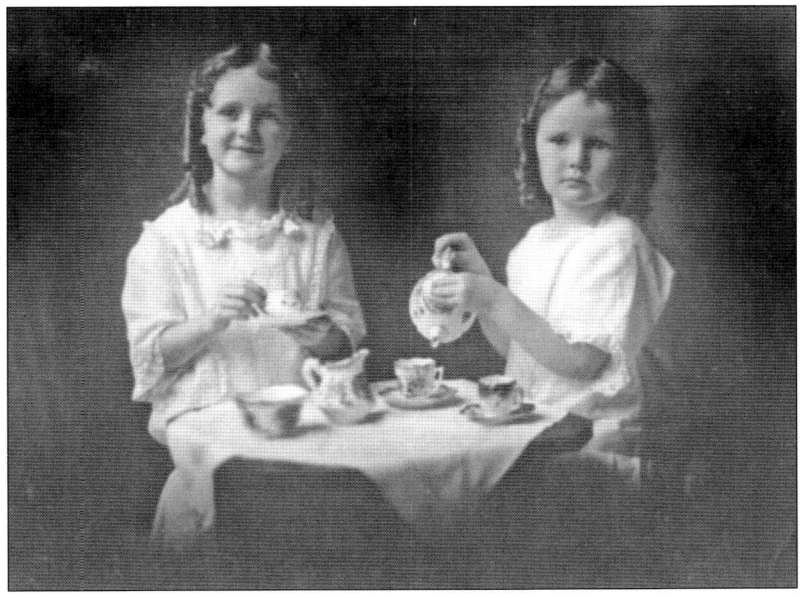

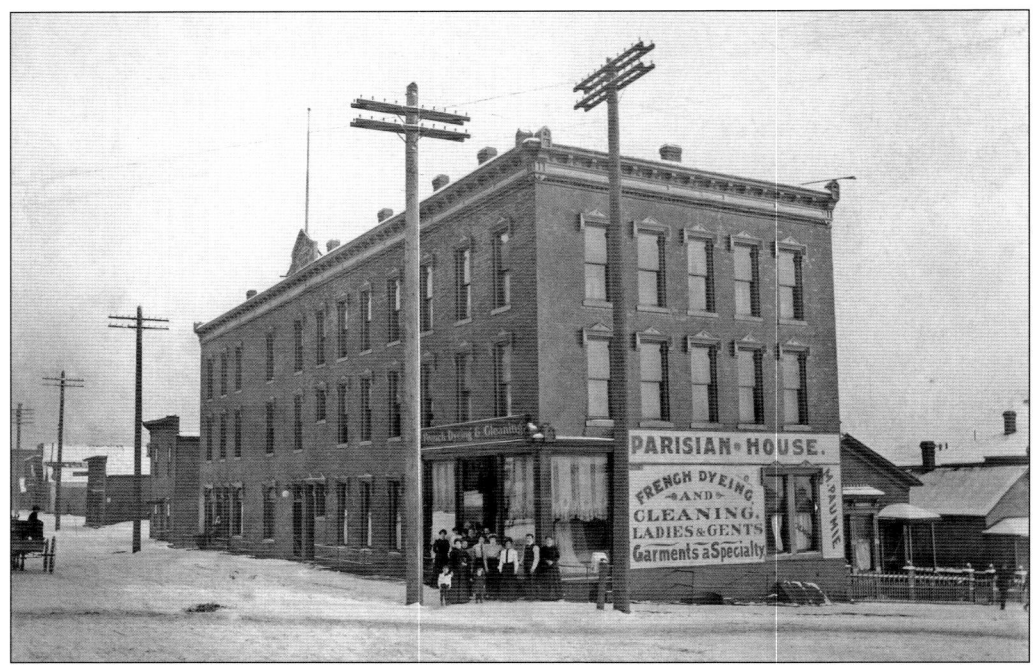

Considering the wealth of the Mining City and many women's efforts to keep up with worldly fashions, the Paumie Parisian Dye House and Cleaners could not help but succeed—and succeed it did for nearly a century. The business was established in 1887 by Camille and Maria Paumie, immigrants from Paris. The eventual location of the business on West Galena Street (a building that now houses a branch of the U.S. Postal Service) provided space for both boarders and the cleaning business. It was a lucrative location because of the number of prostitutes in the area. At that time, prostitution attracted sophisticated young women who dressed well and furnished their parlor houses in satin and lace—a perfect clientele for Mrs. Paumie's shop.

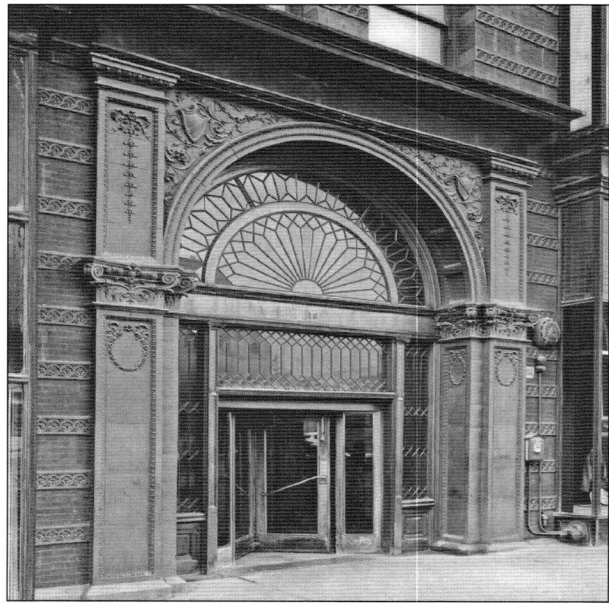

Beginning in the late 1890s, Butte residents expressed their status as the world's greatest copper producer by erecting a host of skyline-altering buildings. Most notable was Daniel Hennessy's magnificent six-story mercantile at the corner of North Main and Granite Streets where the ACM moved its corporate headquarters in 1901. Built in 1898 to offer merchandise to miners and their families, the Hennessy Building is an elaborate edifice with an ornate cast-iron storefront, leaded glass, and wrought-iron grillwork.

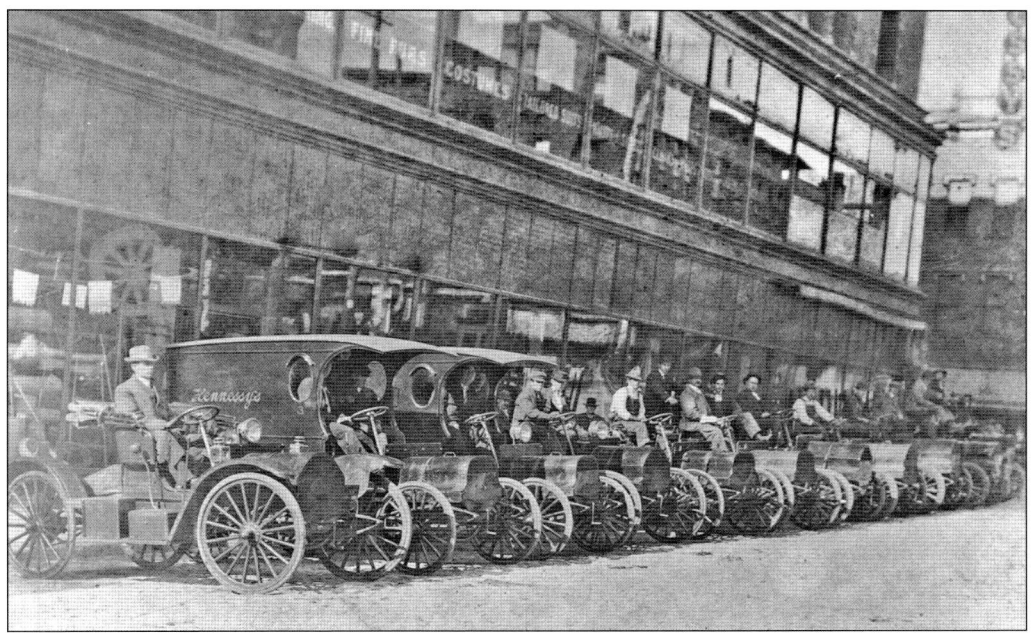

Inside the Hennessy building people were treated to marble staircases, oak counters, and solid bronze balustrades. Hennessy's was *the* place to shop, and people traveled from throughout the state and beyond to purchase men's, women's, and children's clothing; house wares; jewelry; and furniture until its closure in the late 1970s. Here Hennessy vehicles line up to prepare for a day of deliveries.

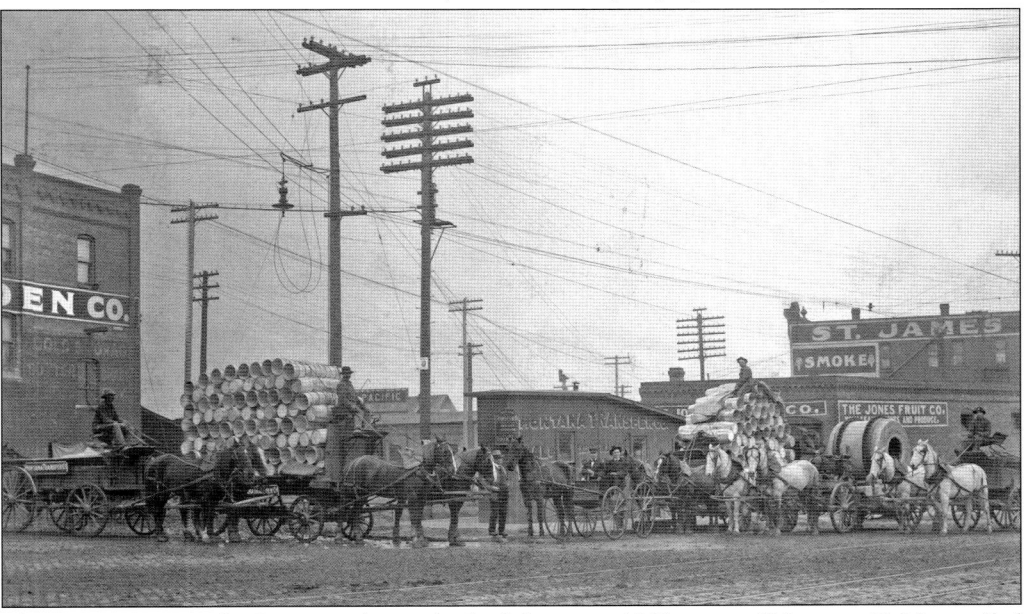

The Montana Transfer Company (center), which began in 1905, is over 100 years old. Now called Christie Transfer and Storage, it was owned and operated by Kenneth Christie, who was also the proprietor of a number of other businesses in town, including a furniture business, a coal company, and an oil-refining business. The building shown here, which today has a second floor, no longer houses the transfer company.

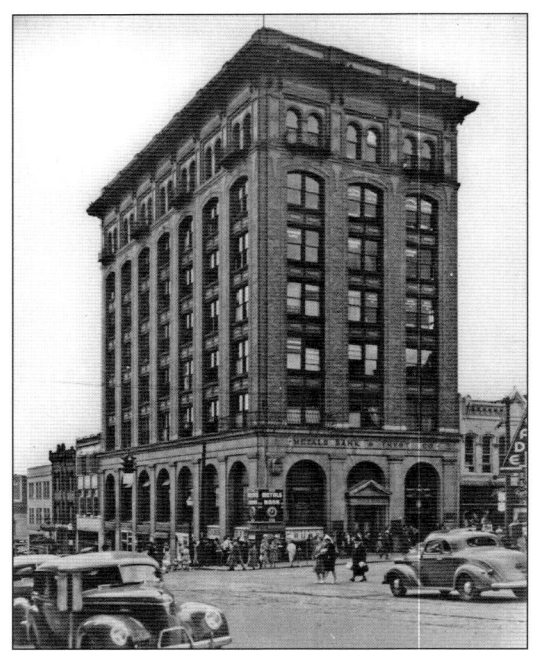

As copper brought Butte to the forefront as one of the most consistently active and financially sound metal-producing cities in the United States, the small banking firm of Hoge Brownlee laid the groundwork for the eventual development of one of the largest banking institutions in the state—the Metals Bank and Trust Company. Like the mines, railroads, timber mills, newspapers, and countless other projects that were the product of Marcus Daly's genius, this bank was to play an early and important part in city and state banking circles.

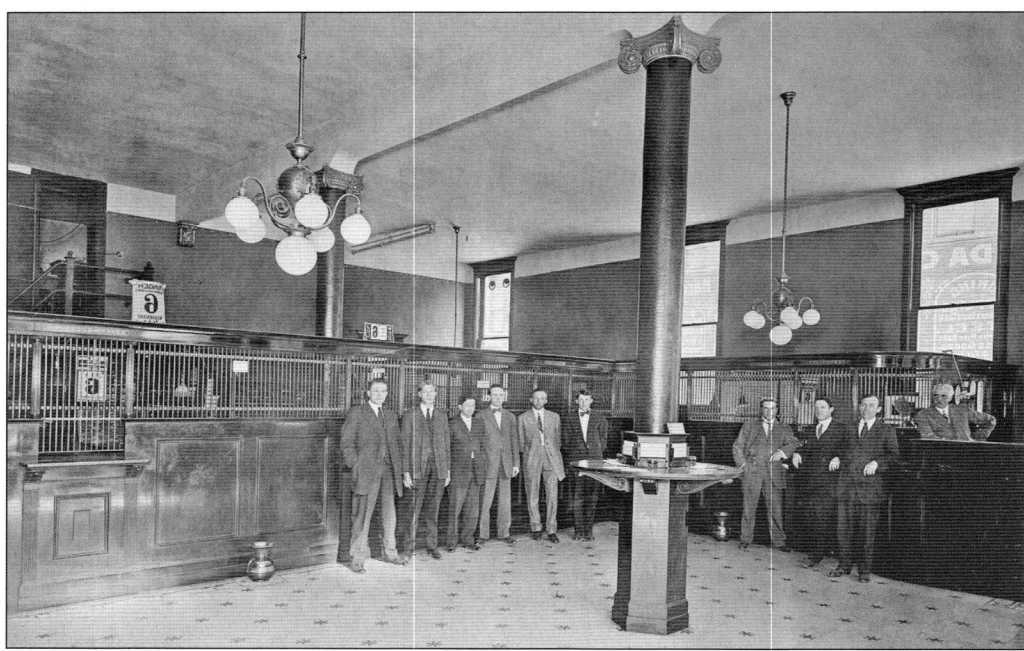

Founded in 1882 by Marcus Daly and several associates, the bank had its start as the Daly Bank and Trust Company. This bank was among the soundest institutions in the United States. From 1882 through 1887, over $15 million passed through this and an Anaconda branch just for labor and supplies of the ACM. The years of Daly's administration were ones of financial unrest nationally, but his bank was one of very few in the country that continued to pay cash for all demands made on it, a considerable accomplishment since payrolls of the district mining companies amounted to several hundred thousand dollars weekly.

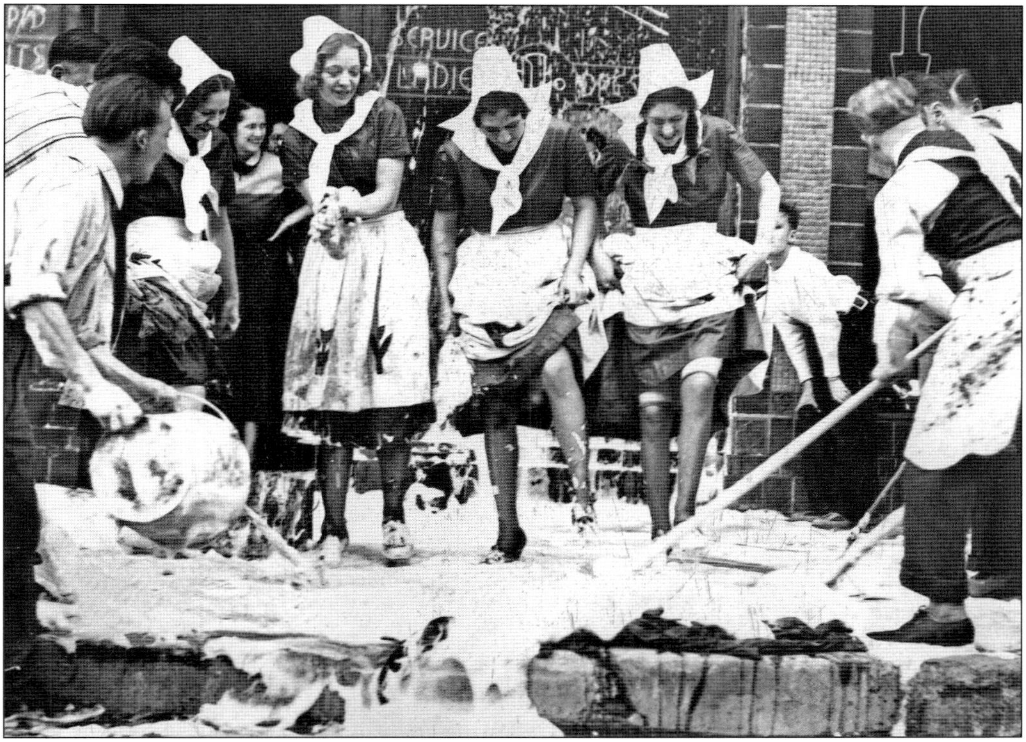

Charles Hauswirth was one of the most popular mayors of the city. In 1937, Mayor Hauswirth initiated a clean-up program that encompassed the entire city. People throughout the community participated, including groups like the Rotarians, businesses, schools, and neighborhoods. It was a wonderful photo op as people cleaned the sidewalks in front of their businesses and cleared vacant lots of rubbish.

Volunteers even scrubbed the statue of Marcus Daly, which at that time was located in the intersection of Main and Copper Streets near the Federal Building. The statue now resides on the campus of Montana Tech on West Park Street.

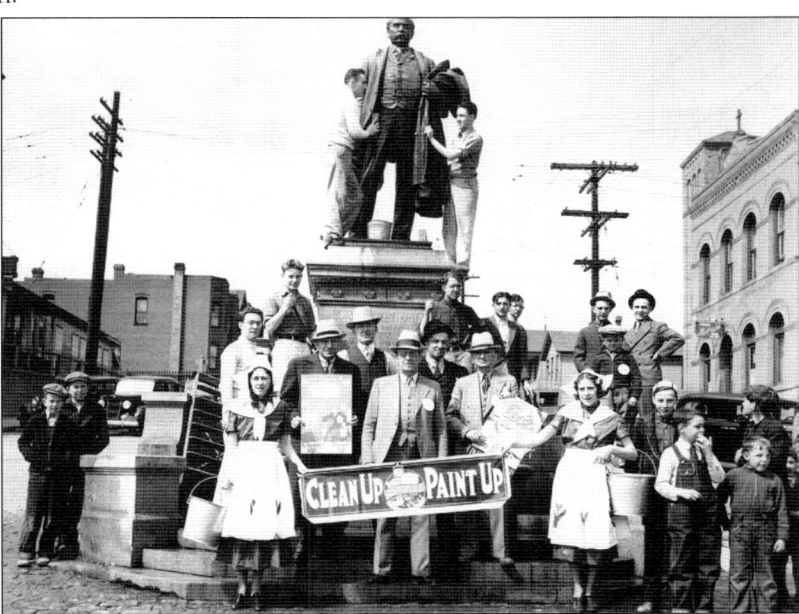

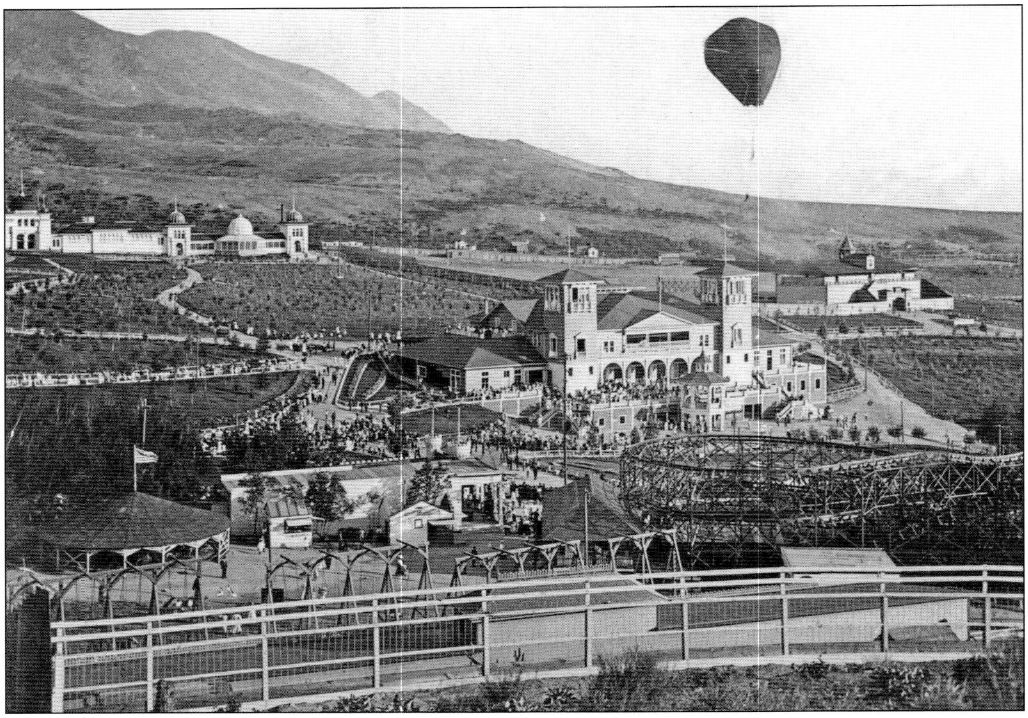

William A. Clark purchased the 21-acre Columbia claim to develop an amusement area. By the end of 1900, Clark had spent $100,000 on the project. Cynics saw the gesture of goodwill as a way for Clark to win a Senate seat, but the children of Butte did not care. By 1928, the Columbia Gardens grew to 68 acres and included a beautiful lake, acres of lush grass, a tri-level pavilion with an 80-foot-by-130-foot hardwood dance floor, a children's playground with elaborate equipment, a zoo, greenhouses with over 150,000 different plants, a herbarium with specimens of every flower and plant native to Montana, a fish hatchery, an athletic field, and a covered grandstand. Clark insisted that all of the children of Butte could have a free day every Thursday in the summer, and this tradition was carried on until the Columbia Gardens was consumed by mining in the mid-1970s.

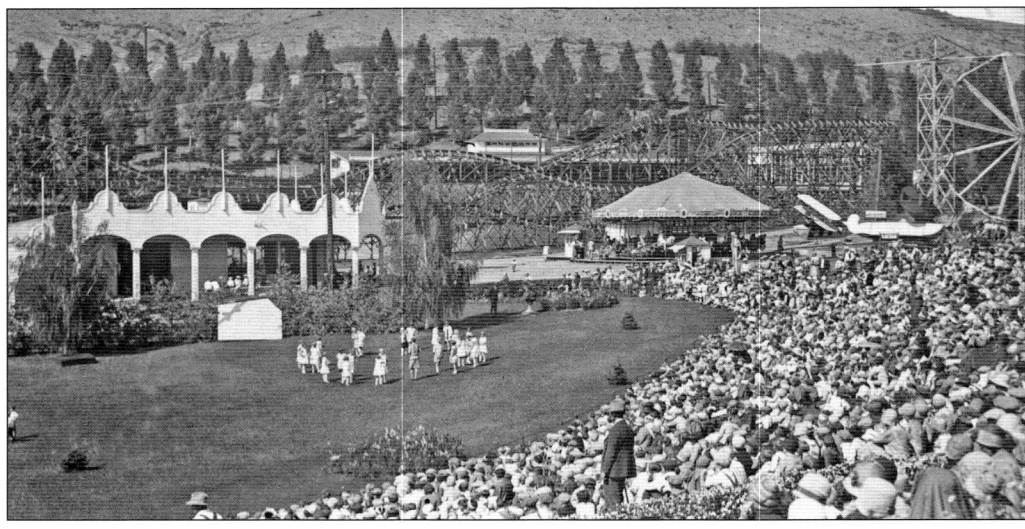

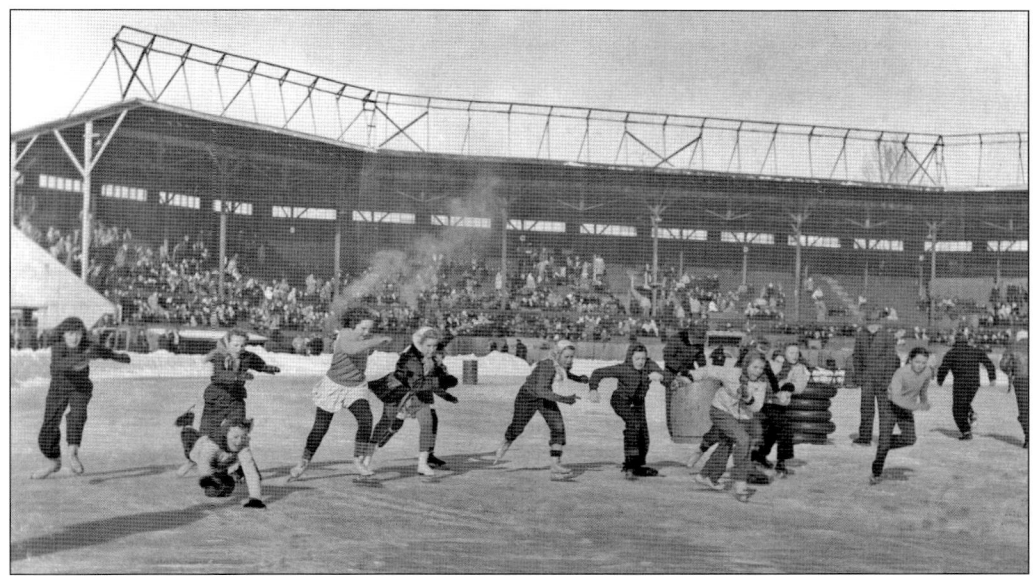

Clark Park was another gift to the people by William A. Clark in early 1905. Once again, many people believed Clark was enticing support for his run for the Senate. That did not deter them though from enjoying the fruits of the supposed bribery. The park was home to the Butte Miners' Baseball League and the Butte Independent Football League. The park also hosted ice events such as figure and speed skating, curling, and hockey. Many community gatherings were held at Clark Park. Charles Lindberg spoke to a crowd of 10,000 in the park on his Spirit of St. Louis Tour in 1927. The grandstand burned in the early 1950s. Today the park serves the city of Butte with picnic and playground areas, tennis courts, and skating activities in the winter.

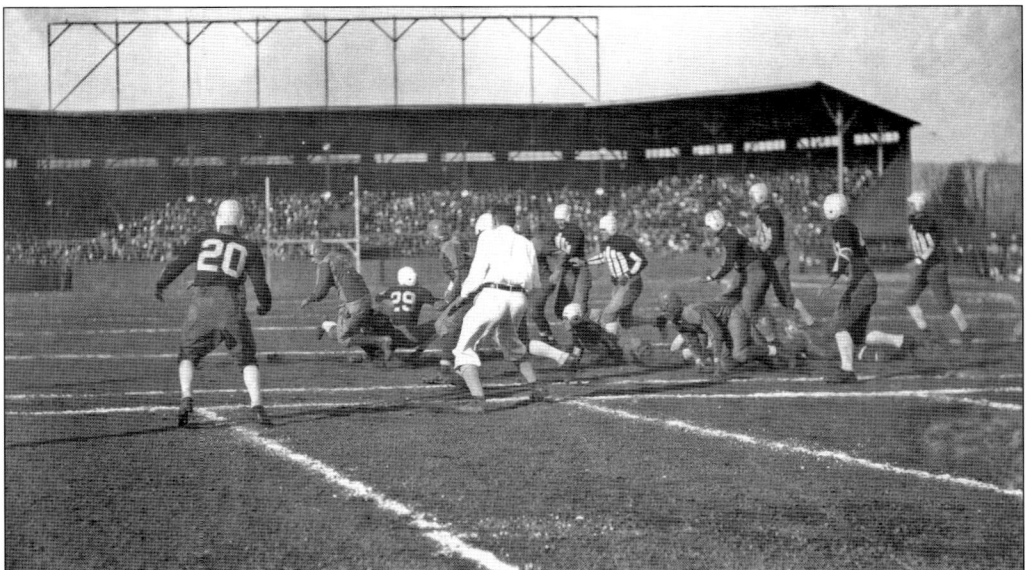

The Bobcat/Grizzly game, an in-state rivalry between Montana State University and the University of Montana, is one of the most popular football events each year. This game was held in Butte at Clark Park because it was the only city in the state at that time to have the facilities to accommodate the large number of spectators it attracted.

Butte celebrates its prosperity boisterously. Independence Day festivities begin on July 3 with a fireworks display from the top of the Big M, the butte after which the city is named. Many family and class reunions are held during this time so that people from out of town and out of state can partake of the marvelous display. The following day, a parade with hundreds of entries thrills young and old alike.

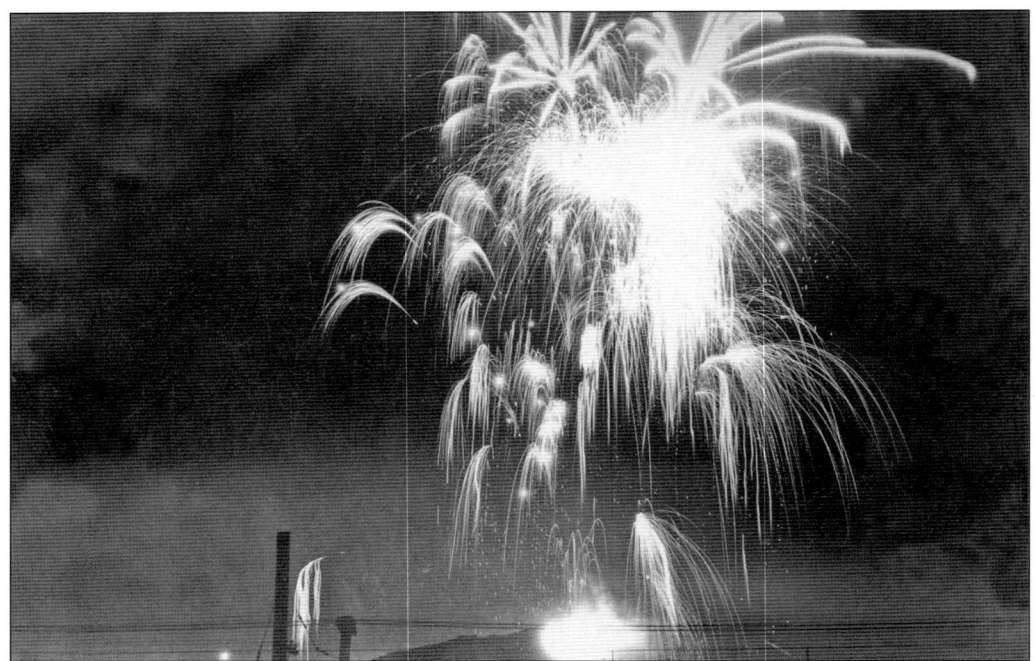

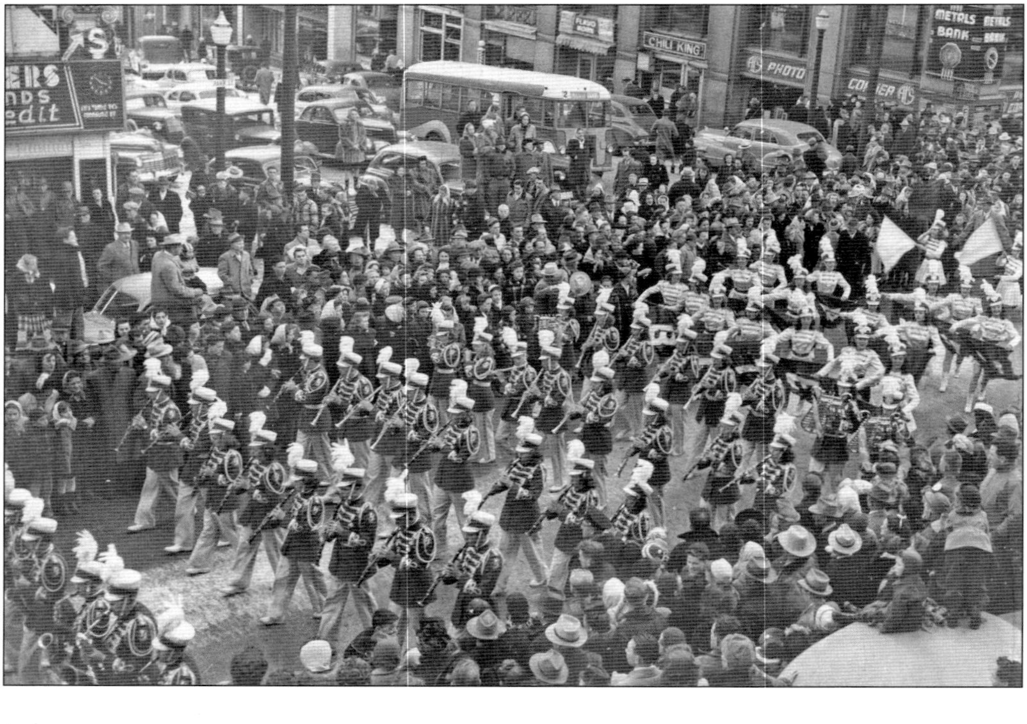

The Homer Club was the first independent women's club in Butte. It was founded by Nettie Casper, who invited women of kindred spirit to her home to gather, read, and sew. The women soon progressed to a study of the ancient Greeks, Homer in particular, and for the next 32 years, they read their way through classic literature, oratory, philosophy, and art history. In 1925, they began reviewing contemporary literature. The Butte Homer Club exists to this day and still follows fairly closely to the original format of the meetings. These photographs depict the Homer Club in 1891 (above) and 1892 (below).

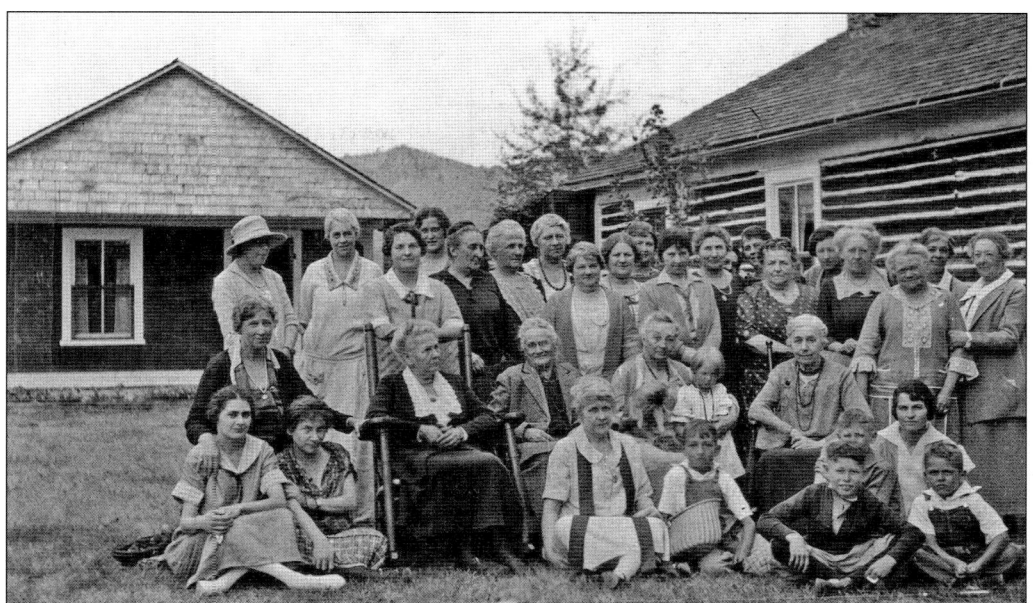

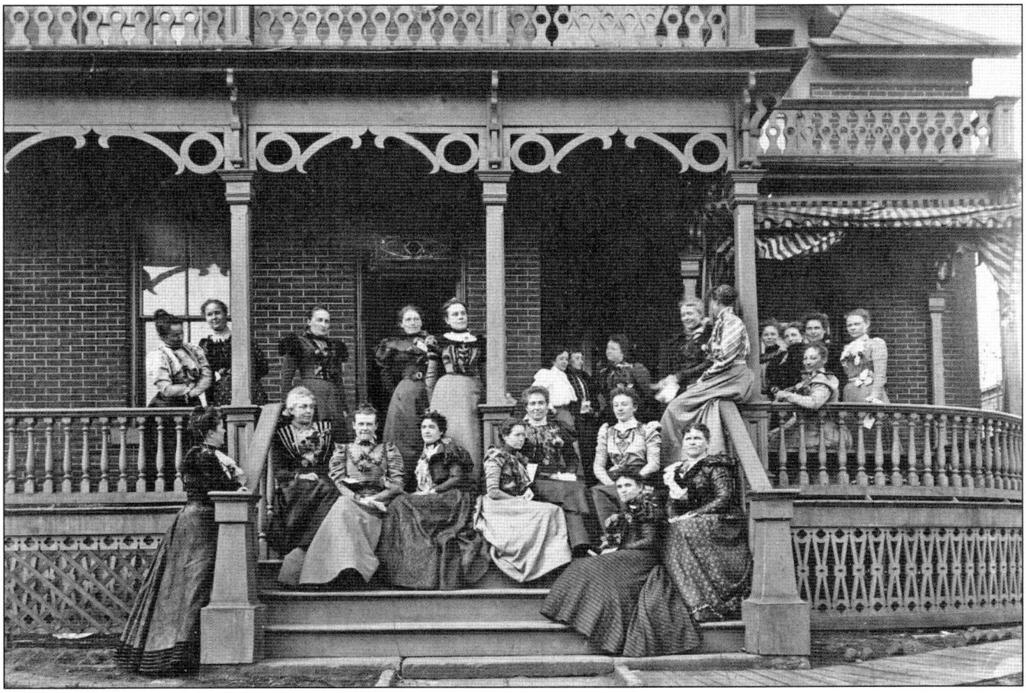

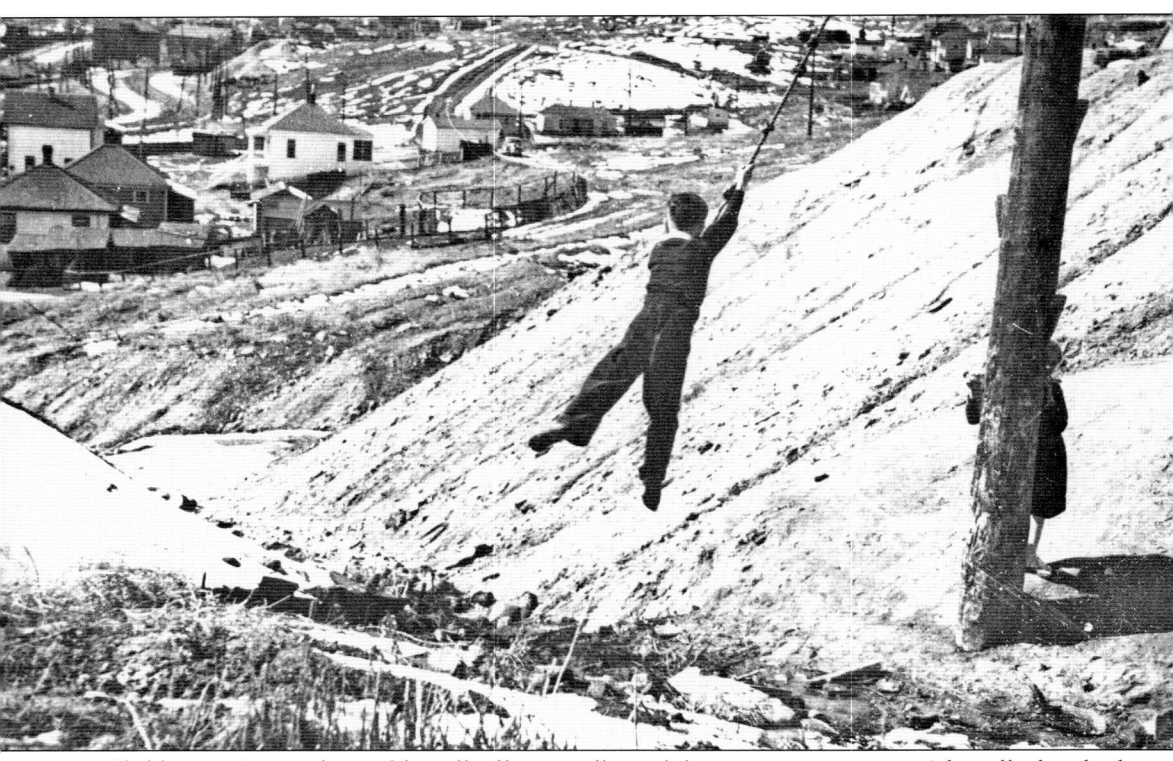

Children in Butte always felt well off—regardless of their monetary status. After all, they had such wonderful playgrounds: the mine yards, the confluence of railroad tracks, the ore dumps, the wooden tunnels that surrounded the steam pipes, and the huge boulders upon which they could climb or hide behind. Their fields were hills of polluted dirt and rolling tumbleweed. Kids ran free with no fear of whom or what they might run into. Into the night, kids would play hide-and-seek in areas that spanned blocks.

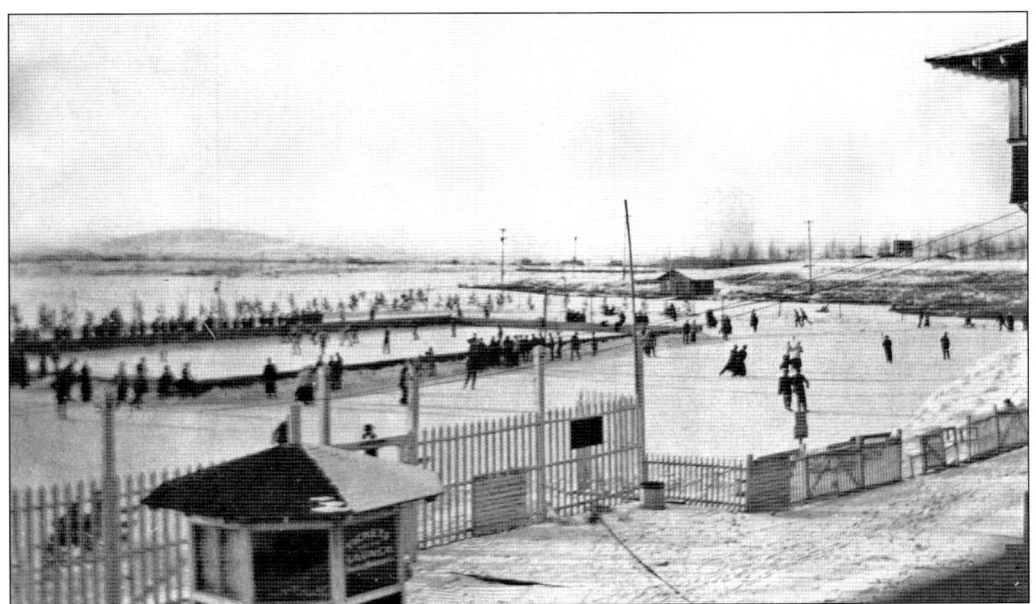

In years past, any empty lot was a baseball field, and any street could host a game of kick-the-can. The steep hills were perfect for sleigh riding, and for hours on end, children would bound down the precarious pathways and streets that evoked joy and fear at the same time. They would brave the frigid temperatures and ice-crusted snow to be outside in the sunshine that generally graced the city even at temperatures of 20 to 30 degrees below zero. Even the poorest children had ice skates. They may have been handed down and may have had tape holding them together, but they worked and were appreciated. In 1936, there were 23 ice-skating rinks in Butte.

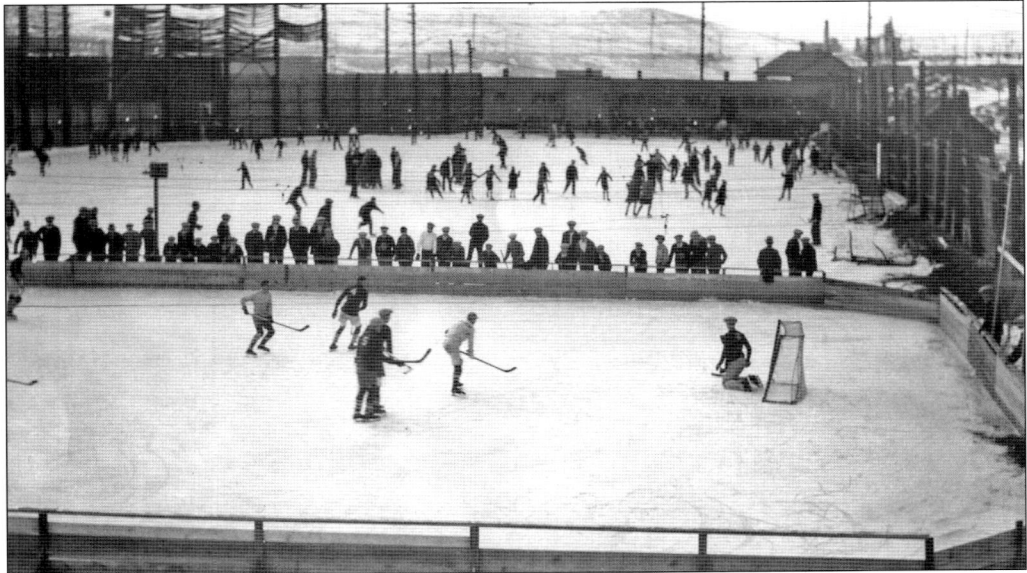

It made sense that hockey was a favorite sport in Butte given the frigid temperatures during the winter. Although the Zamboni machine was yet to be developed, the players and supporters found ways to smooth the ice to make it suitable for the fast pace of hockey. Hockey has seen a resurgence in recent years, and a dedicated facility is maintained near Clark Park by and for the hockey club.

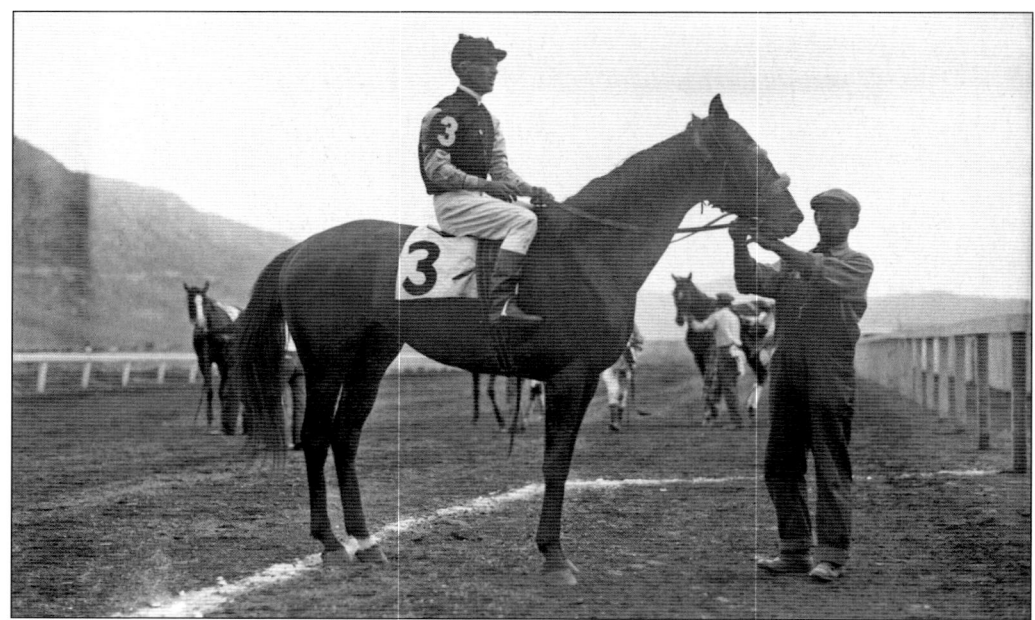

Appropriately, given its wealth, Butte had a massive horse-racing track where horses from all over the country raced. As Burrus Young recounted in an article in *The Western Horseman* in 1890, "Nowhere was the betting higher, the loyalty to local horses more intense, the crowd more cosmopolitan than in the Western mining camp of Butte." In 1896, over $2 million passed through the pool boxes.

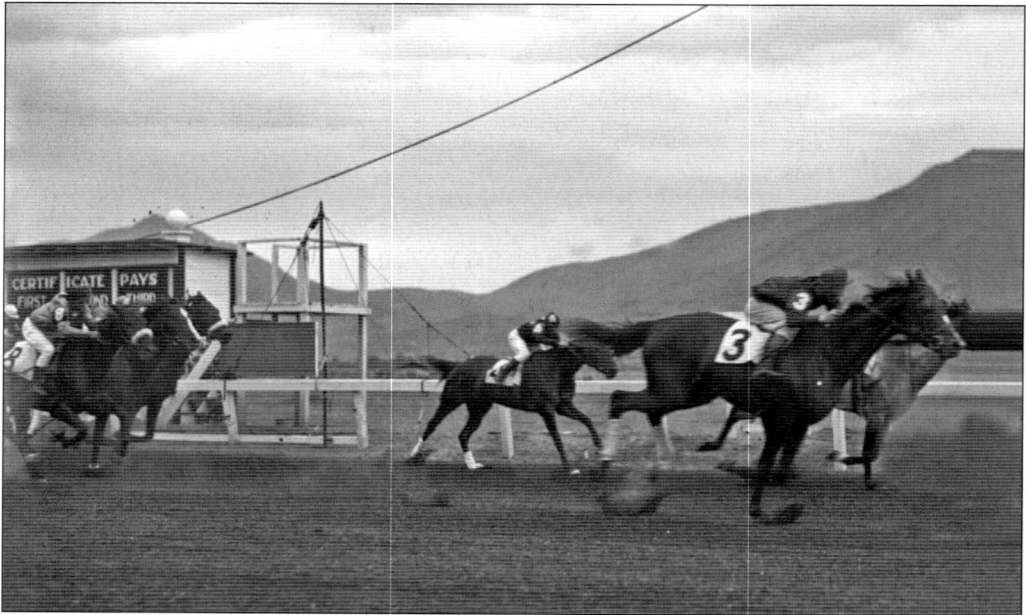

Marcus Daly, one of the Copper Kings, was an avid horse-racing fan and owner. He moved his horses to Montana because he believed that racing at higher altitudes would be an advantage for horses that later raced at lower elevations. Although his horse ranch was elsewhere in the state, Daly's horses often were favored when they ran in Butte.

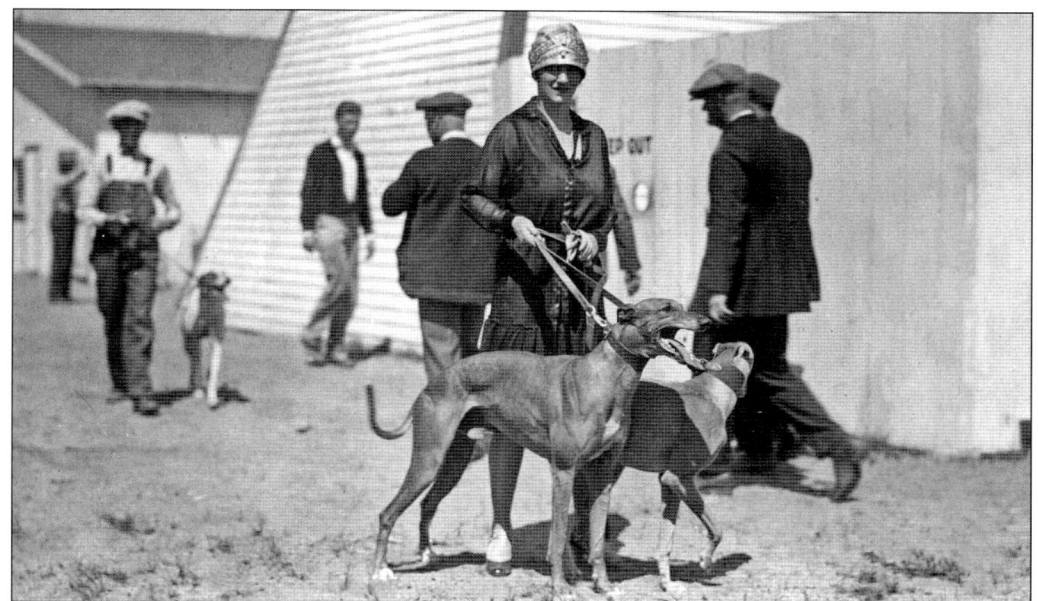

Dog racing was another popular sport from the late 1800s to the mid-1900s. During the 19th century, dog racing was called "coursing," and it was a combination of racing and hunting with live jackrabbits. It was a Cornish sport, and many Cornish immigrants brought their sporting dogs with them from England. A coursing track was established in southeast Butte in 1898 and operated until 1918 when it closed because of legal obstacles.

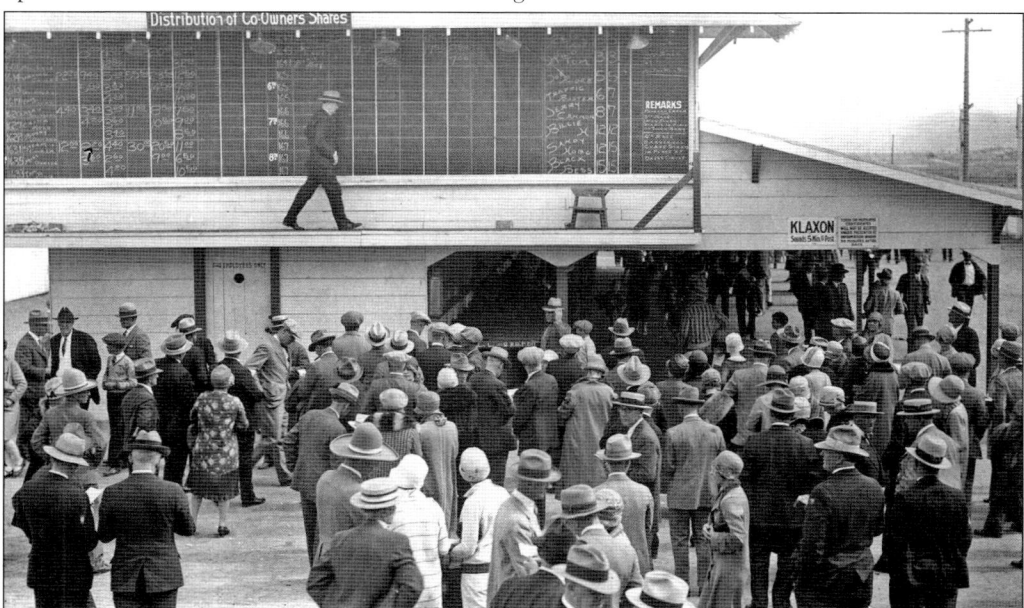

It was not until 1926 when the Highland Kennel Club was formed, bringing dog racing back into style. By then, mechanical rabbits were used, which many Cornishmen felt took the sport out of coursing. Many championship dogs were bred and raced in Butte; however, the Depression and residential development brought an end to dog racing once again. The sport reemerged in 1957 south of Butte but lasted for only two seasons.

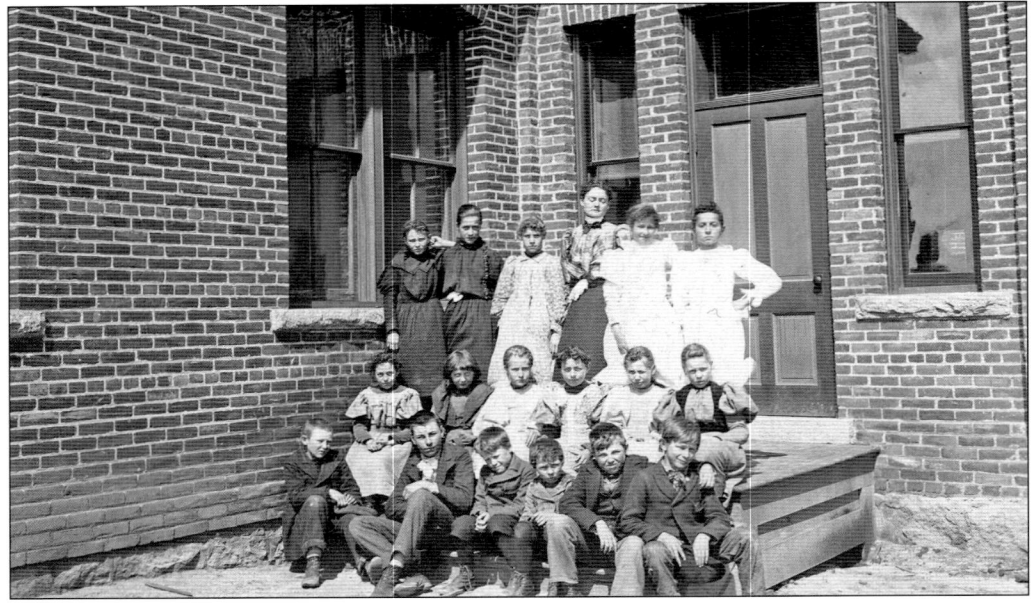

Butte has always valued education for its children. Widowed mothers viewed education as a way to keep their young boys from going underground, new immigrant families learned English and the ways of the new world by sending their children to school, and children found a way to move themselves forward by attending school. Education has always been an important component to Butte's history.

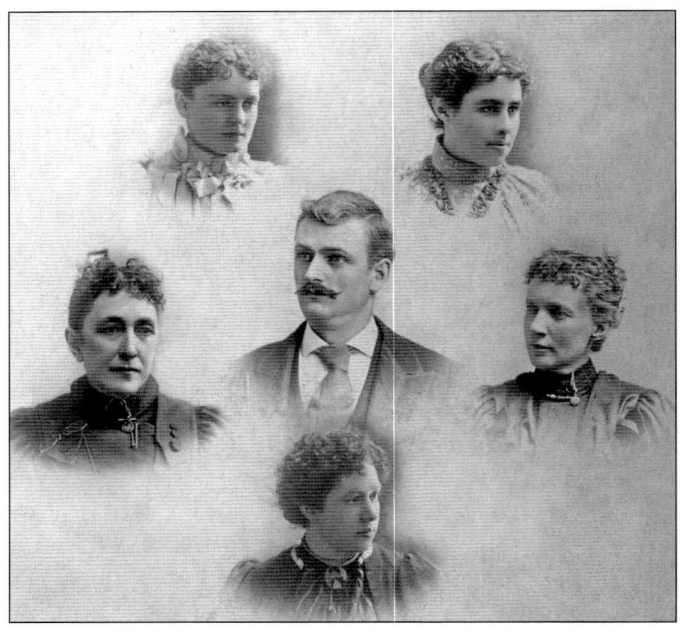

In 1923, there were 28 elementary schools, one public middle school, one public high school, and one Catholic high school. The school system employed over 420 teachers. Butte also had the advantage of the largest business college in the Northwest, as well as schools in telegraphy, music, law, and mechanics. The local college, the School of Mines, was established in 1900. It is now called Montana Tech and is part of the University of Montana system. It is rated as one of the nation's top schools. This photograph shows the teachers and principal in Butte in 1890.

Today Butte benefits from a flourishing arts community, of which the Butte-Silver Bow Arts Foundation is a major element. The foundation wears many hats: maintaining and restoring the Charles Clark Mansion, providing educational opportunities for artists of all ages, operating a coffee shop and arts supply store, and encouraging the adaptive reuse of historic structures. "Economic growth through the arts and humanities" is its mantra. The foundation recently purchased the old YMCA, a classic 1917 building, to provide refuge for artists and to invigorate the community's creativity. (Courtesy of Glenn Bodish.)

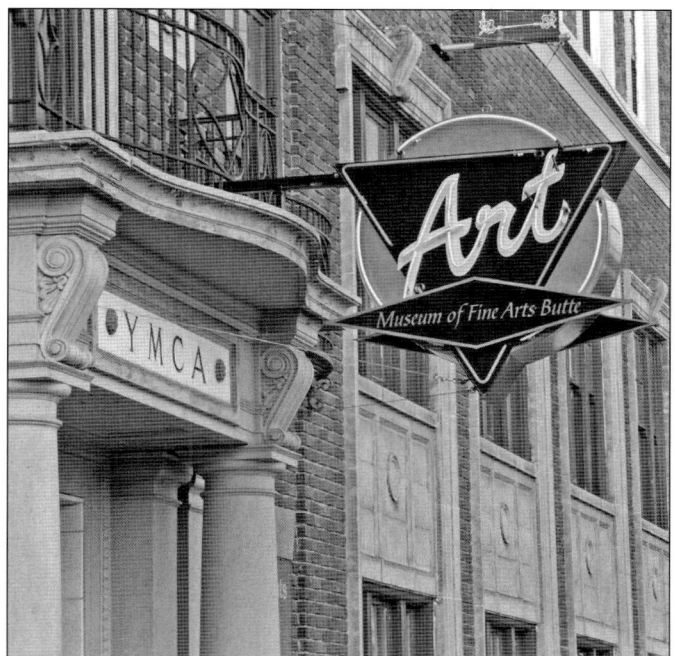

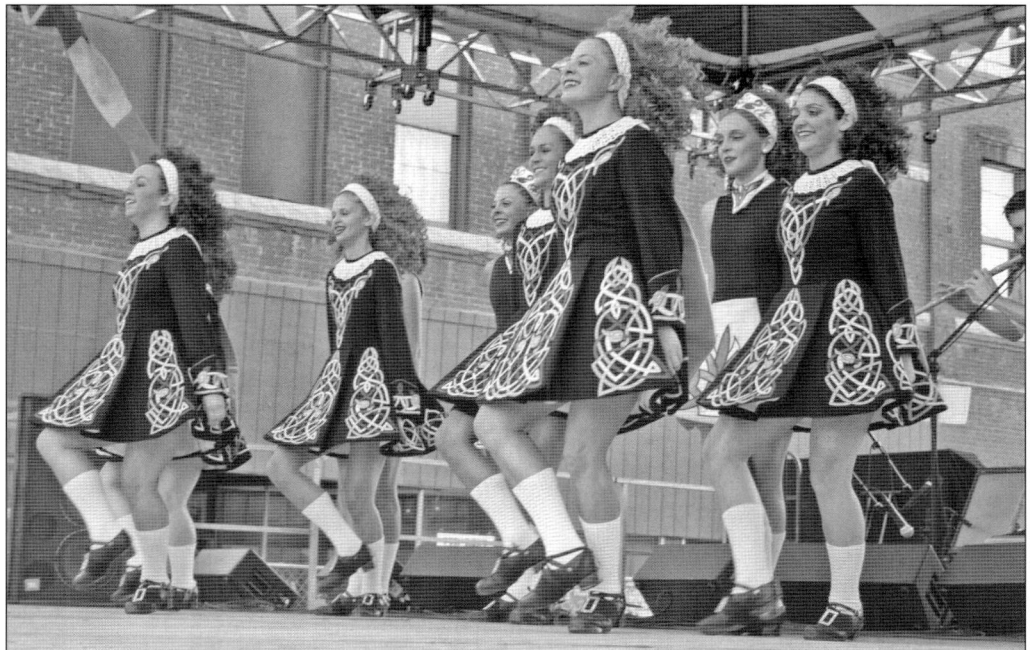

Butte has become known as "the Festival City" of Montana. Although Butte has always been ready for a party, the first national festival to come its way was An Ri Ra, a three-day Irish festival that attracts people from throughout the world. An Ri Ra hosts musicians, dancers, storytellers, and language instructors for a fun-filled weekend in August each year. The festival is hosted by the Montana Gaelic Cultural Society, which was founded to promote and preserve Gaelic culture through language, music, dance, and social gatherings. (Courtesy of the An Ri Ra Committee.)

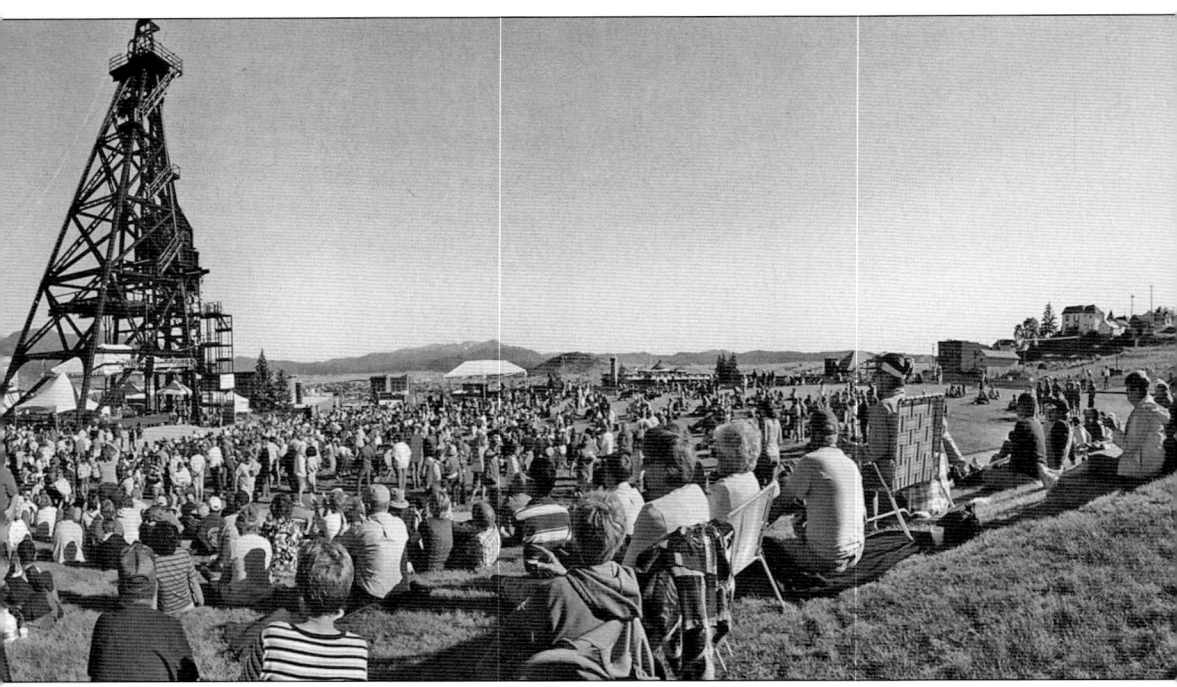

Butte is the proud host of the 70th, 71st, and 72nd National Folk Festival in July. The festival is an outdoor event that brings entertainers from throughout the country to rejoice in the richness and diversity of American culture. In 2008, over 75,000 participants enjoyed the music and dance performances, regional and ethnic foods, storytelling, and juried arts and crafts exhibits. Although the last festival in Butte is in 2010, organizers plan a regional festival in coming years. The festival has several venues over a multi-block area, the favorite being the Original Mine Yard where entertainers perform under the steel headframe with a backdrop of the Highland Mountains. (Courtesy of Walter Hinick, *Montana Standard*.)

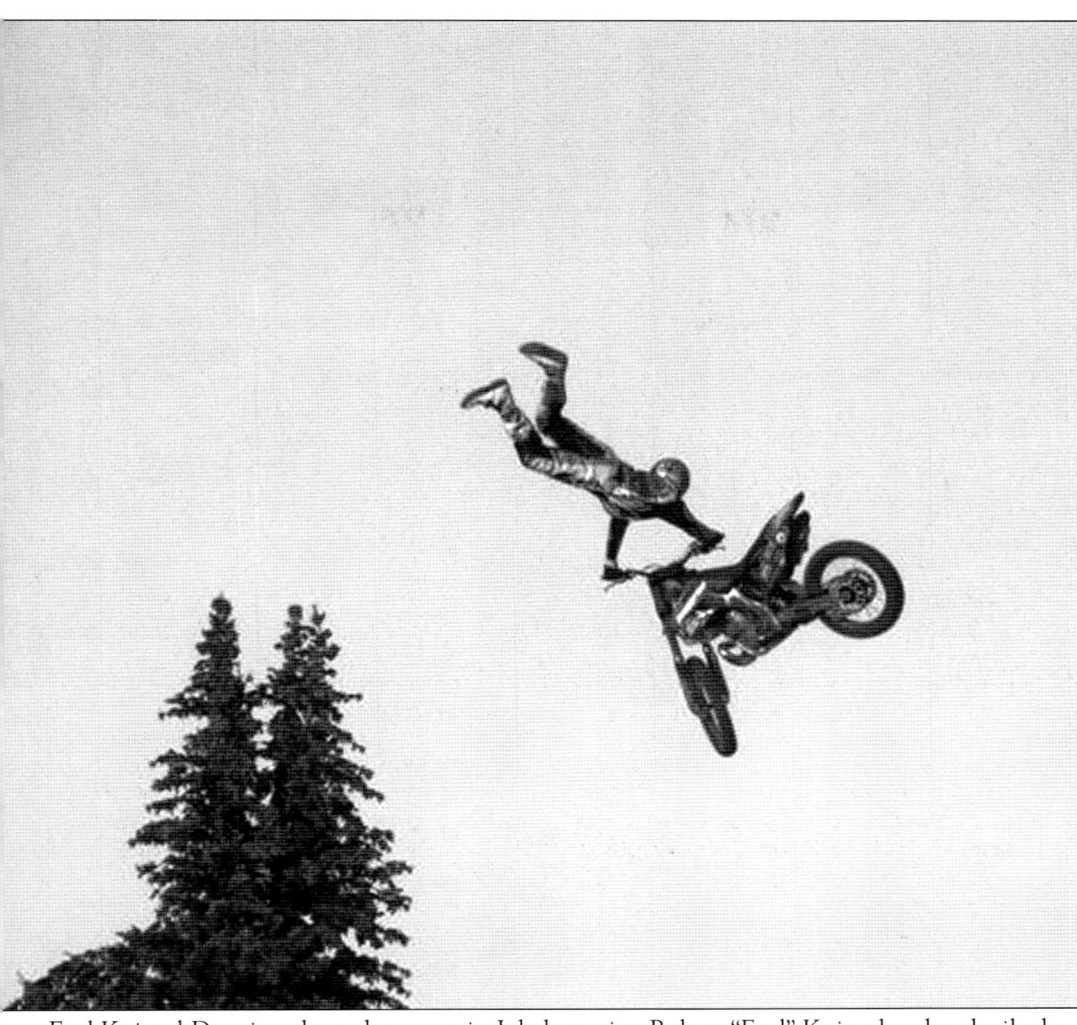

Evel Knievel Days is a three-day event in July honoring Robert "Evel" Knievel, a daredevil who took impressive chances, risking life and limb. Evel Knievel was born and raised in Butte and, like most Butte-born people, never ceased to call Butte "home." He came to be a famous character for performing such amazing stunts as jumping a motorcycle over the fountains outside Caesar's Palace in Las Vegas, Nevada, in 1967. The festival provides the audience with thrills and daredevil antics—events truly fascinating to watch. Started in 2002, the free festival draws thousands of spectators from throughout the world. (Courtesy of the Evel Days Committee.)

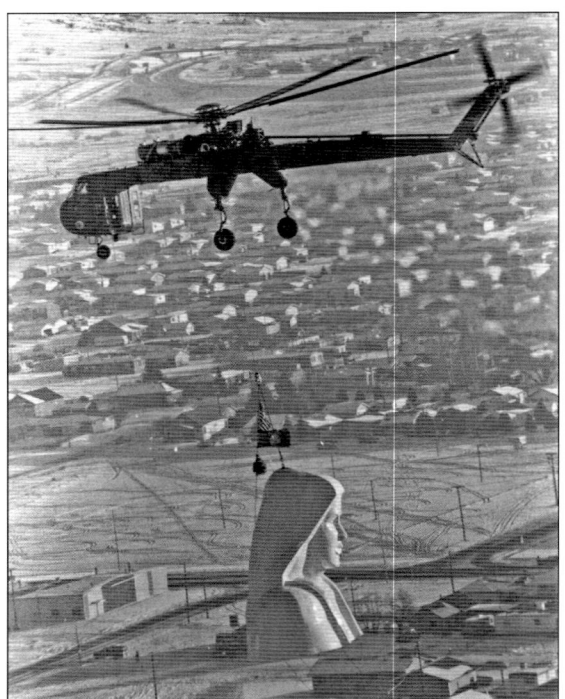

Butte not only comes together for a party, it will also get behind a worthwhile project 100 percent. A prime example is the statue *Our Lady of the Rockies*. In 1979, a local businessman made a promise that if his wife recovered from a serious illness, he would erect a statue in honor of the Virgin Mary. After talking about the idea to a number of people, the concept grew, and before long, a group of volunteers joined forces and created a 90-foot statue that pays tribute to all women. This photograph shows the flight of the head of Our Lady of the Rockies as she is moved by helicopter to her home on the Eastridge. (Courtesy of Sgt. Howard Anderson.)

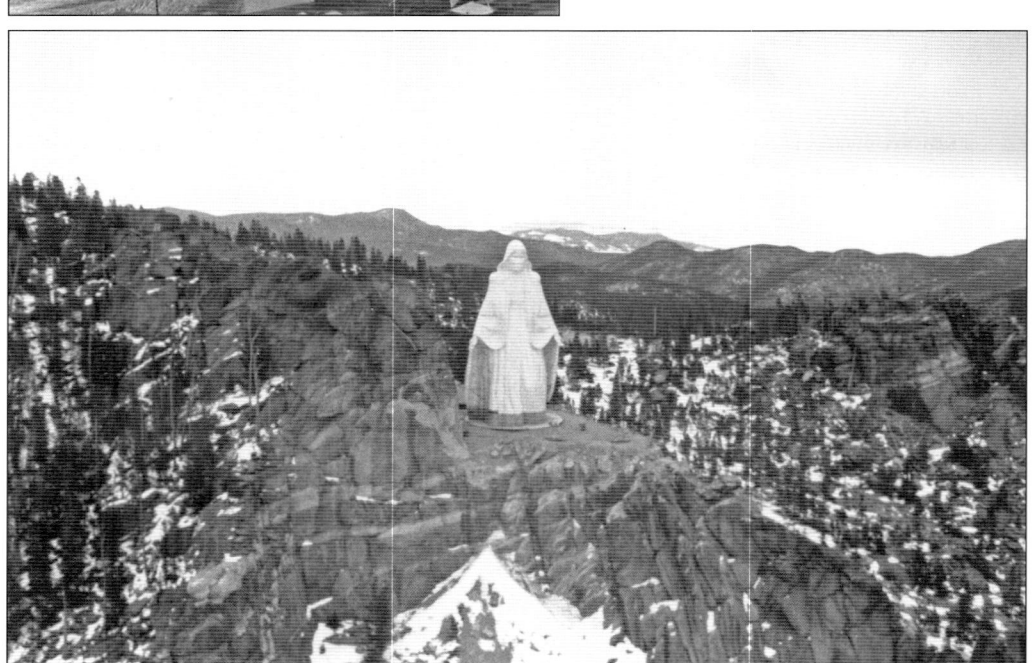

The creation of *Our Lady of the Rockies* took six years, countless hours of volunteer time (many from mining company retirees), financial contributions from throughout the world, and sheer determination. In 1985, the statue became a reality on the Continental Divide. Standing 8,510 feet above sea level and 3,500 feet above town, the statue has become a beacon for travelers and a tribute to the tenacity and determination of Butte people. (Courtesy of Sgt. Howard Anderson.)

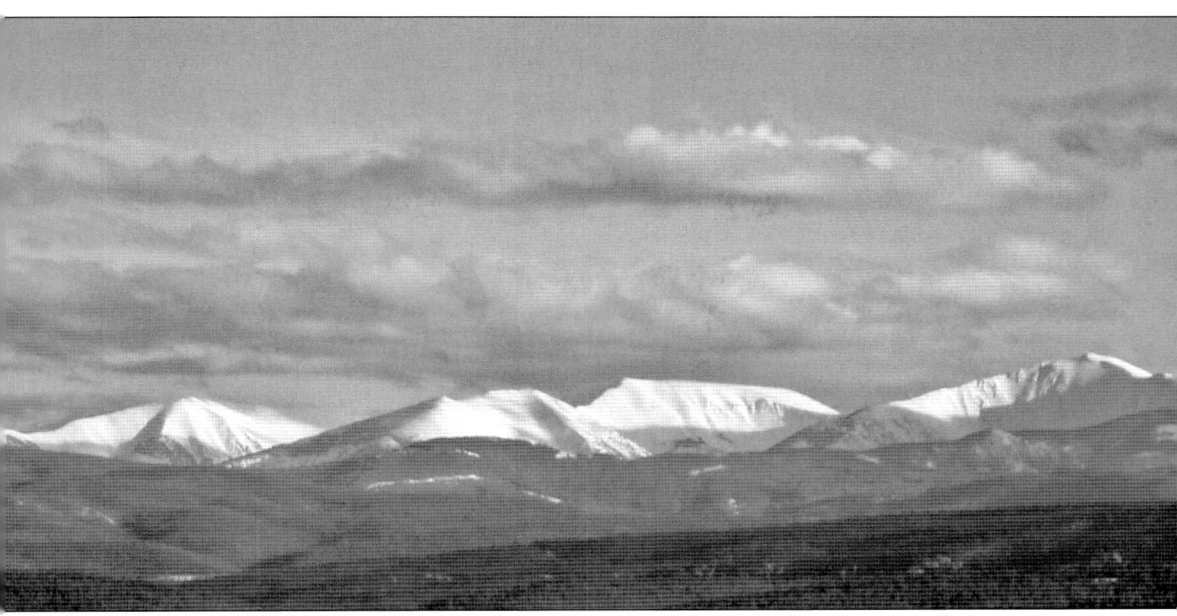

Montana is aptly called "Big Sky Country." Regardless of the season, Butte is blessed with clear blue skies that seem to go on forever and a surround that includes the Continental Divide and the Pintlar Mountains. Shown here are the Highland Mountains, the range south of Butte that can be seen from almost anywhere in the city. As Thomas F. Rooney notes in his article, Butte is "encircled by the everlasting hills that rear their majestic snow-capped peaks to the sky." Today, as in the past, the people of Butte measure their wealth in each other, in the richness of their culture, in the spice of their history, in the panorama of mountains surrounding it, and in the contributions Butte has made to America. Viewing the Highland Mountain Range, one believes the possibilities for the future are limitless. (Courtesy of Gordon Crain.)

www.arcadiapublishing.com

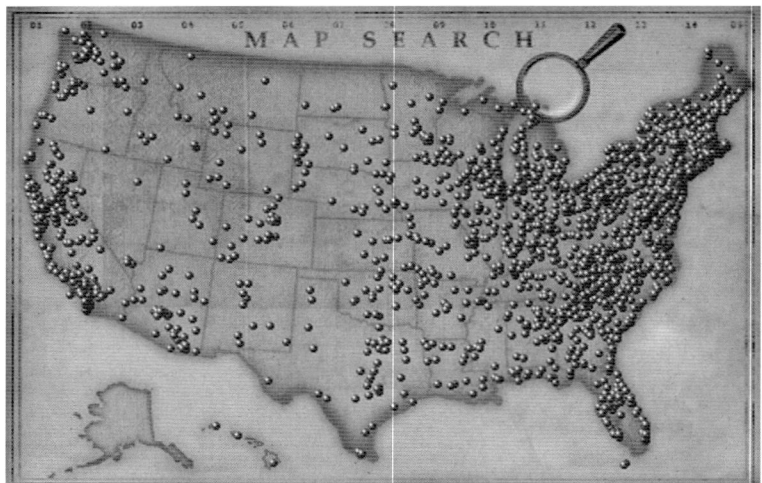

Discover books about the town where you grew up, the cities where your friends and families live, the town where your parents met, or even that retirement spot you've been dreaming about. Our Web site provides history lovers with exclusive deals, advanced notification about new titles, e-mail alerts of author events, and much more.

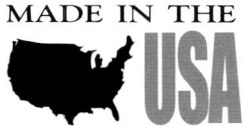
MADE IN THE USA

Arcadia Publishing, the leading local history publisher in the United States, is committed to making history accessible and meaningful through publishing books that celebrate and preserve the heritage of America's people and places. Consistent with our mission to preserve history on a local level, this book was printed in South Carolina on American-made paper and manufactured entirely in the United States.

This book carries the accredited Forest Stewardship Council (FSC) label and is printed on 100 percent FSC-certified paper. Products carrying the FSC label are independently certified to assure consumers that they come from forests that are managed to meet the social, economic, and ecological needs of present and future generations.

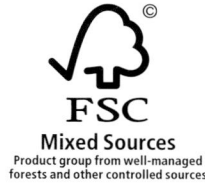
FSC
Mixed Sources
Product group from well-managed forests and other controlled sources

Cert no. SW-COC-001530
www.fsc.org
© 1996 Forest Stewardship Council

Find Your Place in History.